Living Your Spectacular Life

FROSTY WOOLDRIDGE

authorHOUSE®

AuthorHouse™
1663 Liberty Drive
Bloomington, IN 47403
www.authorhouse.com
Phone: 1 (800) 839-8640

Published by AuthorHouse 03/13/2017

ISBN: 978-1-5246-7154-9 (sc)
ISBN: 978-1-5246-7153-2 (e)

To

My mother Vivien Wooldridge

My father Howard Wooldridge

For their profound guidance, positive impact and emotional balance they bestowed upon my brothers Rex, Howard, John and sister Linda. Parents create the single greatest bearing on any child's entire life. I am thankful for my mom and dad's even-keeled parenting that allowed us to sail the tempests of life with confidence, tenacity and joy.

Contents

Section VII—People Choosing Spectacular Lives

Section VIII—NUTS AND BOLTS OF WORLD ADVENTURE

Section IX—PREPARATION IS NINE-TENTHS OF SUCCESS

Section X—MAJOR VENUES FOR
WORLD ADVENTURE

Introduction

The self-discovery journey you chose by reading this book deals with attaining happiness, fulfillment and purpose in life.

This book draws on my five decades of world bicycle travel across six continents. Along the way, I learned a few things about living a spectacular as well as happy life.

Another traveler, Mark Twain said, "Twenty years from now you will be more disappointed by the things you didn't do than by the ones you did do. So throw off the bowlines, sail away from the safe harbor. Catch the trade winds in your sails. Explore. Dream. Discover."

By the time you finish reading this book, expect your self-confidence to expand, your sense of adventure to explode and your sense of your destiny to be in your hands. How can I be so confident? If the truth were told, I arrived on this planet from very poor parents in a farming area in middle Michigan. My tenth grade history teacher told me, "I didn't think you would amount to much of anything."

She gasped when I sent her a postcard with me standing on the Wall of China. When I sent her a postcard from Antarctica, she beamed at one of her students "making it" in this world.

I won't kid you; no one ever gave me a dime. I earned it with hard work. I've lived a million dollar life on minimum wage. Since I did it, you can do it!

Along the way, I learned some compelling ideas on how to discover your life's most rewarding and happiest path. Let's dig into this book together.

You may appreciate this quote from the late comedian Robin Williams speaking as Jack in the movie "Jack." Williams' character ages four times faster than regular human beings. Jack spoke at his high school commencement as an older man. He said, "Please, don't worry so much. Because in the end, none of us has very long on this Earth. Life is fleeting. And if you're ever distressed, cast your eyes to the summer sky when the stars are strung across the velvety night. And when a shooting star streaks through the blackness, turning night into day... make a wish and think of me. Make your life spectacular."

Through my love of travel, reading books, hard work, writing and participating in sports, I live a spectacular life. So can you! This book shows you multiple aspects of being happy in the 21st century in this high-speed, advanced and technological society. You discover in this book dozens of young, middle-aged and older people living spectacular lives through their actions. They share their secrets with you.

Another quote offers you a deeper perspective for your life. Napoleon Hill wrote many books on success such as **Think and Grow Rich.** He presented his students with the metaphor of the horse.

Hill said, "Life is like a horse. Life will ride you, as you become the horse. Or, you can ride while Life becomes the horse. The choice as to whether one becomes the rider of Life or is ridden by Life is the privilege of every person. But this much is certain. If you do not choose to become the rider of Life, you are sure to be forced to become the horse. Life either rides or is ridden. It never stands still."

As you can imagine, I read every single one of Hill's books. They cover every aspect of living a meaningful, fruitful and joyful life. He shows readers how to engage work and play. While his books published 100 years ago, his wisdom applies to the 21st century because of its timelessness.

Another American writer Henry David Thoreau said, "If you advance confidently toward your dreams, and endeavor to live the life which you have imagined, you will meet with success unexpected in common hours. You will pass through invisible boundaries. You will engage new and liberal laws. And you will live with the license of a higher order of beings."

Pretty noble ideas, yes? You betcha'! This book shares with you some of the finest thinking and quotes from such men as Ralph Waldo Emerson, John Muir, Wallace Stegner, Edward Abbey, Henry David Thoreau and women like Eleanor Roosevelt, Elizabeth Gilbert, Jane Goodall, Anne Carson, Donna Taart and Karen Joy Fowler.

This book covers various aspects of being happy from the perspective of my six continents of travel to visit dozens of cultures, languages and ways of life. In my 45 years of traveling, I watched happy people, sad people, dull people, bored people and disengaged people. I witnessed rich people, middle class people, poor people and wretched people. The universe shows no favoritism. I witnessed death at young ages, middle ages and old ages. As a volunteer ski instructor for the disabled at Winter Park, Colorado for 24 years, I saw people with horrible disabilities face life with a smile and joy beyond comprehension. I also saw unhappy, angry and lonely people with riches and opportunities beyond imagination. As a teacher in my twenties, I saw kids destined for joyous lives while others faced difficult lives due to the nature of their personalities.

Interestingly, introverts and extroverts present different aspects on the happiness meter. Each may discover happiness by following his or her passions. Additionally, all of us fall into the nine personality traits of "Enneagram." Whichever aspect of your persona you inherited or you chose—life presents you with different challenges and possibilities depending on how you select your life path. By incorporating various writers and ideas, you give yourself a better chance at happiness. In other words, you may avoid stumbling forward into your life. You may walk or run toward your chosen destiny with confidence.

Furthermore, you will discover that people who love their work enjoy waking up each day to move toward their happiness because they enjoy their work. When they like their work, they love their lives. When they love their lives, they express higher vibrational frequencies, which in turn, attract other people living fulfilling lives. Such optimal vibrations engage the universe in a grand dance of joy, positive attitude and greater satisfaction. You may discover those frequencies in this book. By learning your highest and best, you may laugh with life, live it to the maximum and smile for a lifetime.

You will come away knowing that every new day allows you to choose to live a happy life by your thoughts, choices and actions. You maximize your outcome by your daily choices that nourish your body, mind and spirit. The degree of happiness in your life depends on these three entities working with each other, for each other and toward a greater state of joy and well being in your life.

In this book, you will find suggestions to various works by other authors to enhance your life as to work, play and spiritual connection. Why other authors? They may ring your bells better or inspire you beyond what you read in this book. As to work, how would you like to discover your best life-path at an earlier age or at any age? Wouldn't it be more fun to wake up each day to work at what you love? Or, close to it? Wouldn't it be better for your body, mind and spirit to pursue an activity best suited to your personality propensities and interests? Let's explore these ideas in the following chapters.

What constitutes a spectacular life?

Webster's Dictionary defines spectacular as: striking, sensational, remarkable, stunning and outstanding. He defines happiness as: a state of emotional health, good spirits, cheerfulness and a prospering life. Living with purpose. Enthusiasm. Living in an atmosphere of good fellowship. Accomplishing contentment within one's mind.

When you combine happiness with spectacular, you create an extraordinary life. Does that mean your every moment bursts with incredible high points? Of course not! It means you prepare, work and move toward those spectacular adventures in your life that present you with uncommon experiences that give your life eternal expectation.

Spectacular living along with happiness arrives in different flavors at various times in our lives. A child feels happiness by being held, suckling on a bottle or entertained by playing with a toy. A pre-teen chases excitement through his or her activities on the playground or with a group of friends. A high school student feels sensational moments through academic or athletic achievement. A college student enjoys happiness via the great rush of learning and participating in evolving events of university life.

A person in his or her twenties enjoys life by discovering his or her ability to work or play with others with a mutual goal. Persons in their twenties may find happiness in a meaningful relationship that leads to marriage and children. They may love dancing, sports and riding a bicycle. They may enjoy movies, plays and video games.

People in their thirties may find spectacular living via success on a job or in a relationship with a growing family. Persons in their forties may find happiness being proud of their children achieving excellence in school. People in their fifties may enjoy fulfillment through volunteer organizations or discovering a different career passion. Someone in their sixties may find ongoing happiness reading books, taking a class or discovering an art form such as sculpting, ceramics, painting, playing an instrument or ballroom dancing.

People in their seventies, eighties and nineties may find spectacular living by reading books, watching the Nature Channel or talking with friends.

Although, I knew Ms. Gudy Gaskill, 80, who hiked the 489 mile Colorado Trail every summer until she passed away at 81 years of age. Many eighty year olds roar through life with zest and passion.

At whatever age, a human being chooses sensational living through his or her actions that lead to a purposeful, enthusiastic and meaningful life. That may be their work, their families and/ or their play.

While average people may spend their days in dull jobs or weekends drinking and watching endless TV, they each possess a choice to change their existence toward productive, creative and spectacular lives at any point for any reason.

Highly creative people may participate in exceptionally imaginative and innovative lives. It's their inner fire that burns toward participating in life at their highest and best. Some enjoy an inner spectacular gene while others must work to maintain a certain joy for living.

In the end, life boils down to you.

Did Mozart, Beethoven and Bach live spectacular lives? If you listen to their extraordinary music, yes, they lived passionate lives creating music.

The key: you enjoy the option to live a spectacular life by choosing your thoughts and moving forward with your actions. When you do, you will create experiences that will drop your jaw and leave your eyes glazed over with wonder. Those spectacular moments will become the highlights of your life.

Your Happiness Factor

Depending on your upbringing or lack thereof, your definition of spectacular and happiness may be different from anyone else's in the world. Several things impacted your happiness factor during your youth: your parent's attitudes; whether you enjoyed one set of parents, no parents or blended families; whether you enjoyed smart parents or kind parents or not so smart parents; your personal growth initiatives or your amalgamation of pains. Thus, you may define happiness in any number of ways. In the end, your happiness factor augments your spectacular living factor.

You may recall the adage: "**If one does not know to which port one is sailing, no wind is favorable.**"

Thomas Jefferson, America's foremost writer in the creation of the Declaration of Independence stated that each person must be allowed to enjoy, "Life, liberty and the pursuit of happiness."

Obviously, that word happiness stands up there in the pantheon of human questing toward a meaningful life. It leads to the spectacular aspect of living.

"**Suddenly, you're ripped into being alive. And life is pain, and life is suffering, and life is horror, but my God, you're alive and it's spectacular.**" ~ Joseph Campbell

"**The happiest people in the world are those who feel absolutely terrific about themselves, and this is the natural outgrowth of accepting total responsibility for every part of their lives.**" ~ Brian Tracy

"**Life is spectacular. Forget the dark things. Take a drink and let time wash them away.**" ~ Tim Tharp

Do any of these definitions of spectacular living in conjunction with happiness resonate with you? If not, sit down with your pen in hand and write a sentence about what you think makes you happy or would make you happy if you possessed something or realized a dream or commanded a genie's power to wish for a fabulous life.

Once you define the port toward which you sail, and once you define the parameters that create your happiness, you may proceed toward living a spectacular life.

A Spectacular Moment: Will You Live or Will You Die During Your Spectacular Life?

The fear of death follows from the fear of life. A man who lives fully is prepared to die at any time. ~ *Mark Twain*

On my first bike trip to Alaska as a young adventure-seeker at 24, I woke up in my tent on the Russian River of the Kenai Peninsula hearing a "Grumph, grumph, emph" outside my tent. The Russian River enjoys fame not only for its salmon fishing, but also, its 1,000-pound grizzly bears. They visit the river to feed on millions of salmon racing for the spawning grounds.

I shot upright with a chill ripping down my spine. My brother Rex slept in his tent about 10 feet from mine. All night, I swatted no-see-ums, a tiny biting fly, but the bear posed greater danger. I opened my front flap to see an enormous grizzly looking right at me, not four feet away. As the breeze shifted, I smelled the worst case of halitosis in my life. He stunk worse than a barnyard.

He looked at me and I looked at him. My heart jumped out of my chest from beating so fast. My mouth dried up like a cotton ball in the desert. Strangest feeling of my short life! That bear could kill me in minutes. I wouldn't stand a chance.

Within 15 seconds, he ambled around the side of my tent. As he passed by the sidewalls, he rubbed his muzzle and drooled across the bright orange nylon. The sun shone through the tent to accent the drool-line about three feet long. Seconds later, he grunted some more and started digging at the corner of my tent. I looked back to see his claws rip through the nylon and hit the blue plastic flooring.

My eyes grew wide as I stared at the four-inch claws cutting through my tent. Seconds later, he withdrew them. He walked around my tent to walk right back in front of me. A moment later, he turned toward the Russian River to grab a mouthful of fresh salmon.

My brother Rex said, "Are we gonna' live or die? What's the verdict, bro?"

"Could go either way if he doesn't catch any fish," I said. "I think I just stared death in the face."

Like everything in life, random chance may kill you, let you live or hurt you—depending on the circumstances. That morning, which remains vividly with me to this day, could have turned out ugly. We could have been written up in the Anchorage morning newspaper: "Two cyclists were mauled to death while sleeping near the Russian River yesterday. The bear grabbed one brother and then the other. He gobbled them like a can of sardines. Other campers heard the screams, but nothing could stop the bear from his morning breakfast feast. Services will be held...."

But instead, it wasn't our day to die.

Since my early 20s, through my adventures on six continents—hurricanes, tsunamis, 7.3 earthquakes, 350-pound charging seals in the Galapagos Islands, scuba diving with sharks, mountain climbing, bicycle riding with cars coming up my rear at 70 miles per hour as their drivers text message, Australian bush fires, rip-tides, monkeys raining their feces down on me in the Amazon, moose and grizzly bears—so far, they haven't killed me.

But any of them could have killed me.

Should anyone be afraid of dying on an adventure?

Not on your life! Act like a winner. Accept danger. Agree to the unknown and life on its own terms. Go for it. Never worry about living or dying. Keep moving ahead. Think positive to bring all good to you.

"Let children walk with nature, let them see the beautiful blendings and communions of life and death, their joyous inseparable unity, as taught in woods and meadows, plains and mountains, and streams of our blessed star, and they will learn that death is stingless indeed, and as beautiful as life." John Muir

On a sobering daily note, you read about someone dying in a traffic accident coming home from the big game. You hear of a kid succumbing to cancer. A buddy fell off a ladder. An average of 900 Americans annually die from falling off their bicycles because they didn't wear a helmet. They cracked their skulls. Some live a short time and others make it a long life. It doesn't make any difference if you're rich, poor, smart, stupid, famous or average. I could name hundreds of famous people who died in their 20s, 30s, 40s, 50s or before their time. You may know some dull people living into their 90s. There is no rhyme or reason to any of it. Life happens.

I personally knew a couple that retired after 40 years at the factory. They bought a motor home to travel to Alaska and around the USA to visit 49 state capitals. The morning before their departure date, the husband walked down to the breakfast table. He grabbed the paper. His wife prepared pancakes on the stove. Suddenly, she heard a thud on the table. She looked around to see her husband slumped over—dead. Life and death happen without cause, warning or understanding.

As the saying goes, "Eat dessert first; life is uncertain."

On a logical note, you can avoid being one of the millions of humans who died but never lived to his or her fullest capabilities. You can avoid staring into a television most of your life. One researcher reported Americans watch television for a total of 15 years of their lives. Millions of Americans suffer a mid-life crisis because they failed to live their dreams or they never discovered their life purpose.

Get your butt out there into the wind, onto the road, up that mountain, down that river, through the deep powder, under the stars and sit by that campfire. Live until you die and if you die while you're living a spectacular life, your spirit will smile all the way through eternity.

Section I

Body, Mind and Spirit

Chapter 1

Maintaining Your Body

The most beautiful people we have known are those who have known defeat, known suffering, known struggle, known loss, and have found their way out of the depths. These persons have an appreciation, sensitivity and an understanding of life that fills them with compassion, gentleness, and a deep loving concern. Beautiful people do not just happen. *~ Elizabeth Kubler-Ross*

On your birthday, you entered the world with a perfect body. If you didn't, ensuing chapters deal with disabled living. Your vision, hearing, touch, taste and smell allowed you to interact with the world in wondrous ways. Soon, you discovered your voice by crying when hungry or distressed.

While growing up, your parents fed you healthy foods if they understood the ramifications of proper nutrition. They taught you to speak well, dress well and think positively. They taught you to shower, and brush and floss your teeth. If you enjoyed excellent parents to engrain in you healthy habits for maximum bodily function, you may count your lucky stars.

If you grew up with uneducated parents or incompatible parents or angry parents or fighting parents, you suffered under various challenges such as endless tension, television and junk foods like pizza loaded with everything but a vegetable. You swilled soda pop and other sweet drinks that tricked your intestinal system with synthetic sugars, artificial flavorings and an endless line of additives.

Today, in America, 67 percent of Americans suffer portliness of 20 to 50 pounds of excess weight and 35 percent

3

suffer gross obesity. One look at the "Biggest Loser" TV show illustrates the greatest healthcare crisis in America. Some 150 million Americans or more look like those people struggling on the TV show.

Obesity increased dramatically in conjunction to fast food franchises beginning in the 1960s. Corpulence reaches into China where McDonald's operates today as well as Rio de Janeiro, Tokyo, Canada and much of Europe. This obesity pandemic stems from high-speed work and lifestyles that promote 'instant eating' on the run or while driving a car. Those same food chains introduce chemicals like Monosodium Glutamate, an excito-toxin that causes endless hunger sensations. Instead of one hamburger, the customer feels the urge for a second with more fries. Such an artificial inducement overwhelms our biological capacity to maintain a healthy weight.

Concurrently, our modern environment discourages physical activity at work, at home and in the community. American men watch 4.5 hours of TV nightly seven days a week. This habit promotes sedentary pursuits over active living. If you look at this phenomenon closely, sedentary living dominates American life along with poor eating practices.

The consequences show up with heart disease, high blood pressure, diabetes, aching joints, cancer and a dozen other maladies. Americans choose synthetic chemicals prescribed by their trusted doctors to solve their problems. Doctors diagnose the problem, prescribe symptom stomping drugs and operate when all else fails.

With two-thirds of the American public terribly overweight, it may seem normal. Obesity stems from childhood traumas via poor parents, poor food choices, lowered self-esteem, poor self-concept and junk food paradigms ingrained in all American youth via the television.

If you find yourself in the death-grip of obesity at whatever level, take a look at yourself in the mirror. Happy with what you see? Not happy? Who can you blame?

While reading this book, you may choose to come to terms with taking care of your body as the first order of happiness. A person who loves to look at his or her body in the mirror because he or she maintains it, lives a happy life when stepping out of the shower, daily. Looking like a god or goddess isn't the point. You desire to maintain a lean, fit and functioning body.

No matter how your parents raised or didn't raise you, today, you may choose fitness, health and wellness by your own hand. You may choose a basket of excuses for devouring junk food like pizza and cheeseburgers along with soda pop. You may avoid exercising, but in the end, it comes down to your daily choices. You may find help via organizations that show you how to eat correctly, how to exercise and how to retrain your mind toward healthy living.

In the end, it's up to you. Excuses won't cut it. Blaming your parents, your past or the pizza maker won't solve it. Giving up only causes more misery.

You may find a support group for proper eating. If you can afford one, hire a personal trainer at the local recreation center. If you enjoy average wages, hang out with people who visit the gym five and six days a week. They exercise and eat healthy foods. Their energy expands into your energy field. Join a weight loss system.

If you utilize food for comfort of your sorrows, traumas and low self-esteem, seek counseling to discover the source of your emotional duress.

Weight loss:

www.JennyCraig.com

www.WeightWatchers.com

www.Sensa.org

www.LifeVantage.com

Personal trainer:

Every recreation center and gym in America features certified personal trainers. Find one, work with him or her, and learn how to love athletic endeavors that fit your style.

Personal Trainer Certification - American Council on Exercise

www.acefitness.org/fitness-certifications/personal-trainer-certification/

Outdoor activities:

Try www.Meetup.com You may join "meet-ups" across the country that feature men and women who love outdoor activities such as bicycling, hiking, swimming, rowing, climbing, backpacking and just about every activity to engage your body toward peak fitness, trimness and overall health.

When you hang with those who cherish healthy eating and fitness, it rubs off on you. It pulls you along into living a dynamic lifestyle.

While you must accept the face and body-type giv
you at birth, you enjoy the total choice to maintain your body at
its highest and best. Oh, and by the way, if you're not handsome
or beautiful, join 90 percent of the human race. Most of us look
average. So what! Make the most of your life with total acceptance
of your looks and get your butt out there with an engaging
personality, ability to dance or play a musical instrument. In the
end, your personality delights people more than your looks. Your
heart maintains friendships long after the beauties of youth subside.

One added note: you may face disabilities from birth. You
may face any number of accidents during your life that change
your health picture: loss of a limb, loss of sight and loss of hearing.
If you read some of the stories about people with no arms, no
legs, sightless and a variety of horrific challenges—you find that
they never gave up in their quest to live a spectacular life. One
man I met in 1984 while bicycling across the United States, Bob
Wieland, walked across the entire country coast-to-coast on his
hands. Why? He lost his legs in the Vietnam War. Did it stop him?
No! In fact, years later, he hand-cycled across the USA coast-to-
coast three times. He completed the Ironman Triathlon in Kona,
Hawaii. He holds the world record in the bench press in his weight
class. You may read about handless artists that paint with their feet
or mouths. You may follow the totally blind man who backpacked
the Appalachia and Colorado Trails by himself. Whatever you
choose, a spectacular life awaits you.

The Buddha said, **"Every human being is the author of
his or her own health or disease."**

Powerful books to move you toward your success:

The Slight Edge by Jeff Olson
The Compound Effect by Darren Hardy
**Success for Teens: Real Teens Talk About Using The Slight
Edge** by John Flemming
Body, Mind Mastery by Dan Millman

Bird Tracker on Bicycle: Dorian Anderson

"Have you ever observed a hummingbird moving about in an aerial dance among the flowers? It's a living prismatic gem. It is a creature of fairy-like loveliness as to mock all description!"
~ W.H. Hudson, Green Mansions

Individual passions glide on America's highways in different forms. Some folks pursue their quests of visiting all our National Parks within a summer. Others carry kayaks to challenge rivers from Maine to Oregon. Still others climb mountains in pursuit of their Holy Grail. Fly-fishermen-women pursue that speckled trout in high mountain streams. Somewhere out there on the roads that crisscross the planet, an adventure-seeker pursues his or her individual dream with an exceptional sense of determination.

When you meet them, they look normal, they seem normal and they may act normal. That's where normal ends! Those "outliers" carry a nonstandard, burning passion within them that surpasses normal imagination.

One such individual graced our door in Golden, Colorado. Talk about high energy! New York City could harness his high-voltage life to their power grid to run it for a full year.

Dorian Anderson, lean, black-haired, with brilliant smile and replete with a vigorous personality, set out on January 1, 2014 on a cold, snowy day in Boston, Massachusetts to bicycle 18,000 miles around America in search of every bird species in the lower 48 states. He called his quest "The Big Year" which allows him to seek out and photograph as many of the more than 700 species of birds thriving in America.

After Stanford, he attended New York University where he completed a Ph.D. in Developmental Genetics. He studied how cells in the early embryo polarize and how this polarization event functions to control subsequent morphogenetic movements during gestation. Ironically, it was in the most urban of environments that his birding interest became obsessive.

After NYU, he accepted a post-doctoral position at Massachusetts General Hospital and Harvard Medical School in Boston to investigate the molecular mechanisms that control neural plasticity.

He offers brilliant bird photographs from his bicycle pursuit of our fine-feathered friends. His daily updates relive his adventures in bird watching.

Since we are members of www.warmshowers.org, Dorian picked us out as hosts after he climbed Guanella Pass and summited 14,100-foot Mt. Bierstadt on the Continental Divide. At that altitude, he captured a ptarmigan at 13,500 feet. At 8,000 miles into the journey, he registered that bird as number 488 on his list.

He rolled into our house in the evening for a hot shower, conversation and bed.

Next morning, we bicycled five miles up to the top of Genesee Park, near our house, to seek out a specific dead tree that housed a family of Williamson Sapsuckers. We heard the hungry brood calling out to their parents for more food. Within minutes, a beautiful male appeared carrying grubs in his beak. He sported black back feathers, yellow/white underbelly and red tuft on his neck. His leg feathers looked like an Indy 500 finishing flag.

Anderson pulled out his 200 mm camera lens for the perfect shot. Later, the mother sapsucker appeared with another beak-full of grubs. Andersons registered a Williamson's Sapsucker at number 489.

As I sat there with this bird-watching enthusiast, I felt his reverence for the natural world. He spoke about preserving birds, butterflies and all living creatures.

Anderson said, "I read about folks who spend hundreds of thousands of dollars to fly to places where a particular bird has been spotted. One fellow flew 200,000 miles during his "Big Year" to gather as many sightings as possible. I would like to see bird-watchers and all Americans avoid expelling so much carbon exhaust into the biosphere. That's why I came up with the idea of bicycling around America to find all these bird species and not pollute the planet."

Why take such an enormous trip?

"During a 'Big Year', a birdwatcher attempts to see or hear as many bird species as he or she can in North America in one calendar year," said Anderson. "This endeavor begins on January 1st and, depending on the level of commitment, can require the birder to visit all corners of the continent during the subsequent 364 days. The most ambitious Big Years typically record between 700 and 745 species of birds while logging well in excess of 100,000 miles of plane, car, and boat travel.

"Biking for Birds is my completely crazy and hopefully fantastic twist on the traditional North American Big Year. During 2014, I will travel only by bike, foot, and kayak as I move about the continent in search of birds. My movements will be unaided by petroleum, natural gas and electricity. I will not have a support vehicle; everything I need will be carried on my person and my bicycle. This Big Year permutation will certainly add an unprecedented level of adventure to the endeavor, and it should set a new standard for environmentally sustainable travel.

"The immediate goals of this endeavor are three-fold. First, I want to find as many bird species as possible. If I can complete the proposed route, I should find between 550 and 600 species. I hope my efforts to achieve this goal will promote heightened interest in birds, bird watching, and bird conservation. Second, I hope "Biking For Birds" will showcase the bicycle as a healthy and environmentally sustainable form of transportation. Third, I have partnered with both The Conservation Fund and the American Birding Association. I hope to raise $100,000 (or more!) on behalf of these organizations that focus on land conservation and promotion of bird-watching."

After spotting and photographing the sapsucker, I felt an enormous sense of adventure with Dorian Anderson. He elevated my appreciation for our fine-feathered co-travelers on planet Earth.

When you visit his site, you may enjoy lively adventure chatter, brilliant bird photography and a place to send your donations to The Conservation Fund and American Birding Association.

Later in the day, we visited Buffalo Bill's Grave. Soon after, we traveled on our loaded touring bikes down the fabled "Lariat Loop" on Lookout Mountain into Golden, Colorado. After lunch at a sandwich shop, Dorian headed north on Route 93 toward Boulder.

He waved, "Live well my friend."

"May the birds be with you," I said. "Thanks for the memories."

Dorian Anderson completed his bicycle-bird quest in extraordinary physical shape on December 31, 2014. He photographed over 600 bird species.

Visit his website: bikingforbirds.blogspot.com

Email: bikingforbirds@gmail.com

Harriet Anderson: 78 Year Old Ironman Champion

In 2013, Harriet Anderson raced the Ironman Triathlon in Kona, Hawaii. No big deal if you're 25, full of muscle, pep and vinegar!

You can power through the 2.4-mile swim in ocean water. You can jump on your 27-speed carbon bicycle to ram through 112 miles of hot, dry pavement. Finally, you slip into a pair of shorts for a 26.2-mile marathon. Thousands begin the race and many fail to make the finish.

But if you're 78 years of age, the game changes dramatically. You must deal with aching muscles thin with age. You must maintain training that exhausts 25 year olds. You must deal with the pounding of your hip joints and knees already "rusting" with age.

Not Anderson! She completed 21 Ironman Triathlons since the age of 53. She wins her age division each time. In 2013, no one else could match her "Wonder Woman" power to cross the finish line—first in her age group.

You may ask the question, "Why would a 78 old woman want to race in one of the world's most grueling competitions with people one-quarter her age?"

That may be THE question for the ages.

In October 2009, at age 74, she finished in 11 hours and 53 minutes. That's just seven minutes before the cutoff. How did that happen? During the bicycle portion of the race, another cyclist bumped her off her bike causing her to break her collarbone. She taped it up and pedaled the last 32 miles of the bike portion before placing her arm in a sling and walking the entire marathon to finish the race under the limit.

Anderson said, "I guess I was just born with the endurance gene."

Speeding into her 50s, Anderson tried Master's Swimming and excelled. She raced 10 K's. She cycled in local races. In 1989, she signed up for a half-Ironman. Voila! She won her age group. Her win qualified her for the Kona Ironman in October.

She rose early each morning for a bicycle spin of 30, 40 and 50 miles. She swam endless pool laps. She ran, ran and ran some more. She maintained a sense of balance so as not to injure herself.

She eats like a vacuum cleaner on high speed. She devours cereals, fruits and lean protein. She loves Cliff Bars.

"I'm really kind of amazed, because I wasn't an athlete growing up at all," Anderson said. "So I would never have thought that I would still be doing something like this. So each year I keep thinking, 'Oh my God, I'm still doing this?'"

Eleven times, she claimed first place in her age division. Lately, few race in the over-75 age group.

"For the last few years I've been the only one in my age group," she said. "So the only thing I have to do is just finish."

At 5'6", 120 pounds, a former registered nurse who enjoys marriage to the same guy for 50 years, she remains lithe and agile. She's easy going with a ready smile. One of the things I noticed in her video interviews: completely happy with her life.

One item blows me away about her: I run short-course triathlons and have run three half-Ironman's. It takes guts, gumption and true grit. The training nearly kills men half her age. In the case of Harriet Anderson, I couldn't hold a candlestick to her physical accomplishments. Running an Ironman breaks most men down to physical misery and exhaustion. To do what she does at age 53 all the way to 78 defies my imagination. If you are a man or woman, look her story up on the Internet. She will motivate you, cause a sense of awe in you and bring out the best in your body, mind and spirit.

A full Ironman triathlon is not about finding your limits; it's about finding out what lies beyond them. For Harriet Anderson, she lives with no limits.

Robert Sweetgall: Forrest Gump's mentor

Robert Sweetgall once carried the nickname "butterball" because of his rotund stature. While facing middle age with high blood pressure and a history of heart disease, Sweetgall set out to change his life for the better.

Today, Sweetgall stands in the **Guinness Book of World Records** as the only man to walk all 50 states, 11, 208 miles, in 365 days. That's an average of 31 miles per day. With such credentials, he's known as the "Real Forrest Gump" from Tom Hanks' movie of the same name.

In 1982-1983, he marched 10,600 miles around the perimeter of the U.S. His grandest journey began on Sept. 7, 1984 through September 7, 1985 to cover 11,600 miles and touch all 50 states.

"Robert is compressing a lifetime of walking into a year," said Dr. Rippe, his doctor back in his hometown in Massachusetts. "So far, he's tested clean, and he's in great all-around shape. He's an unusual athlete, but we've found that even he can get his heart rate up to training range from walking in a relatively short time. For the average person, 45 minutes of determined walking three or four times a week will provide all the exercise his heart needs without the sweat or injury hazard of running."

When not out walking around the planet, Sweetgall walks 30 miles per day to keep in shape. At five miles per hour, that's six hours a day. While most would count that mileage as excessive, Sweetgall notes that the average American male watches 4.5 hours of TV every day of the week.

Before he quit his job as an engineer with DuPont Corporation, he lived a sedate life with bowling as his only sport. Ironically, within a short timespan, his father and several friends died of heart attacks. He took up jogging and then, running and finally ran a marathon. That led to ultra-marathons and triathlons.

Sweetgall decided to undertake his 'around the USA' trek in 1982-1983.

During his trek, he braved freezing temperatures in Washington State, 60 mile per hour headwinds in North Dakota and snow in Colorado. After his treks, he speaks to high schools, civic clubs and colleges.

"Kids make the best audiences," he says. "A trip like mine tickles them, and they love the idea of walking as an achievement."

Older people like his message. "I met a man in 1984 in Toledo," said Sweetgall. "He shook the hand of Edward Payson Weston, the greatest American walker ever."

As history would have it, the young Weston walked from Boston to Washington DC to shake hands with Abraham Lincoln at his 1861 inaugural. Weston continued hiking his entire life.

Today, at 68, Sweetgall has logged over 70,000 miles. He's written 17 books on fitness and walking. He loves skiing, snowshoeing, swimming and jogging. You may contact him at www.CreativeWalking.com

Chapter 2

Uplifting Your Intellect

The crowning fortune of a man is to be born to some pursuit, which finds him employment and happiness, whether it is to make baskets, or broadswords, or canals, or statues, or songs. *~ Ralph Waldo Emerson*

By engaging your intellect through reading books, taking classroom or online courses and/or learning a language, musical instrument or playing chess—you uplift your mind to its highest and best.

As you can see by the position of the first three chapters, much like a three-legged stool, you maintain equilibrium and vitality by taking care of your body, mind and spirit. Each aspect of your total health depends on these three entities working with each other, for each other and toward each other.

To create your highest and best intellectual excellence, study diligently in high school to maximize your intellectual abilities. From there, vocational school or college promotes you to your best positioning for jobs that fit you. Your education provides you with skills, talents and abilities to succeed in this society. If you fail to try your hardest during your education, you set your feet and life in cement in the coming years. You guarantee your life at the bottom rung of the economic ladder. It's not fun. Try to maximize your intellect throughout your life for maximum positive results along your life path.

History records dozens of men and women who destroyed their lives by omitting a balance with their bodies, minds and spirits.

For example: the late comedian Robin Williams commanded millions of adoring fans, mega-dollars in his bank account, loving wife and kids and endless movie contracts. However, he drank profusely throughout his life. He snorted cocaine, smoked dope and tried many other drugs to alter his mental and emotional circuits. He enjoyed extreme "highs" that only drug-intoxicated moments could provide. During those years, he re-wired his brain in ways that we cannot imagine. He suffered accelerating depression. Essentially, he lost the balance in his mind. Ultimately, he killed himself August 11, 2014.

Lindsey Lohan, another rising female actress—addicted herself to alcohol and drugs, so much so, she sat in prison for periods of time. From there, she attended drug rehabilitation clinics. Consequently, she lost acting parts. She lost friends because healthy people flee from individuals on self-destructive paths. She lost her freedom, her money and, for the most part, her mind. No telling what her ending might become from rearranging her brain with drugs instead of balancing her intellect with educational opportunities.

One of my favorite singers, Elvis Presley became world famous, rich beyond measure, married a beautiful woman, fathered a child and commanded millions of adoring fans. Unfortunately, he didn't take care of his body, mind and spirit. He became drug addicted and enormously obese. At 43, Presley died of a heart attack.

You may look around you with endless examples of your father, mother, grandfather, grandmother, uncle, aunts and friends dying from ill health, lack of purpose, alcohol or smoking. Every family suffers a story of members who deteriorated from their poor choices.

What if they all engaged their minds in the pursuit of knowledge instead of the next drug or alcoholic high? What if they read books or attended movies or Shakespearean plays to enhance their minds?

As stated, American men watch 29 hours of television weekly. That equates to 4.5 hours a day, seven days a week. Women average 24 hours of television a week, or 3.4 hours daily.

Can you think of any greater waste of time, mind and intelligence than watching that many hours of TV week-in and week-out? Watching TV deadens your mind, softens your body and annihilates your spiritual balance. Television watching separates you from living.

If you ask anyone who watched all those programs for a week what they remember from any of them, it's a good bet they couldn't tell you a single meaningful aspect of any of the blur of junk being played out on American television weekly. Television gears everyone to buy something, but to learn little.

As an aside, yes, television offers "The Nature Channel" and other positive programming. You decide. Choose wisely and intelligently to add to your intellect.

In the meantime, if you read a book, attend a class or create a painting, sculpture or write a manuscript, those activities enhance your mind, expand your intelligence and carry you toward your most creative possibilities.

Your choice! A lifetime of stupid, inane and meaningless television/and or video games that dull your mind and kill your intellect—or, a life filled with your creative mind expanding and growing to your highest and best!

Powerful books to enhance your mind:

No Ordinary Moments by Dan Millman
The Four Purposes of Life by Dan Millman
Everyday Enlightenment: The Twelve Gateways to Personal Growth by Dan Millman

Move Your Mind Toward Learning to Create a Healthy and Vital Life

Life Is Too Short: Get Off Your Cell Phone

During my youth, my dad took me fishing. My mom took me on bicycle rides. My dad shouldered me with a small daypack for hikes in the woods. He pointed out chattering squirrels. He helped me see my first deer. He pointed out a fox on a ridge. He guided me into Glacier National Park to see my first grizzly bear. Later, he taught me how to paddle a canoe. My mother showed me how to press flowers. My dad taught me how to play baseball.

The first time my parents took me for a hike into Yosemite National Park, my eyes bugged out at the stupendous Half Dome along with Yosemite Falls and Mirror Lake. Years later, my parents offered the Grand Canyon, Yellowstone and Arches National Parks. During the moments we shared at Niagara Falls; words could not express my wonder at the natural world. Everything I saw, I soaked into my being. Every moment I experienced the natural world taught me lessons that inspire me today.

In high school, I engaged in sports and seven service clubs plus a seven-day-a-week paper route. I worked my way through college. I played numerous sports that enriched my life, body and spirit.

My dad said, "Study hard and study often to grow your intellect. After all the sports, all the girls and all the parties, your intellectual prowess will be your greatest asset in American society."

That single point drove me to study seven days a week in high school. It drove me to write an English paper on Friday night instead of waiting until the last second on Sunday night. His wisdom caused me to study weekends in order to be prepared for tests and pop quizzes.

One of the greatest pieces of advice he gave me: "Read books from every realm to give you a broad foundation of understanding."

His wisdom plays in my mind to this day. I nourish my mind along with my body and spirit.

Like my dad treated me, I took my boys mountain climbing, river rafting, bicycle touring, fishing and a host of outdoor activities. Nothing beats a night under the stars with a blazing campfire! It must be the closest thing to heaven.

As the years add up, I am astounded at how fast life races along. With each birthday, I cherish every adventure afforded me during my time on this planet.

But what I see today exasperates me. I see mothers tapping on their smart phones while their kids swim, play in a sandbox or do their homework. No attention to their kids! Teens tap out 3,300 text messages a month according to a National Public Radio report. That's over 100 per day! I see hikers in the woods with their ears plugged into I-Pods, which silence the sounds of birds, bees, coyotes, whitewater streams and weather.

When my wife and I go dancing at the Stampede in Denver, I see 50 women with white lights glowing up into their faces as they sit around the dance floor. Clear message: "Don't bother me. I'm not here to dance. I'm addicted to my cell phone."

While on bicycle rides, I see people talking on their smart phones while pedaling, when they stop for snacks and even in bathrooms. I see kids at school at lunch totally absorbed in their cell phones instead of talking with classmates.

During the snowy months, I ski weekly at Winter Park Resort, Colorado. I see guys and gals talking on their cell phones riding up the lift, while eating lunch, and as soon as they reach the parking lot at the end of the day.

Why aren't they listening to and enjoying the sights and sounds of Mother Nature, the falling snowflakes and the winter wonders before them—instead of gluing their ears and lips to a cell phone while they talk to someone who must be as disconnected as themselves?

My take: cell phones may prove to be the loneliest form of unemotional, unattached and inhuman communication on the planet. Cell phones negate human contact, interconnection and fellowship. They destroy any sense of joy, sorrow, happiness or ability to make human contact. Cell phones turn their users into a droid much like R2D2.

Just for the record: your time on this planet consists of 80 years at the most in America. You enjoy 15 to 40 as your youthful years with your friends and kids. Your 40s to 60s become the years when your youth slips past and your old age harkens. From 60 to 80, you're ready to exit the planet. Those decades rip past faster than Warp 9 on the Starship Enterprise. How do I know? I've seen more rock stars die in the past several years from my era of the 60's than I care to relate.

Who can you be with today and tell them what they mean to you? Who else can you schedule to see, versus call or text? Reach inside yourself and realize who matters to you and show it, personally.

What book can you read or class can you take to enhance your mind? Alas, get off your cell phone! Get into life! Become friends with another human being and communicate with them eye to eye, emotions to emotions and feelings to feelings.

When you go for a hike, listen for the distant woodpecker or squirrel chattering in a tree. Watch hummingbirds suck nectar from a flower. Gaze at the clouds and listen to the chirping of the crickets. Listen to the trees. Hear the magic.

When riding a bicycle, enjoy the living world at your fingertips. Inhale the scents of summer, the flowers in the field and the birds flying along with you. Watch the horses in adjacent fields prance with you. Gallop your own iron steed into the wind to feel your life on fire.

In the end, live your life to its fullest without a cell phone. Yes, use it for emergencies, but refrain from addiction to a cold, cruel piece of technology. Create and cherish friends, family and colleagues on a personal level of your humanity. As you grow older, you will cherish your conversations with friends much more than your smart phone's emptiness.

Chapter 3

Feeding Your Spirit

Camp out among the grass and gentians of glacier meadows, in craggy garden nooks full of Nature's darlings. Climb the mountains and get their good tidings. Nature's peace will flow into you as sunshine flows into trees. The winds will blow their own freshness into you, and the storms their energy, while cares will drop off like autumn leaves. ~ *John Muir*

Today in America, you face a high-speed, technological society like nothing in human history. You may live in a large city replete with endless concrete, steel and glass. You face horrific traffic, noise and overcrowding. Such amenities cut you off from Mother Nature. Such cities cut you away from touching the earth, swimming in a lake or walking through a forest.

How do you feed your spiritual life when everyone lives on a smart phone, Facebook and Twitter? How do you feed your spirit with a job that pushes you, torments you and/or you endure or abhor?

Does attending church fulfill your spiritual needs in this Warp 9 speed society? Can you keep your spiritual balance when you want to knock your boss' block off or smack a co-worker for being distorted or nasty?

Ralph Waldo Emerson said, "Man is conscious of a universal soul within or behind his individual life, wherein, as in a firmament, the natures of justice, truth, love and freedom—arise and shine. This universal soul, he calls Reason: it is not mine, or yours, or his, but we are its; we are its property and men. And the blue sky in which the private earth is buried, the sky with its eternal calm, and full of everlasting orbs, is the type of Reason. That which, intellectually considered, we call Reason, considered in relation to nature, we call Spirit. Spirit is the Creator. Spirit hath life in itself. And man in all ages and countries, embodies it in his language."

Emerson's writing attempted to describe spirit one hundred years ago. Today, we know more about spirit and religion. We know ancient religions fail to apply to this modern world. Myths and magic cannot stand up to the test of reality.

Thus, you may be confused on different levels. You may be asking tons of questions that cannot be answered to your satisfaction.

Generally, you may look toward religion to show the way of spirit. Many people define religion as the way to everlasting understanding of humanity's purpose on this planet.

Many say religion explains unknown intellectual mysteries. Not really! Religion explains strong and abstract emotional feelings. It may be used to oppress people. It connects societies. It explains suffering. It's been called the opiate of the masses. Today, our new opiates—television, smart phones and video games.

Ancient religions based everything on conjecture, myth and some spiritual god or messiah to lead ethnic groups out of their misery.

If you find that a particular religion works for you and your spiritual path, then, by all means, follow it. However, if not, I discovered some pretty neat ideas as to spiritual philosophy in my travels through multiple cultures. You might like the following definition of religion or not. You might like some new ideas by 21st century spiritual leaders. You might find more evolved spiritual paths mesh with yours. It's called "New Thought" philosophy. It compiles all the ancient truths into a digestible spiritual paradigm for the 21st century, while deleting the myths.

Dr. Ernest Holmes wrote: **Science of Mind and Spirit**. He uplifts spiritual orientation to a new concept of God as a spirit that expresses through all living and non-living matter in the universe. www.MileHiChurch.org

Eckhart Tolle wrote: **The Deepest Truth of Human Existence.** You might like this man's understanding of spirit. He nails it. www.Eckharttolle.com

Dr. Roger Teel wrote: **This Life Is Joy.** Dr. Teel leads this nation in "new thought" spiritual understandings. Watch his weekly sermon via streaming your computer. I can tell you this; he will shake your rafters and inspire you beyond any preacher in the land. www.MileHiChurch.org

Thomas Troward wrote: **The Creative Process in the Individual.** This spiritual thinker will knock your socks off with his command for living a spiritually uplifted life. www.DivineWaves.com

Spiritual Balance

You may or may not appreciate any of the writers suggested herein for discovering spiritual balance. Therefore, conceive your own. Write your own thesis. You possess every quality and intellectual talent to define your spiritual path.

Henry David Thoreau presented a gracious understand of maintaining spiritual balance in his epic Walden essays:

"We need the tonic of the wildness—to wade sometimes in marshes where the bittern and the meadow-hen lurk, and hear the booming of the snipe; to smell the whispering sedge where only some wilder and more solitary fowl builds her nest, and the mink crawls with its belly close to the ground.

"At the same time that we are earnest to explore and learn all things, we require that all things be mysterious and unexplorable, that land and sea be infinitely wild, unsurveyed and unfathomed by us because of unfathomable.

"We need to witness our own limits transgressed, and some life posturing freely where we never wander."

You might incorporate into your daily life an activity called: grounding. Take a walk into the woods or into a park or your own back yard. Take off your shoes and socks. Stick your feet into the soil or grass for 20 to 30 minutes. The vibrational frequencies of the planet run up through your feet to re-harmonize your own vibrations and frequencies with the planet. You might consider it equal to tuning a guitar or truing a bicycle wheel or flying with a chevron of geese. You come back into vibrational harmony with yourself and the planet.

Finally, the health and wellness of your body, mind and spirit depend on you. Discover that balance throughout your life by turning to the wilds and a campfire by a lake. Once you find your own equilibrium, maintain it, stick with it and enjoy it.

Spiritual books that may inspire you:

This Life Is Joy by Roger Teel
Frequency: The Power of Personal Vibrations by Penny Peirce

Section II

Jobs, Relationships, Friendships

Chapter 4

Finding Work That Fits Your Style

Your work is going to fill a large part of your life, and the only way to be truly satisfied is to do what you believe is great work. And the only way to do great work is to love what you do. If you haven't found it yet, keep looking. Don't settle. As with all matters of the heart, you'll know when you find it. And, like any great relationship, it just gets better and better as the years roll on. So keep looking until you find it. Don't settle. ~ *Steve Jobs, CEO of Apple*

While balancing your body, mind and spirit in this grand trek through life, work becomes your defining daily purpose. It consumes most of your days. It leads you to many satisfying friendships or stimulating rivalries. Work commands your attention to detail or immerses you in boredom. It brings you joy or frustration.

As Steve Jobs noted in the above quote, "Keep looking until you find the right job for you."

Ironically, my son Dan, one of the three CEOs of a computer start-up in Denver, Colorado, spent 80 hours a week developing the computer software as the CTO. After five years, he daily faced a fellow owner of the company who caused Dan a great deal of grief. While my son enjoyed tremendous financial gain, a beautiful house and fabulous girlfriend, he couldn't tolerate his fellow CEO who became a walking megalomaniac. The guy ruined Dan's daily experiences at the office.

At his 32nd birthday dinner, he spoke of his experiences with work and why he resigned.

"Quit when you're bored with the job or it causes you too much grief," said Dan.

Dan chose personal growth and the ability to strike out on his own. Today, as the CEO of his own company, he hires people that work on his positive vibrational level. He loves his work, play and travel. He plays in his own band. He writes and arranges music. He created his own recording studio.

What about you? Staying in a job that bores you or with a boss who sucks? How long do you expect to endure such conditions?

No matter how much money you command, no matter how much status you enjoy, no matter how big your house or how handsome your automobile—it's not worth it to work in a job that brings you daily angst. Millions work for money with no understanding of their long-term consequences.

Notice Americans suffer 1.4 million heart attacks annually. Notice the 67 percent obesity levels. Over 29 million suffer from diabetes and 80 million suffer from pre-diabetes. Notice 50 percent divorce rates. Obviously a whole lot of people suffer from unhappiness.

To follow that thought up, I open my soul to you. After I finished my undergraduate degree at Michigan State University and my second degree program at Grand Valley State University, which included a teaching certificate, I rode my motorcycle out to Colorado to secure a teaching job in math-science. While I loved climbing the mountains, tons of skiing and bicycling—I found myself poverty-stricken at $5,400.00 a year in teaching salary back in the 1970s. Additionally, teaching drained me emotionally, physically and spiritually. Students sucked me dry daily. After five years, I chose another path.

What to do? I moved to a run down, cheap farmhouse in Michigan to pursue what I truly loved: writing. For two years, I lived in that 100-year-old farmhouse. I wrote eight books that never published. I sat by a campfire near my pond under a starlit sky many summer nights. In autumn, I watched colorful leaves flutter to the ground. I cross-country skied in the winter. I listened to no radio or television, but I read two to three books a week from the local library. I carried my own firewood to heat the house. I exercised daily and lived simply.

I discovered what Henry David Thoreau revealed when he wrote his book: **Walden.**

"I went to the woods because I wished to live deliberately, to front only the essential facts of life, and see if I could not learn what it had to teach, and not, when I came to die, discover that I had not lived. I did not wish to live what was not life, living is so dear; nor did I wish to practice resignation, unless it was quite necessary. I wanted to live deep and suck out all the marrow of life, to live so sturdily and Spartan-like as to put to rout all that was not life, to cut a broad swath and shave close, to drive life into a corner, and reduce it to its lowest terms."

While you may or may not be able to return to the woods or a farmhouse, you may choose to re-examine your life at some point. You may choose to question your work as to whether or not it sustains you.

When I ran out of money at the farm, my brother offered to teach me how to drive an 18-wheeler furniture truck for United Van Lines.

Rex said, "You can make five times more money in three months of hard work than you can in nine months teaching school."

Sure enough, that first summer, I made more money than I did in five years of teaching. Yes, hard work, long hours and endless white lines. So what!

"You don't seem to be a truck driver," many customers said to me.

I answered, "I am not a truck driver; I am a writer temporarily working a second job."

In other words, I always defined myself as a writer. Trucking allowed me the freedom and money to travel. Six continents later, 13 published books and thousands of articles, I continue on my chosen path.

You may ask yourself at the end of this chapter, "How will I find the perfect job in my life?"

What do you do in your spare time? What turns you on as to activities? Do you love to raft rivers? Do you like to teach skiing? Do you find yourself painting pictures? Do you love writing poetry? Do you repair engines?

Generally, whatever you do in your spare time equates to what really interests you in life. You will find in this book a dozen examples of men and women who changed their lives by changing their work. Continue your education with night classes and other learning, but this much holds true: move toward your chosen destiny by your own actions.

Possible avenues to your perfect job:

Clyde Lowstuter wrote: **In Search of the Perfect Job.** The reviews of this book on Amazon show this book elevates you to a job that fits you.

Dr. Paul Tieger wrote: **Do What You Are: Discover the Perfect Job for You Through Secrets of Your Personality Type.** Move toward a job that fits your style, your energy, your personality, your way of moving in the world.

Elizabeth Wagele wrote: **The Career Within You: How to Find the Perfect Job for Your Personality**. This lady hits the nail on the head. Again, some authors may resonate with you so read until you find the one that hits the spot for your quest.

Robert Bittner wrote: **Your Perfect Job: A Guide to Discovering Your Gifts, Following Your Passions and Loving Your Work for the Rest of Your Life.** Once again, you may discover your skills, gifts and work propensities within the pages of this book.

Create Your Own Job

Chad Pregracke: Cleaning Up The Mississippi River One Piece At A Time

The Mississippi River sweeps millions of bottles, cans, tires, oil, chemicals, plastic bags and containers, along with junk of every description into the Gulf of Mexico 24/7. From Minnesota, where it starts as a six-foot-wide, 15-inches-deep stream, it travels 2,552 miles and drops 1,772 feet through nine states until it rushes into the ocean. At its mouth, the Mississippi River creates a 10,000-mile "dead zone" where most vertebrate marine creatures cannot live because toxic waters contaminate their habitat.

How do I know? Over 15 years ago, my friend Gary and I canoed the Mississippi River, beginning at its humble source in Lake Itasca, Minnesota. At first, perfect beauty greeted us until we hit the first homes and towns along the river. From there, bottles, cans, plastic bags, plastic containers, cars, sofas, tires, machinery, paper, cups, used diapers and hundreds of other pieces of trash passed by my eyes. We carried two large plastic trash bags and filled them every day. We dumped them at trashcans in the small towns we passed along the way.

At the end, I wrote a commentary asking the Minneapolis Star Tribune and the Pioneer Press to engage civic leaders, Girl Scouts, Boy Scouts, high schools, Rotary and Lions clubs to form teams to clean up Old Man River. I asked them to consider a 10-cent deposit-return law for all soda pop, beer and liqueur bottles like Michigan's successful law.

The editors and publishers of both papers refused to publish my commentary. Hard fact: 70 percent of Americans refuse to recycle anything. A large percentage of them toss anything, anywhere, at any time. McDonald's and Pizza Hut customers throw the most trash out their car windows. Plastic water bottles, beer and soda containers litter the landscape by the trillions!

Last week, my preacher spoke about the Herculean efforts of Chad Pregracke on his quest to clean up the Mississippi River one piece of trash at a time. Americans along the river toss their debris one piece at a time and Pregracke intends to pick it up "one piece at a time." Pregracke ran into the same roadblocks with his efforts to engage government and civic clubs: they ignored him.

"At the age of 17, he started making calls to government agencies to notify them of the problem, assuming someone would take care of it. Year after year passed by and the problem only worsened. In 1997 Chad decided that, if no one else was going to clean up the river, he would."

Since 1998, Chad engaged 60,000 volunteers to retrieve 6,000,000 (million) pounds of trash of every description. He expanded his work to the Ohio and other rivers.

His website notes: "Chad's vision, charisma, non-stop work ethic and natural leadership garnered him an abundance of awards and honors over the years. Most notably, Chad was the recipient of the Jefferson Award for Public Service, America's version of the Nobel Prize, in June 2002. Chad accepted this award in the United States Supreme Court in Washington D.C. with other award recipients: Rudolph Giuliani, Bill and Melinda Gates, and Lilly Tartikoff."

Chad's teams picked up 13 football fields worth of one-foot thick Styrofoam; 8,800 feet of barge cables; 1,095 chairs; 19,700 balls; 63 250-gallon drums; 83,900 bags of trash; 5,800

55-gallon drums and thousands of other articles tossed by mindless Americans. The list runs down the page like a ticker-tape parade of embarrassment.

Chad Pregracke authored: *From the Bottom Up: One Man's Crusade to Clean America's Rivers.* To purchase a copy of the book, please call his office at (309) 496-9848.

This brings up the most important point: we Americans must begin to clean up our country "upstream" by changing ourselves from a "throw-away" society to a "recycling-return" society. All the cleanups in the world won't solve the core problem: millions of Americans tossing their containers and trash.

We need to help Chad expand his work into the deposit-return container laws like the State of Michigan. We need to transform from using plastic bags to using cotton bags. It's evident that millions of Americans don't care where they toss their trash. Economic incentives change that behavior very effectively. Michigan's rivers, lakes and roadways remain pristine because an army of kids scours the landscape for 10-cent return containers.

If you're the kind of person who cares about North America's environment and beauty, sign on with Chad Pregracke's team. Start your own team in your own city or state. Expand your powers by forming groups that create change. Model your work after Chad's work. He will help you.

Finally, where you engage your heart, you infuse your life with energy, purpose and passion. Follow Chad's lead and become a leader in your state, city and community. Your efforts will give the Mighty Mississippi a chance to run clean again along with all the other rivers in America. In the process, you will preserve Tom Sawyer, Jim and Huckleberry Finn's legacy.

Visit his website: www.LivingLandsandWaters.org

"Rivers flow not past, but through us; tingling, vibrating, exciting every cell and fiber in our bodies, making them sing and glide."~ John Muir

Angela Haseltine Pozzi: Salvaging Our Plastic Oceans

Cultures have long heard wisdom in non-human voices: Apollo, god of music, medicine and knowledge, came to Delphi in the form of a dolphin. But dolphins, which fill the oceans with blipping and chirping, and whales, which mew and caw in ultramarine jazz - a true rhapsody in blue – are hunted to the edge of silence. ~ *Jay Griffiths*

In 1963, I began scuba diving in the Caribbean. For 50 years, I explored the marvelous waters off the Great Barrier Reef, Galapagos Islands, Hawaii, Great Lakes, Mediterranean, Atlantic, Pacific and Indian Oceans.

I personally watched the oceans turn from pristine perfection to rolling garbage piles ebbing and throbbing with the tides as humanity tossed trillions of pieces of plastic of every description, glass, tires, chemicals, nets, nylon, canvas and worse into the oceans of the world.

No doubt, you heard about the 100 million tons of plastic floating 1,000 miles off San Francisco, the size of Texas, known as the "Great Pacific Garbage Patch." It runs from 30 to 60 feet deep with plastic in places. It's gigantic, it's sickening and it grows by 3.5 million plastic containers 24/7. Fact: 46,000 piece of plastic containers float on every square mile of the world's oceans.

To see it grow over a lifetime sickens me to no avail. Yet, after Oprah Winfrey exposed the "Great Pacific Garbage Patch" twenty years ago, not one single world leader or American leader or even citizens of the world stepped up to work for a 25-cent deposit-return law on all plastics coming out mercantile stores worldwide.

Oceanographer Jacques Yves Cousteau said, "Water and air, the two essential fluids on which all life depends, have become global garbage cans."

As we poison, plasticize and acidify our oceans 24/7, we will pay dearly at some point.

Enter artist Angela Haseltine Pozzi, director of www. WashedAshore.org, who lives on the beach in Brandon, Oregon. She makes art out of all the plastic that washes ashore from the vast Pacific Ocean at her doorstep.

Enjoy this four-minute video of her work:
http://www.karmatube.org/videos.php?id=4168

"The Washed Ashore Project is a non-profit, community-based organization with a mission of educating and creating awareness about marine debris and plastic pollution through art," reads her website. "Washed Ashore is a project of The Artula Institute for Arts & Environmental Education, whose mission is to provide opportunities to express and teach environmental issues through the arts.

"Under the leadership of Angela Haseltine Pozzi, community members of all ages work together to clean up our beaches and process the debris into art supplies to construct giant sculptures of the sea life most affected by plastic pollution. This has resulted in thousands of pounds of debris removed from local beaches and turned into works of art. These unique art pieces are part of a traveling exhibition that includes educational signage and programs that encourage reducing, refusing, reusing, repurposing and recycling.

"As lead artist, Angela Haseltine Pozzi orchestrates the construction of these towering, aesthetically striking sculptures of marine life with the assistance of many volunteers and a dedicated staff. Angela has been an exhibiting artist and educator for more than 30 years and now chooses to use art as a powerful tool to encourage community and environmental action about her true passion…cleaning up the world's oceans."

"A frightening 90 percent of the debris we collect is petroleum-based: plastic items, nylon ropes and net. We are able to use 98 percent of this trash to create sculptures, including a walk-through replica of an ocean gyre, a Styrofoam coral reef, Henry the fish, a plastic bottle sea jelly, an oil-spill replica, and a musical sea star (tuned to an e-flat scale!). An interdisciplinary environmental arts curriculum and a feature-length documentary are in progress to accompany this work."

"Many of us ask what can I, as one person, do, but history tells us that everything good and bad starts because somebody does something or does not do something." Sylvia Earle, Oceanographer

Pozzi stated, "300 million pounds of plastic is produced annually and less than 10 percent of it is recycled."

Where does it end up? Answer: humanity considers the oceans as its ultimate toilet.

In her plastic ocean art, she produces seals, starfish, birds, turtles and dozens of other creatures. Ironically, the "Great Pacific Garbage Patch" kills millions of those critters and seabirds via suffocation, starvation, snaring them under water, gut stuffing and worse.

At some point, we humans must ask ourselves if we possess moral responsibility and ethical choices toward preserving all life on this planet by respecting its right to exist alongside us. As of today, we fail miserably.

What can you do? Answer: get involved. Work in your state for 25-cent deposit return laws for all plastics leaving every store in the USA and around the world. It takes you at the local level to create "consciousness shift" which leads to "critical mass shift" that moves into "tipping point" whereby give our home planet a chance to function biologically along with all its animals. With strong deposit laws, if anyone throws their glass, metal plastic containers, kids of every description cover the land to pick-up debris.

"I had fought on behalf of man against the sea, but I realized that it had become more urgent to fight on behalf of the sea against man." Alain Bombard, Biologist

"If man doesn't learn to treat the oceans and rainforest with respect, man will become extinct." Peter Benchley, author of **Jaws.**

As a lifelong scuba diver, I attest to those statements.

Contact Pozzi at her website and ask her how you can chip in with money, volunteer and/or make a difference in your own area. www.washedashore.org

Boyan Slat: Cleaning Up 300 Million Tons of Ocean Plastic

"Once there was the Stone Age, then the Bronze Age, and now we are in the middle of the Plastic Age," said teenager Boyan Slat. "Every year, we produce 300 million tons of plastic. Much of it reaches our oceans."

At 16 years of age, Boyan Slat scuba dived off Greece in the Mediterranean Sea to see more debris floating on and under the surface.

He said, "At first, I thought I was swimming through strange jellyfish. Instead, I swam through more plastic bags than fish."

Seeing all the ocean trash, he asked himself, "Why not clean it up?"

Slat quit his Aerospace Engineering studies to create www.TheOceanCleanup.com in order to fund his research on how to pick up all the plastic trash floating on the oceans of the world. Researchers discovered that 46,000 pieces of plastic float on every square mile of Earth's oceans. That plastic debris stems from billions of humans around the planet tossing their plastic into rivers, streams and directly into the oceans. Thousands of ships, boats and luxury cruisers toss millions of pieces of plastic day in and day out across the globe. Plastic does not break down. It oxidizes slowly into smaller pieces, but it never degrades.

Today, we find plastics in the tissue of birds, fish, whales, turtles, dolphins and just about every creature that feeds in the world's oceans. Plastic debris constitutes a biological nightmare whose consequences reach decades into the future.

Additionally, with the five major gyres revolving in the oceans of the world, in excess of 100,000,000 (million) tons of plastic gather in giant ocean-going garbage patches. You may Google "The Great Pacific Garbage Patch" the size of Texas in the Pacific Ocean 1,000 miles off the coast of San Francisco. It grows from 60 to 90 feet deep in places. It kills millions of sea birds, turtles, sharks, dolphins and whales.

Slat said, "We stuff the oceans with enough plastic to equal the weight of 1,000 times the Eiffel Tower. It ranges from plastic nets to miniscule pieces. It's doing tremendous damage to our marine life, reefs and all ocean creatures."

Being a brilliant as well as naive teenager, Boyan Slat decided to construct designs of some contraptions that would scoop up millions of tons of plastic floating on our oceans. Because of his enormous ideas, TED TALKS invited him to bring his ideas to a wider audience. Enjoy the 11-minute speech below. You will be shocked at what you see happening to our oceans:

https://www.youtube.com/watch?v=ROW9F-c0kIQ

Because of my worldwide scuba diving experiences, I saw the progression of plastics since 1965 when corporations first initiated plastics into the biosphere of this planet.

The plastic pollution problem

- Millions of tons of plastic have entered the oceans.
- Plastic concentrates in five rotating currents, called gyres.
- In these gyres there is on average 6 times more plastic than zooplankton by dry weight.
- 1/3 of all oceanic plastic is within the Great Pacific Garbage Patch.

Slat's brilliant strategy combines his love of diving with his love of the biology of the oceans. He created a solar powered trawler in the shape of a manta ray that sweeps through the gyres 24/7 to pick up surface plastic, chew it up and store it in huge bins for collection. He also created floating booms that allow the oceans to sweep the plastics into their lairs for efficient pickup.

"If we want to do something different to save our oceans," he said. "We have to think differently. Ironically, those who throw their plastics face consequences. Ocean going ships spend $1 billion annually in repairs from plastic clogging their propellers and intakes."

Ecological effects

- At least one million seabirds, and one hundred thousand marine mammals die each year due to plastic pollution. It's probably much higher.
- Lantern fish in the North Pacific Gyre eat up to 24,000 tons of plastics per year.
- The survival of many species, including the Hawaiian Monk Seal and Loggerhead Turtle, could be jeopardized by plastic debris.
- Plastic pollution is a carrier of invasive species, threatening native ecosystems.

Health effects

- Toxic chemicals (including PCBs and DDTs) are adsorbed by the plastic, increasing the concentration a million times.
- After entering the food chain, these persistent organic pollutants bio-accumulate in the food chain.
- Health effects linked to these chemicals are: cancer, malformation and impaired reproductive ability.

Boyan Slat, a teenager, stands at the head of his class in creating solutions for the folly of humanity. He needs your support. Join him.

If ever humanity needs leaders to stand up and be counted, we need more Boyan Slat's to lead us out of our ransacking our planet home toward a biologically healthy future.

Meloti and Isabel Wijsen: Bye, Bye Plastic Bags on Bali

Ten and 12 year old sisters, Meloti and Isabel Wijsen noticed plastic bags clogging the beaches, streams, streets and highways around their tiny island of Bali. They read reports from local scuba divers complaining about plastic trash clogging the reefs and mingling with seaweed around the island.

What they witnessed appalled them. Ironically, Bali tourist organizations sang praises about Bali's palm trees, white sandy beaches, blue waters, stunning mountains and plentiful wildlife.

In reality, hotels, businesses and villages added to the plastic bag trash at stunning speeds. Under the water, scuba divers could not pick up enough plastic bags to keep up with the ones being discarded by thousands of people every day of the year.

What bags didn't get tossed ended up in incinerators that created toxic smoke and ash that blanketed the island.

The two sisters created an army of determined school kids who wouldn't take "no" for an answer. They knocked on doors all over the island. They created petitions for people to sign at the airport when tourists landed on the island. They formed beach cleanups, created T-shirts, a website and organized legions of kids to follow them.

At first, they met severe resistance from the Bali government and many businesses. Undaunted, they traveled to India to the home of Mahatma Gandhi, the man who ejected the British from his country. His legacy and tactics inspired the girls. The late Princess Lady Diana also inspired them concerning her work to ban landmines worldwide.

Meloti said, "We don't have to wait until we are older to make a difference."

They gave talks at schools across Bali and held beach cleanup days.

"Being kids, we thought if we get one million signatures, they cannot ignore us, they will have no choice," Maloti said. "Who would have guessed one million signatures is, like, a thousand times a thousand?"

At that point, they discovered that 16 million visitors landed at the Bali airport annually. They walked into the airport manager's office with a bid to set up a booth.

He said, "I can't believe I'm letting you do this, but I am."

They collected a million signatures within weeks. After months of trying, they walked into the president of Bali's office with the petition. They brought facts about plastic waste: a study by the University of Georgia of 192 countries found that Indonesia tossed the second largest amount of plastic trash behind China, at 3.2 million tons of plastic waste in 2010, about 10 percent of the world total. The amount humans toss plastic trash into the oceans annually: 8,000,000 (million) tons. China, India and America discard the most plastics of all countries. All totaled, researches estimate that the Earth's oceans house 5.25 trillion pieces of plastic and counting.

After their appearance on Ted Talks, the sisters inspired legions of teens worldwide to start their own organizations to make positive change in the world.

Through the sisters' tireless efforts, Bali will be plastic bag free in 2018.

Isabel said, "Don't let anyone tell you that you're too young or you won't understand. We're not telling you it is going to be easy. We're telling you that it's worth it."

Contact them: www.byebyeplasticbags.org
Email: byebyeplasticbags@gmail.com
The two sisters spoke on Ted Talks: www.tedtalks.com

Chapter 5

Relationship Choices Equate To Joy

It seems to me that the best relationships, the ones that last, are frequently the ones that are rooted in friendship. You know, one day you look at the person and you see something more than you did the night before. Like a switch has been flicked somewhere. And the person who was just a friend is...suddenly the only person you can ever imagine yourself with. ~ *Gillian Anderson*

Once you gain self-mastery of your body, mind and spirit, life feels wondrous. By working a job that fits you, life becomes glorious. Those may be the easiest factors in living a happy life.

In order to live a spectacular life, your choice of a life-mate as well as your friends constitutes the most challenging quest of your life.

Why? Answer: in this swiftly changing world, everyone arrives on your life's doorstep from everywhere else in the world. Everyone stepping into your life whether a man or woman, comes to you with different ideas, different religions, different cultures, different areas of the USA, different backgrounds and different expectations.

Let's take buddies or girlfriends first. Friends come into your life and blend into your circle because you enjoy similar activities. Usually, your job puts you into contact with other men and women. You find a few of those people "work" for you. You like them and they like you.

Guys like sharing sports or watching pro games with buddies. Guys meet friends on the tennis court or at the recreation center or at a "Meet-up" for skiing, cycling and mountain climbing.

Later, they share a beer and talk about everything on their minds—usually, women.

When it comes to girlfriends sharing time with girlfriends, they talk about the latest make-up, fashion styles, shoes, movies and, of course, men. Since I'm not a woman, I really don't know what they talk about. Whatever makes their friendships—probably stems from the same things that men share in friendships. That equates to similarities of thought, activities and intimate conversations about feelings, fears, hopes and insecurities.

In today's world, with TV driving women to drink, consume drugs, and live in hyper-activity along with comparisons to the Victoria Secret models—it's difficult to appreciate how they keep their balance.

Unfortunately, many don't. An average of 13 teenagers die every hour from drug overdoses 24/7. Another 18 commit suicide daily in America. Men kill three women every day in America via domestic violence. Millions take billions of pills for every kind of ailment known to humanity. Most of the pill solutions stem from our accelerating mental instability in this society. In the end, pills mask or stomp symptoms of emotional and physical problems.

Therefore, friendship may be your most profound connection to leading a balanced and happy life.

"The glory of friendship is not the outstretched hand, not the kindly smile, nor the joy of companionship; it is the spiritual inspiration that comes to one when you discover that someone else believes in you and is willing to trust you with a friendship." Ralph Waldo Emerson

As you gain friends, be certain to nourish your friendships. Compliments help. Regular times together cement emotional feelings. Keep your friendship circle to the number that you can sustain on a regular basis. Listen to them and be a sounding board. A friendship of a week on a vacation, or a year back home or a lifetime breathes energy into your life.

Friendships can cause you great pain when they head south. Learn ways to engage in communication. Learn the pitfalls that lead to friendship breakup.

One note: if a friendship turns sour, try to face your friend. If he or she doesn't coalesce with you, but causes more irritation, you may choose to end it in order to return to balance for yourself. You don't have to become angry or vengeful. No faultfinding! No character assassination! Simply terminate a friendship that doesn't work for you any longer.

How to deal with loss of a friendship:

How to Cope with Loss of a Friendship by Dr. Irene Levine. You will lose some dear friends in this life over arguments, over male friends, over disagreements as to politics, religion and wives-husbands who don't like you.

How to Deal with Losing a Friend by Wikihow.com. These 13 steps give you a good path to follow in recovering from the loss of a friend.

Losing Your Best Friend: Vacancies of the Heart by Frosty Wooldridge. I lost several best friends in my life that ripped my heart out. I interviewed others who lost their best friends, both male and female. This book offers you ways to nourish your friendships and several ways to avoid spouses who can't stand you.

Significant Other, Life-Mate or Marriage Leading to Happiness

Finding and keeping a life-mate or marriage partner today in the United States of America must be the most aggravating, difficult, dangerous and rocky path to happiness in the history of humanity. Our society races beyond the emotional/ biorhythmic/ stress limits of just about everyone.

Every man and woman faces countless variables in making a relationship work. That's why you see 50 percent divorce rates. Another 25 percent stay married only for the kids. The last 25 percent enjoy reasonable marriages. Those statistics prove "not so good odds" for most people.

How can you change it for yourself to a "happily ever after ending" storybook romance?

Of course, you can read a dozen books on successful marriage. I recommend for women and men: Barbara DeAngelis' book: **Are You the One for Me?** She offers a brilliant checklist for women to discover whether or not a guy might work for them in the long run.

For men and women, you might consider: **How to Deal with 21st Century Women—Co-creating a Successful Relationship** by yours truly. While it's an "edgy" title, this book offers up-to-date, reasonable processes for finding and maintaining a positive relationship for both men and women. Today, women dynamically grow in education, stature, financial competence and sexual equality. They won't tolerate being trashed by their husbands or significant others. They demand equality.

Men must come to terms that they no longer own all the money, property, buildings, political power or sports trophies. Men need to slide over in the front seat and appreciate their lady when she wants to drive or go to her favorite movie.

In that book, my friend and I discovered the best ways to create a successful relationship. Not by earning a PH.D. in relationship understanding, but by our living and loving our way through divorces—to learning how to meet our best matches. You may enjoy a few of the parameters below from one of the chapters.

First of all, utilize the "two year courtship" minimum format before you step to the altar. Secondly, engage the "one year living together" for a total of three years invested in your lifetime marriage vows. Thirdly, wait to get married after your 26th birthday because of the reasons explained in the book. Go out and sow some wild oats for heaven sakes. Most folks don't realize the limitations to living with the same person for the rest of their lives.

In your twenties, give yourself a few experiences before settling for the white house with picket fence. By getting down to the nitty-gritty of daily living, loving and getting along (or otherwise), you may make rational decisions whether or not you might survive 30, 40 or 50 years of marriage.

The keys to the long-term viable relationship

Let's say this woman at the city park turned your head and looked in your direction. She's not a one-night stand. At this point, you're looking for a long-term relationship. You want a steady squeeze and a comforting companion—maybe a wife or significant other. What things do you want to do before you romance her?

We assume at some point, you want to settle down to one woman and a family. When you exit the "sex for the sake of sex" stage of your life, you need to employ your wisdom and experience to search for and find a suitable life-mate. First of all, take your time and develop a solid foundation to your relationship. Sure, you're aching to bed him or her, but that's not the way it works in the long run. If you're a woman, you can't wait for him to love you like Brad Pitt and Angelina Jolie (opps, that didn't work out so well) or George Clooney and his 36-year-old child bride. You need to evaluate how you both matchup. Check these keys to a viable long-term relationship:

Emotionality

Do you both enjoy even-keeled emotional make-ups? Do you talk out your differences? Do you discuss your mutual challenges rather than fighting? Do either of you suffer from jealousy? If jealousy rears its ugly head from either partner, you face tremendous conflict at the drop of a hat. Jealousy stifles any relationship and foments tension like few other emotions. What about envy? Do you envy your partner? Do you envy your friends? Envy breeds discontent. In the end, two people must connect like rails on a railroad track. You're both separate human beings able to stand on your own, yet connected by the ties of love, respect and honor toward one another as you travel in the same direction. If one of you suffers from jealousy, envy and insecurity, you will infect the relationship to its ultimate demise.

Sexuality

Let's make it exceedingly clear that sexuality can make or break a relationship in the long run. If she loves intimacy because she loves the frolic, play, closeness and orgasms, you've got a lifelong playmate. If she's got hang-ups, insecurity problems, lack of orgasms, and fear of closeness—you've got problems. If you possess high-energy sexuality and she carries a low sexual drive, you've got problems. Do not let this factor slide just because you're in love, lust or in need. Solution: keep searching until you find a lady or man who loves intimacy as much as you. Sexual compatibility sets the foundation of your physical, mental and emotional relationship. This information applies to women searching for a compatible man.

Spirituality

In the long run, you need a life-mate who feels her own spiritual-religious path runs along the same tracks as yours. If she requires church every Sunday and you don't, you need to figure it out with her. If you're both off-kilter on this issue, you may find your relationship derailed at some point in the future. Most women seem to need religion more than most men. You both need to talk this one out to make sure you both live on the same page. How will you bring up your kids as to religion and spirituality? If she goes for Jesus and you go for Buddha or the Great Spirit, you may reconsider your relationship and its chances. Believe us, it will become a bigger and bigger issue if you're both on separate religious or spiritual paths.

Interests

Find a lady or man who loves what you love. When talking and sex cool down, it's your mutual interests that keep you moving together into the future. Again, your similar activities bind you jointly over the years. We think you both need to enjoy at least a half-dozen activities that you both can share: bicycling, camping, dancing, movies, running, canoeing, rafting, skiing, mountain climbing, motorcycling and dozens of other outdoor sports. For the less athletic, you may like bowling, fishing, hunting, tractor pulls, walking your dogs, bridge parties, video games and many other less physical activities. If you enjoy being a couch potato, find yourself a plump female or male couch potato. When you love playing sports and keeping fit, find a lady or man who loves those same sports and loves to eat nutritionally and maintain his or her sexy body.

Values

You will discover whether or not you possess the same values together over a 24-month courtship period. Especially living together for 12 months! If you exhibit slob-like behavior, she will discover it. If she lacks your values as to neat and clean, integrity, educational growth, dressing well and keeping the car washed, you will discover it during the two-year courtship. Of course, you could compromise if you find suitable ground. Values represent the ethics and style of your life. Your mate needs to be in the same ballpark if you're going to be cheering for the same team throughout your lives together. Additionally, she will be checking you out over the 24-month courtship to see if you fit her needs in the "values" category. Additionally, plan to live together for a year to make your total courtship of 36 months. By the end of that period, you will enjoy a clearer picture on whether or not you want to spend the next 30, 40 or 50 years together.

Lifestyle

Do you love to travel and she loves to mend socks? Are your eyes glued to the television 29 hours a week, which is the American male average? Are you a slob and she is fastidiously neat and clean? Does she love to go dancing every Friday and Saturday night, but you would rather attend drag races? Is she high energy and you low energy? Are you both quiet and you like it that way? Do you like to scrimp and she loves to spend lavishly? Figure out your true lifestyles before you hitch up at the altar.

Personality compatibility

Do you both get a big kick out of each other, daily? Do you find comfort in sharing time with each other? We call it the "mutual likability" factor. When you both share personality compatibility—you get along, you enjoy each other, you have fun together and it's easy on your daily romp through life. By finding a mate that matches you in the personality compatibility category, you will not have to "work" at your marriage. You will "click" naturally. Please note: most couples suffer disagreements at times. That's life. Talk through them. At the same time, when you enjoy mutual compatibility, your daily lives together flow with greater ease and grace. Refer to the Barbara DeAngelis book, Myers-Briggs and Taylor-Johnson Temperament Analysis tests.

Listening

Women complain that men don't listen to them. You watch skits on sitcoms that dramatize the fact that men don't listen to their women. The former "Married with Children" sitcom depicted a husband unable or unwilling to listen to his wife. The sitcom "According to Jim" ranks at the top as to a husband who didn't listen to his wife. As soon as the wife starts complaining, boyfriends or husbands try to solve their loved ones' problems. We offer you a secret to a long and healthy relationship: listen to your wife, lover or significant other. Just listen. Keep quiet. Listen with fixed attention and with your heart. At the most you might utter the sacred words, "I understand." When a woman discovers a man who listens to her, she feels like she's elevated directly into heaven. Remember this one piece of advice and you will walk around with a smile on your face most of the time.

Goals

Are you both looking down the tracks of life with similar goals? Do you want kids? No kids? Will you raise them with corporal punishment? Will you raise them with gentle behavior modification? Check "Love and logic" as to raising kids. www. LoveandLogic.org What religion or philosophy will you teach them? Will you live in the country? Live in the city? Do you want to be rich? Do you expect to be average? Can you support each other's aspirations?

If you avoid living together, you cannot and will not discover your compatibilities. Even more important, you will fail to discover your incompatibilities. You would never buy a car without driving it to see if you like the way it fits, feels and performs. You wouldn't buy a set of golf clubs until you checked out the fit, style and performance of the clubs. You wouldn't buy a bicycle without making sure it fit your needs, your height and your style of cycling. Same with a long term relationship: you need to try each other out to see if you like each other's fit, feel and performance. Living together for 12 months gives you a pretty good idea for your long-term success.

How do you discover all those factors needed for relationship success?

First, you talk. You spend more time talking and sharing your ideas about life than you do hugging, kissing and trying to get into each other's pants. You need to find out whether you like her and/or if she likes you. You need to respect her values and hers must be similar to yours in core areas. Take time to learn about each other in various situations such as stress, angry moments, playtime, health crisis and a family quarrel. Discover how you treat her and how she treats you during that time.

Secondly, if you're serious about this woman or man, realize that you might fall into love. If you do, would she be a good mother for your children? Would you be a good father? Does she smoke or drink? Do you? Would she stop smoking and drinking during the pregnancy for the child's health? Is she a fitness nut? Is she a vegetarian? If she's already been married with kids, do you want her to have more with you? Do you want to be an instant stepfather? Or stepmother? Get down to the gut level reality of what you're dealing with in this potential relationship.

We knew a guy who fathered two kids by his wife. While she carried his second kid, he cheated on her. After the second kid was born, he walked away from his wife. However, he wanted to be a part of his kids' lives, so he obtained twice-weekly visiting rights. He proved to be a lazy schmuck who couldn't make enough money to pay child support, so finally, his ex-wife took him to court to force him to pay back child support. The judge made him pay, but he still paid less than sustaining money for his two children.

The twit started living with another lady who had two girls from a previous marriage. Before he knew it, she became pregnant with his child.

At 46 years of age, his own ignorance or ego trapped him. He earned little money. He became the stepfather to two girls. His ex-wife took him to court for more money for his first two girls. He married his girlfriend pregnant with his new child. Thus, he tried to be a father to his first two girls plus his new child and his two stepchildren. In addition to that, he and his new wife fought regularly and their relationship became a chapter out of an "angry wives" novel.

This happened to him because he didn't talk it out and make any plans. Instead, life made plans for him. Those plans weren't what you might call a lot of fun—all the way into his 60s with burdensome emotional and financial responsibilities.

Besides that, he caused a lot of pain and anguish for all those affected by his unfortunate choices and actions.

Keep your horse in the barn until you know what kind of pasture you're letting him gallop around during the night. From the get-go, use a condom. Use it every time and use it intelligently.

One final note for living a spectacular life

If you really want to live a compelling life also known as a "Peter Pan" existence, consider staying single. Most women won't sleep in a tent for a year in South America. Most women want comfort and security. Most don't do well by endlessly traveling the globe out of a backpack. I stayed single until age 55 in order to travel and command my options. If you do find a lady who loves world travel and living out of a tent, grab her before another adventuring soul snatches her.

For any women pursuing a spectacular life living style, you possess all the power of taking your life toward any direction on the planet. If you desire or enjoy a male companion, hang out where guys windsurf, Para-sail, scuba dive, rock climb, kite surf, backpack, mountain climb, mountaineer-skiing, alpine skiing, bicycle touring and dozens of other wild and crazy life-adventures.

Books to enhance your opportunities for a spectacular life:

The Traveler's Gift: Seven Decisions That Determine Personal Success by Andy Andrews
The Young Traveler's Gift by Andy Andrews (teens)

Chapter 6

Self-Discovery

The energy of imagination, deliberations and inventions, which fall into a natural rhythm, which are totally one's own, maintained by innate discipline and a keen sense of pleasure— these are the ingredient of style. And all who possess it enjoy one thing: originality. ~ *Diana Vreeland*

You manifest the only *you* in the universe. Your unique life won't be repeated throughout all of eternity. Therefore, direct your life toward your highest and best by testing, trying, experimenting and expressing yourself. Try everything as to jobs, as to friends, as to styles of dress, as to athletics, as to whatever charges into your life at any time during your lifespan.

Key point: to discover your true nature, to enter into your true self-appreciation and to find your purpose—that's self-discovery. Along that path, make no comparisons as to money, status, height, weight, build, voice, eye-color, hair or anything. You are unique beyond comparison.

Today, as in the past, most humans compare themselves to others who might be attractive, rich and athletic. Once you discover that you cannot be compared to anyone, you grow in self-discovery.

Agreed, in this modern day American world, you face an endless stream of comparison on television, radio and advertisements. Media shows you how to be richer, smarter, better looking and famous. You could drive yourself nuts with comparisons.

Let's share a story about a young man, in a very comfortable middle class family, who screwed off during high school to the point of poor grades, hanging with other goof-offs and barely graduated with minimum achievement. I remember him telling me, "I've never done any homework." He sounded proud of himself, even boastful. I remember getting into his face, "Young man, do you realize that life speeds toward you like a brakeless train? Do you realize that your free ride with your parents ends at high school graduation? Are you prepared for anything resembling a successful life?"

He blew me off with his apathy, "Whatever!"

Twelve years later, I maintained contact with him. He flunked out of junior college. He worked as a roofer, delivery boy and drug store assistant. He lived in his brother's house. He used his credit card to create $10,000.00 in debts. He felt depression from his endless failure cycle. He couldn't afford a date. What would he tell a woman about his successes? He remained on the edge of meaninglessness by playing endless video games.

Finally, in his 29th year, he abruptly quit his job, secured a non-paying position at a resort spa in Europe and become the chief cook and bottle washer. He said in a Facebook post, "I am happier than words can explain." Nonetheless, he returned home in debt, without a job and a resume qualifying him for further low-paying jobs.

At age 30, he spoke to me, "I'm 30 years old, live in my brother's house and work a crappy job that I hate. I'm depressed most of the time. And, here I am at 30, and I haven't done anything with my life."

Which brings me to this understanding: no matter your looks, brains, social status at birth, financial benefits or lack of them—you must choose your life path at some point. You can screw off. Or, you can apply yourself and your talents to discover your optimum life's work. You can fall into a job or create a job. You may create a lifestyle or craft one that fits your life energy.

To repeat—Napoleon Hill said, "Life is like a horse. Life will ride you as you become the horse. Or, you can ride while Life becomes the horse. The choice as to whether one becomes the rider of Life or is ridden by Life is the privilege of every person. But this much is certain. If you do not choose to become the rider of Life, you are sure to be forced to become the horse. Life either rides or is ridden. It never stands still."

I said to him, "Please understand this reality: at least half your high school classmates got married and divorced in the past 12 years since graduating. They pay child support and suffer weekend visits with their kids. Another quarter of your classmates endure lethargic marriages with kids, bills and uninteresting jobs. In terms of your life, you've only lived your adult years of age 20 to 30. You still enjoy choices as to jobs, education and a compatible life-mate. If you live to 80, that leaves you with 5/6th of your adult life span. At any point, you may choose further education in college, trade school, vocational tech school and hundreds of jobs. You may create your own job. Instead of remaining a victim of your choices, you may become a champion of your ideas and opportunities. Remember! Never compare yourself to anyone."

He said, "I never thought about it that way."

In this game of life, you remain the captain of your destiny. Set sail toward it by your actions, your enthusiasm, and your complete acceptance of your responsibilities to yourself. Once you decide to live on the positive side of life driven by your actions, your path grows with greater energy and opportunities. In other words, you accelerate toward living a spectacular life.

Section III

Foundational Concepts for Spectacular Living

Chapter 7

Thoughts Thicken into Things; Things Become Reality

I will not die an unlived life. I will not live in fear of falling or catching fire. I choose to inhabit my days, to allow my living to open me, to make me less afraid, more accessible, to loosen my heart until it becomes a wing, a torch, a promise. I choose to risk my significance; to live so that which comes to me as seed goes to the next as blossom and that which comes to me as blossom, goes on as fruit. ~ *Dawna Markova*

CONVICTIONS LEAD TO EXPERIENCES

As the Greek philosopher Aristotle said, "You must possess an idea of something before you can bring it into form."

He might have said, "Thoughts thicken into things. Things become reality."

That means invisible ideas come to visible form.

Ask the inventor of the light bulb, Thomas A. Edison, about his ideas. He brought 100 ideas to form as inventions. What about the uncommon architecture of Frank Lloyd Wright? His buildings still elicit wonder. How about Bill Gates or Mark Zuckerberg with their work in the computer realm as to software and Facebook? They started with an idea. How about science fiction writers with amazing stories of other worlds? You all know about Gene Roddenberry and *Star Trek*. We have all flown around the universe with Jean-Luc Picard and his crew on the starship Enterprise. Before him, Captain James T. Kirk explored the galaxies.

Everything we enjoy today started with imagination. Your creative energy works within this universe of ideas. As a human being, you are the only species on the planet that can engineer creative thinking.

CONCEPTS FOR LIVING YOUR INTENTIONS

1ST Concept—Thoughts thicken into things

Your thoughts and ideas or choices, acted upon, become your new reality. While attending school, if you choose to attend class, participate in discussions, study hard and take the tests—your intelligence and comprehension of the world grows. You not only earn top grades, you advance your intellectual talents toward higher learning, athletics and personal improvement.

Your thoughts, which drive your actions, make you an excellent employer or employee. However, if you choose to be late to work or goof-off on the job, you will become another kind of employer or employee and soon be out of business or unemployed. When you come to work on time, perform with excellence and exhibit your talents, you will experience trust, better pay and added opportunities. In other words, your thoughts on how you conduct yourself—thicken into your actions—and result in your becoming an excellent addition to any organization with all of its rewards.

On the other hand, if you exhibit lazy behavior, become chronically late, irresponsible and other poor choices, your thoughts thicken into a lifestyle of your choosing. Life treats you commensurately as to your thoughts and actions.

Positive thoughts lead to positive actions

Let's say you and your buddies decided to go camping on the weekend. Your thoughts thickened into the idea of going camping. From there, you made preparations to pack the car, filled it with gas, brought food, consulted a map and finally, traveled to your destination. Your thoughts thickened into a camping trip that you fulfilled.

All human beings possess minds with choices. We think. We decide. We change. We desire. We sense. We feel. We understand. We choose. We dream. We chase. We touch. We hear. We see. We smell. We react. We perceive. We extrapolate.

With all those amazing attributes, we find ourselves in a giant ocean of choices, possibilities and entanglements. We may organize those choices as we direct our minds to personal success of our dreams or intentions.

We drive our lives forward by thinking positively. Watch out! Very quickly, people will notice a spring in your step, a smile on your face and an energy bubbling up from within your body, mind and spirit.

Essentially, you begin working with the "Law of Positive Energy Exchange." That means the more positive energy you express daily toward yourself and others, the more that energy and human responses reverberate back to you.

"Creative living means optimizing your environment. Enthusiastic, successful people realize that life is a game; the hand they've been dealt is their environment, the result is optimization and their edge is creativity. They understand that overcoming obstacles is the natural state of human existence and represents the challenge that keeps life exciting." Ed Scott

When you read books that interest you and watch instructional movies, you will see your thought patterns change.

Over time, your actions will evolve. Your mind and body will respond in ways you couldn't have imagined in the past.

Once you engage creative thinking, your thoughts thicken into things, skills, adventures, relationships and just about anything you can imagine.

KEY POINTS FROM THIS CHAPTER

1. Re-script your brain to positive thinking.
2. Thoughts thicken into things; sporting events, camping trips, good grades.
3. Begin practicing positive thinking for positive outcomes.

Chapter 8

Reality Starts in Your Mind

This is the beginning of a new day. You have been given this day to use as you will. You can waste it or use it for good. What you do today is important because you are exchanging a day of your life for it. When tomorrow comes, this day will be gone forever; in its place is something that you have left behind...let it be something good. ~ *Unknown author*

2nd Concept—Reality starts in your mind

What you perceive through your senses gives you an idea of what exists out there in the world. What you see is what you get. You've heard that statement dozens of times from others.

Most humans think that reality is visible and that visible reality is the only reality. As we discussed earlier, ideas create new realities and ideas change reality. Our minds create ideas. In fact, all reality started with an idea.

Therefore, your reality stems from your thinking processes and how you see or understand the world. It's called a "worldview." Your culture and parents along with your life experiences thrust it upon you. Have you ever noticed that successful people tend to come from successful parents?

Successful parents imprint their children with positive self-concepts via their actions and their words. Children of loving parents gain security, sense-of-self and a worldview that allows them to go forth like a crusading knight to do battle with life and expect to triumph.

However, as an inner-city teacher, I saw the exact opposite of positive self-concepts in the children I taught. Many inner-city kids find themselves hammered by negative self-concepts from their parents and other kids with the same programming. Why? Their parents instilled in them negative self-concepts on multiple levels—because their parents succumbed to the same parent scripting.

"You're dumb! You're ugly! You're useless!" Those statements have been repeated millions of times in many homes. Additionally, because of unfortunate food choices, many children suffer obesity, diabetes and poor self-image. With violence, drugs and other negative behaviors, many children find themselves in uphill battles as to education, personal well-being and future outlook.

I won't sugarcoat their reality. It's unfortunate.

Nonetheless, some kids, no matter what their background, carry the spark of life in them that allows them to triumph over enormous difficulties. Oprah Winfrey provides a positive example.

Yes, you have read about rich kids whose lives turned to broken shambles because of drugs, sex and rock n' roll. Hold it! I like rock n' roll and I turned out okay. You have read about movie stars falling into despair. Many celebrities must enter drug rehab numerous times. You may have discovered that perfect marriages shatter in a blink. You will discover that life guarantees us nothing. Not happiness, not money, not love!

Life only allows us opportunities. Those opportunities may yield positives or negatives. It's how we handle them that counts. You may have heard, "In life, we're all dealt a hand to play from the same deck of cards. Good or bad, it's how we play that hand. It's our choice."

INTENTIONS, INTENTIONS, INTENTIONS

If you experienced a hard luck past as some folks call it, you may change that past by rewriting your immediate life. Is it difficult? It depends on your courage, your intentions and your will to overcome. Finally, it depends on your will to succeed at whatever level you expect. You can rewrite the poor scripts of your past into a newer opportunity-filled reality of your present. Everything stands in the here and now. Your life begins anew each day.

Assume or accept that your intention has already manifested. Whether you are taking a test, working on a project, sewing a dress or building a car, think in your mind that you have already succeeded. As you travel adventure highway, act and see that you raised your hand at the top of Mount Denali in Alaska or walked on the Great Wall of China or canoed the Mississippi River or skied a whole winter in Colorado or painted a stunning piece of art...anything that you intend as your passion to accomplish.

Your dreams become true via your intentions. Intentions move the world, move with the law, move with your thoughts and take you wherever you intend to go.

YOU MAKE YOUR REALITY BY YOUR THOUGHTS AND ACTIONS

Finally, your mind creates your reality, good or otherwise. For a powerful example, I once lived near a lady named Elizabeth who loved to complain. When she didn't like the heat, she said, "I hate these hot days, day after day."

When it rained, she said, "I hate rainy days. They are so gloomy, so dark and so depressing." When the winter arrived, she said, "I hate snow. I just hate it."

One afternoon, on a fine summer day, I stood out in her front yard talking with her as she complained about the coming winter.

"I dread the cold and snow," she said.

I responded, "Elizabeth, have you ever thought about moving to Florida where it's warm all year around?"

"Oh, the humidity and bugs down there would just kill me," she said. "I just can't take the heat let alone the people."

Her mind created her reality. No matter where she lived, misery followed her and the world was a negative place.

How can you handle where you live in a positive way? If it's sunny, hot and humid, you can still take your bicycle ride in the morning and a shower afterwards. When the winter snowstorms arrive, you can trade your canoe, bicycle, hiking shoes or kayak for cross country or downhill skis.

"Whatever the weather, I enjoy myself," says my friend Bob.

Fortunately, if you're reading this book, you probably enjoy a much more positive self-concept. Nonetheless, I wanted you to see the difference. Why? As you travel around many parts of the world, you will witness some nasty and ugly aspects of humanity.

At first, their reality will knock your socks off when you see people starving and children dying with flies crawling all over them. You will see harsh realities not imagined in the United States and other western countries. You will see living conditions more brutal than any pictures. Such sights may drive you to despair and even depression. However, you will find a way to buck-up your emotions and accept what you cannot change. If you are affected enough, you may join the Peace Corps and change the world for the better. Every person reacts differently to his or her world experiences.

You cannot change the world; however, you can change your sphere in the world to move it toward a more positive future.

By living your adventures, you will find yourself exploring creative avenues. Your limits keep extending until you feel limitless. Your view of the world and your reality begin to grow to greater dimensions.

Remember this concept. Reality starts in your mind. Your thoughts create your reality. Your positive choices and actions make for a spectacular life.

KEY POINTS FROM THIS CHAPTER

1. You create your reality via your perceptions.
2. Changing your perceptions takes practice.
3. Work on self-concepts that push your limits.
4. As you see yourself living a spectacular life, you take actions toward that reality.

Chapter 9

Engage Your Creative Subconscious

Invariably, when big dreams come true, and I mean BIG, there is a total metamorphosis of one's life. Their thoughts change, their words change, decisions are made differently, gratitude is tossed about like rice at a wedding, priorities are rearranged, and optimism soars. Yeah, they're almost annoying. You could have guessed all that, huh? Would you have guessed that these changes, invariably, come before, not after, their dream's manifestation? ~ *Mike Dooley*

3rd Concept—Engage your creative subconscious

This concept operates on all thought and executes the will of your mind to bring your ideas to form.

You must engage the positive creative process of your subconscious mind. To put it clearly, you must, in your conscious mind, create an idea of what you intend. Once you complete that task, your subconscious mind works on the particulars.

For example: when an architect draws plans for a building, he writes his ideas down on papers, which are known as blueprints. He places those instructions into the hands of the work crews, which act as his subconscious. They build the house. His ideas manifest as a building, bridge or skyscraper. In other words, his conscious and subconscious activities come to form or reality.

In the early part of the last century, a farm kid had to fetch water by walking outside the house to a big hand pump that sat on top of a deep well. He or she brought a full pail of water and an empty pail to the pump. Why? If the farm kid expected to pump water, he or she had to use the full pail of water to prime the pump. The farm kid poured the pail into the pump to create the necessary suction and sealing of the parts to begin drawing water up the long pipe that was sunk 100 feet into the ground. Once primed, the farm kid filled both pails and walked back to the house.

In other words, the farm kid had the conscious idea to procure two buckets of water. The kid primed the pump (subconscious) to secure the final result of two pails of water, which is the final product or end result stage. Even in the 21st century, if you visit a park with a hand pump over a water well, you will have to pour water into the top of it to prime it before you can pump any water out of it.

If you are an artist, you may think of a fantastic painting one evening. Your conscious mind thinks of the theme of the painting. That night, your subconscious mind dreams up all the extras that will make that painting your grand work. Once you conceive of an idea, you must let your subconscious prime your brain to work on the idea to bring it to fruition. The next day, you bring it to form by painting the actual work of art.

The same process works for any kind of an adventure that you hope to bring to reality. You first consciously think of what it is that you intend to bring into form. As you sleep at night, your subconscious brain fills in all the blank spots. In the days ahead, you fulfill your conscious and subconscious work by taking action to bring the adventure to reality.

This tells you that nothing can be anything unless you first conceive the idea in your mind. Your thoughts become the activities of your life whether you choose to paint, write, play sports, compose music or any other life activity.

Always accept your own creative talents and abilities with no comparison to others. You captain your own boat. The key to your success is to live your life at your highest creative energy and enjoy every second of it. Your thoughts give you a ticket to the future of your life.

"Your thoughts and your thoughts alone will set you in motion," said author Mike Dooley. "Your thoughts will yield the inspiration, creativity and determination you need. Your thoughts will orchestrate the magic and inspire the universe. Your thoughts will carry you to the finish line if you just keep thinking them. Never give up! Never waiver! Never doubt! Aim high!"

KEY POINTS FROM THIS CHAPTER

1. Allow your creative subconscious to work for you.
2. Intentions drive everything followed with action.
3. What you think is what you get.

Chapter 10

Believe It, See It, Do It, Live It

A large volume of adventures may be grasped within this little span of life by individuals who interest their hearts in everything. *~ Sterne*

4ᵗʰ Concept—Believe it and you will see it

Imagine it, intend it, believe it and work toward it. You will realize it. Creative law operates by your imagination and as you think.

You may read a slew of self-help books and a few may possess these concepts. Some may capture your attention better than this book. You might read them to receive a different angle on these concepts. That's a good idea. Another writer may turn your crank better to provide you other compelling metaphors in a more logical or even emotional manner. That's why you will find a library of books inside this volume that will give you a leg-up to realize your dreams.

Additionally, read books by adventurers in your area of interest. They expose themselves without shame, without hesitation and without guilt. Whatever got them onto their adventures also bubbles out in their writing or pictures or poetry.

The eminent photographer Ansel Adams said, "I respect everything changing and the solemn beauty of life and death. I believe man will obtain freedom of spirit from society, and therefore while man walks amidst the imminent beauty of objective bodies, he must possess the capacity of self-perfection and must observe and represent his world with full confidence."

In many ways, Adams saw what he photographed before he took the shot. He waited, he pondered and he fidgeted with his camera settings. He took good shots and poor shots. He gleaned his good shots from his average shots. He learned from the mediocre shots and made adjustments. With each outing into the wilderness, he fine-tuned his talents.

You do the same thing as you work toward your dreams. You fidget with your life to make it work so you can see the picture you want to live. You may make any number of mistakes as to choices, friends and work. As you make those mistakes, honor your learning process. Every failure broadens your mind and allows you to proceed by making better choices in the future.

Adams talked about an energy or creative process that moves through all of us. We can engage it for our own needs.

"My private glimpses of some ideal reality create a lasting mood that has often been recalled in some of my photographs," said Adams.

Adams shares with you his visions while working in the wilderness. You enjoy the same capabilities. Like him, engage them in your own ways for your own interests. You are working with the creative human spirit inside you. The more you practice creative thought, the more it works for you on multiple levels.

SEE IT, DO IT, LIVE IT

In my own life, while not knowing my path in my early years, I stepped forward with idealistic enthusiasm. I made a number of mistakes. You will, too. So what! Not a single great man or woman in history enjoyed a perfect life, perfect path or perfect approach.

The great thinker, artist and inventor Leonardo da Vinci incorporated the seven principles of a creative life: curiosity of the mind, demonstration of ideas, expression of the senses, willingness to embrace uncertainty, development of art, logic and imagination, cultivation of grace, fitness and poise, and finally, recognition and appreciation for the interconnectedness of all things and phenomena.

All of us struggle, stumble, tussle and move along the same path he walked. We each carry our own challenges.

The key is to believe in you. Believe in your project. Believe that you will succeed. Then, get your nose into the wind. Move toward your dream with eagerness and curiosity. Move away from the shore and safety. Move toward the unknown until it becomes known. The more you see it—the more you do it—the more you live it.

Pretty soon, you will understand and know the unknown territory. You will learn to feel at ease in it at all times.

"Tentative efforts lead to tentative outcomes. Therefore, give yourself fully to your endeavors. Decide to construct your character through excellent actions and determine to pay the price of a worthy goal. The trials you encounter will introduce you to your strengths. Remain steadfast and one day you will build something that endures; something worthy of your potential." Epictetus, Roman philosopher

How long does that take? It depends. However, the best way to get your feet wet stems from living small adventures. Later, you can move up to bigger adventures.

1. Create weekend adventures.
2. Create weeklong adventures.
3. Create two-week adventures.
4. Create a summer adventure.

5. As you create your smaller adventures, they will prepare you for your longer adventures and you will gain confidence to expand your horizons.

6. Please note that this process works for anyone who wants to play the piano, paint a picture, sculpt, draw, sing, dance or seek other life activities. You begin with baby steps until you are ready to advance.

For example: join a mountain club and climb a mountain with someone who will show you the ropes. Go camping with someone who knows the rules of the wilderness. If you want to learn windsurfing, you need instruction. If you don't take instruction, you will keep falling with no idea of how to correct your deficiencies. That applies to snowboarding, rock climbing or any sport as well as any creative process that requires a learning curve.

CREATIVE PROCESS CANNOT ACT ON A HOPE, WANT OR WISH

Creative process requires expectation and action.

You may have heard your friends lament, "I wish I had good grades...I wish I had a million dollars so I could live a great life...I wish I was smarter." Others have said, "I want a new car...I want to make the team...I hope to get a new bike...I hope the world stops being unfair."

Here's the kicker. The creative energy of the universe (creative realm) cannot act on a wish, want or hope. It can only act on intentions and actions. What happens with wishing, wanting and hoping? If you live in that realm, you become a victim, prey or quarry for life's vagaries.

When you switch gears, much like Ansel Adams talked about, you kick your mind into action, which in turn requires activities to ensure your intentions move toward fruition.

KEY POINTS FROM THIS CHAPTER

1. Intend your dream, see it, believe it, live it.
2. The universe, also known as the creative realm, cannot act on a wish, hope or want.
3. Make no comparisons of yourself with anyone. Such comparisons rob your energy.
4. Strive to make intentions reality in your life.

Chapter 11

The Action Ticket

The sea is dangerous and its storms terrible, but these obstacles have never been sufficient reason to remain ashore. Unlike the mediocre, intrepid spirits seek victory over those things that seem impossible. It is with an iron will that they embark on the most daring of all endeavors. To meet the shadowy future without fear and conquer the unknown.
~ Magellan

5ᵗʰ Concept —You must engage the action concept

We live in a causal universe. Advancement toward your dream(s) depends on ideas transformed into action. Once you create a plan, idea or image, creative energy works on it through you.

Bestselling author Dan Millman said that in order to enjoy ultimate success, "It takes effort over time."

You must kick into gear the "Action Concept." It may be an idea for an invention, trip, project, painting, cartoon, thesis or anything that excites you. Always remain true to your passions. At the same time, be open to ancillary activities and people who may add to your life adventure. Remember, too, that as you grow into your own adventure-filled life, you will mentor others who come into your sphere.

You must maintain a personal determination and persistence to see an effort through to the end.

"If I had to select one quality, one personal characteristic that I regard as being most highly correlated with success, whatever the field, I would pick the trait of persistence. The will to endure to the end, to get knocked down seventy times and get up off the floor saying, "Here comes number seventy-one." Richard Devos, successful businessman.

On my corkboard, a card reads, "The Idea Fairy may strike at any time. Make sure to be alert and write down her ideas, so she will visit often."

You probably remember years ago when some guy got the idea to manufacture rubber shoes with holes in them. He decided to manufacture them in a variety of colors. His main goal was to make them comfortable and reliable.

Naysayers said, "That idea is a crock!"

You got that right. But his idea became one of the largest selling summer shoes in the world. You will see countless people wearing colorful Crocs in the summer. They even sell fur-lined winter Crocs today. It all happened because of an idea. From the idea, he moved into action.

IDEAS MOVE THE WORLD—CLIMBING YOUR MOUNT EVEREST

George Mallory, believed to be the first man to climb Mount Everest, but who died on the descent said, **"The first question which you will ask and which I must try to answer is this: what is the use of climbing Mount Everest? My answer must at once be: it is no use. There is not the slightest prospect of any gain whatsoever. Oh, we may learn a little about the behavior of the human body at high altitudes, and possibly medical men may turn our observation to some account for the purposes of aviation. But otherwise nothing will come of it. We shall not bring back a single bit of gold or silver, not a gem, nor any coal or iron. We shall not find a single foot of earth that can be planted with crops to raise food. It's no use. So, if you cannot understand that there is something in man**

which responds to the challenge of this mountain and goes out to meet it, that the struggle is the struggle of life itself upward and forever upward, then you won't see why we go. What we get from this adventure is just sheer joy. And joy is, after all, the end of life. We do not live to eat and make money. We eat and make money to be able to enjoy life. That is what life means and what life is for."

Let's look at regular people that lived or are living spectacular lives by taking action. Once they latched onto an idea, they carried through with the action concept.

Charles Lindbergh started with flying airplanes. Soon, as a barnstormer, he flew all over the country. Later, he flew the mail. Then, an idea struck him, "I will fly across the Atlantic Ocean."

The rest is history. He loved flying and he loved adventuring. After his historic flight, he barnstormed all over Mexico and South America in the Spirit of St. Louis. Visit the Smithsonian in Washington, DC, in the Air and Space Museum, to see stickers on the cowling of his plane from all the countries he explored.

Leonardo da Vinci, an exceptional adventurer, not only painted, he dissected cadavers to see how the human body worked. He invented flying machines, jet engines, weapons and a prototype for the bicycle. He generated those ideas out of the fertile soil of his mind. He engaged the action concept.

Jack Hamilton, a police officer from Ohio, loves bicycling. On one of my rides across America, I met him riding his bike across the country. He told me how lucky I was to do it all in one trip because I enjoyed three months off to ride. Because he could only get two weeks off a year, he pedaled two weeks and then, returned home, but came back to the same spot where he left off the previous year and the next year to ride another two weeks. It took him five years to ride his bicycle across America. But, he can stand tall in any crowd with the knowledge that he bicycled across

America. How? He worked his idea into smaller parts to create his final victory.

Amelia Earhart loved flying. On May 20, 1932, Amelia Earhart took off from Harbor Grace, Newfoundland, and landed the next day in Londonderry, Northern Ireland. She became the first woman to fly solo across the Atlantic.

"The most difficult thing is the decision to act; the rest is merely tenacity," said Earhart. "Please know I am quite aware of the hazards. I want to do it because I want to do it. Women must try to do things as men have tried. When they fail, their failure must be a challenge to other women."

Andrew Skurka skied, rafted and backpacked 4,600 miles across Alaska and the Yukon Territory in 2010. He stood his ground against charging grizzly bears and endless mosquitoes. He faced loneliness. Nonetheless, he pushed toward his ultimate destination. Was it easy? Try shouldering a 50-pound backpack for 4,600 miles to find out for yourself. In total, he has backpacked 30,000 miles through many of the world's most rugged backcountry and wilderness areas—the equivalent of traveling once around the planet at the equator. www.andrewskurka.com

In 2011, Anne Miltenberger of Boulder, Colorado, rowed her rowboat across the Atlantic Ocean. She competed in the Woodvale Challenge Atlantic Crossing, but her larger vision was to bring attention to the predicament of our oceans being polluted and fished to death by humanity. The enormity of her task boggles my mind. That's over 3,000 miles of monster ocean waves, treacherous storms, mind-numbing loneliness, physical challenges and the incredible expanse of the ocean. However, she rowed for the environment. She cares about this planet and she wants to make the world better for future generations. Her journey started with an idea. She put it into action. www.rowingfortheenvironment.com

Susan Butcher won the Alaska Iditarod dog sled race three years in a row against a mighty field of men. She suffered from dyslexia, which dissuaded her from veterinary medicine. She took up dog sledding. After more experience, she decided to race in one of the toughest endurance races in the world. One thousand miles of cold, mountains, ice, harsh weather and danger confronted her, but she succeeded in her intentions. It all started with her passion for animals and an idea to race in the Iditarod. She engaged the action concept.

KEY POINTS FROM THIS CHAPTER

1. You must move on your plan by taking action.
2. Work to fulfill your idea with persistence.
3. Moving toward your "Mount Everest" takes determination.
4. Improve your plan by being open to new ideas that you write down.

Practices Leading To Spectacular Living

Chapter 12

Growing Your Self-Confidence

**Self-Confidence creates your foundation for spectacular living. You gain it by choosing it. You own it by living with enthusiasm. You enjoy its power by accepting yourself. You feel it by your quest toward your passions. You move toward everything in your life by your single-hearted intensity of joy.
~ *FHW***

1st Practice—Growing your self-confidence

During my lifetime and my brothers' lifetimes, especially during our high school years, fellow students and friends said, "You're too self-confident, too self-assured, too cocky."

Why would anyone choose to be insecure? Why would they want to be known as timid, afraid or milk toast?

If you think you can climb a mountain or you think you won't make it; you're going to end up by the way you think.

In my middle years, friends warned that I would get killed by bicycling, mountain climbing and scuba diving for a year in South America. They feared I might die by traveling across the Outback of Australia. It confounded them that I wanted to backpack into the Himalayas. For certain, a shark would eat me somewhere in the Indian Ocean. And, there's no question, I could be killed at any moment during my bicycle travels around the world with just one driver who might roll over me with his or her 4,000-pound vehicle.

No question! It happens. Yes, I could have been killed many times. I still feel fortunate not to be eaten by a grizzly bear that stared at me, not four feet away, while I awoke in my tent by the Russian River in Alaska in 1977. He could have used my brother Rex and me for dessert after gorging on salmon. But he didn't.

For the record, I continued my continent-jumping adventures anyway. I didn't buy into fear. I didn't compare. I didn't think about dying. I pursued living.

I maintained my most powerful passport to a spectacular life: self-confidence.

Please realize this reality: you can play it safe your whole life in order to avoid the travails and dangers of living. If the Nature Channel takes you to as close to adventure as you wish, by all means, click the remote. Me? I'd rather smell an elephant in India, catch a salmon out of the Russian River in Alaska and backpack the Inca Trail in Peru.

Yes, it's true, my brothers and I enjoyed a mom and dad who instilled in us a sense of self-confidence. Once you possess it, you carry it for life.

If possible, use the people in this book to develop your own self-confidence. They're just like you, no more and no less. They've got their own fears, too. That includes me!

But you decide to pursue your dreams, anyway. Once you make your little dreams come true, the bigger ones become easier. In time, they become normal.

It's all there for you, too, no matter what your age.

KEY POINTS FROM THIS CHAPTER

1. Accept yourself at all times.
2. Work on your abilities, talents and skills.
3. Choose "I can do that" with every challenge.

Chapter 13

Delete Self-deprecating Feelings

Life is known only by those who have found a way to be comfortable with change and the unknown. Given the nature of life, there may be no security, but only adventure. ~ *Rachel Naomi Remen*

2nd Practice—Delete self-deprecating words, feelings or thoughts about yourself

Years ago, my college roommate chastised himself whenever he made a mistake, spilled a glass of milk, tripped or fumbled something. He would scream at himself, "You stupid...." At other times, he would say, "You dumb...."

"Jack," I said after taking a psychology class. "My instructor said your brain is like a computer. It can't tell the difference between a positive word or negative word about you. If you keep telling your brain that you're dumb, stupid or clumsy, guess what dude, your brain will respond by becoming dumb, stupid and clumsy. How about after you make a mistake, you say something like, "I'm going to get better at this...I'm improving...I'm going to change this for the better."

Jack, a math major and always logical, said, "Frosty, good point. I will always speak highly of myself no matter what kind of mistakes I make in the future. Think well, be well. That's me. Thanks, dude."

From that day, he never said anything negative about himself again.

I have brought that practice to many people in my life after asking them for permission to present an idea for them to ponder.

Once people stop berating themselves, it frees their minds to become productive on multiple levels. It brings serenity to their minds, bodies and spirits.

What's the lesson here? You can choose to move beyond self-deprecating concepts. Think positively. Act positively. Feel positively. In the end, you will become a positive, productive and happy person.

If someone came up to you and asked, "Can you name five positive things about yourself?"

Could you? Would you? I hope so. It's good to possess a positive self-image. It carries lighter in your life backpack and it thrusts you into greater possibilities. So, yes, answer them with, "I'm having a great day, I'm funny, I'm excited, I'm smart, I'm interesting, I love life…."

If you look out on our society and you watch all the inane television programs where the scenes show guys and gals in petty group situations, it shows you extraordinarily trivial and mean-spirited tit-for-tat conversations. The guys get into yelling matches. Later, the girls break down in sobs, apologizing and suffering from guilt.

They solve nothing and walk away having learned zilch. But they all leave with one thing intact: their negative self-concepts.

As a young man, I read a book by Thomas Harris: ***I'm OK, You're OK.*** He described four ways people feel about themselves. I'm OK, You're OK. Such a person lives a balanced life and enjoys a healthy outlook. I'm not OK, You're OK. Such a person feels negative self-concepts, but everyone else is OK. I'm OK, You're not OK. Such a person sees himself OK, but everybody else as negative. I'm not OK, You're not OK. Such a person sees himself and everyone as all screwed up. According to that book, many Americans live their lives with an "I'm not OK feeling."

You see them in bars drinking themselves into oblivion. You may see them eating themselves into their own torment. Look at the obesity epidemic in this country for a harsh dose of unhealthy self-concepts. They may smoke, drink endless coffee and watch countless hours of television. Others visit shrinks for $100.00 an hour for years to try to find themselves.

Many people never move to self-acceptance. What constitutes self-acceptance? It means you accept your height, weight, size, looks, mind, abilities and everything about you. You compare yourself to no one. You move through the world on your terms with a sense of self-confidence and enjoyment of the very fact that you're alive, healthy and living. You feel equal to every other human being on earth and you wish all humans and other creatures good will.

How do you get to self-acceptance? You make choices based on new knowledge. This book provides you with opportunities. At the same time, I am offering many other writers that may resonate with you better with their ideas for self-acceptance and success. Either way, you win.

My dad used to say, "I don't care how tough it is or what it takes or how hard you think it is, you can do it. You just decide to stand your ground. Stand tall and speak up or speak out. Accept who and what you are. Just realize that there are hundreds of others too afraid, too timid or too fearful to try. So, decide to do it, make your plans and make it happen."

From this point onward when facing challenges, you may say, "I can do that, I will do that, I am doing that."

KEY POINTS FROM THIS CHAPTER

1. Delete negative self-concepts.
2. Accept yourself as a whole, complete and capable person.
3. Enjoy every potential moment for a positive life experience.
4. Finally, you can say, "I can do that."

Chapter 14

Choose Your View

It is not the critic who counts, not the man who points out how the strong man stumbles, or where the doer of deeds could have done them better. The credit belongs to the man in the arena, whose face is marred by dust and sweat and blood, who strives valiantly. Who knows the great enthusiasms, the great devotion; who spends himself in a worthy cause; who at best knows in the end the triumph of high achievement, and who at the worst, if he fails, at least fails while daring greatly, so that his place shall never be with those cold and timid souls who knew neither victory nor defeat. ~ *U.S. President Teddy Roosevelt*

3ⁿᵈ Practice—Choose your view

No one else but you chooses your mental perspective or your life view. You may choose a positive, negative, neutral, fearful, dull or bored life attitude. You could choose an outlook such as, "I don't care." You can choose an outlook such as, "I will make a positive difference." You may become involved in life or uninvolved. It's up to you.

Please examine two basic views that will lift you toward an extraordinary life experience or an average life path.

Will you choose a worm's eye-view or an eagle's eye-view? Okay! I know what you're thinking. Worms don't have eyes to see. Work with me here. Which will you choose? If you think below the surface or think limitations or wallow in your muck from past conditions—your world will remain that of a worm's reality.

When I attended high school, I studied every night. I attended every class. I played sports. I joined clubs to connect with other students. I learned how to swing dance. I pitched newspapers to 80 customers on my paper route at 5:00 a.m. seven days a week. I kept my eyes on the prize.

WORM'S EYE-VIEW

At the same time, quite a few of my classmates hung out in the parking lot—smoking, drinking and wasting time doing nothing. They didn't complete their homework assignments. Many dropped out to work as tire changers, janitors or stock boys. None of them advanced to college or trade schools.

They guaranteed themselves mediocre lives. They chained themselves to the lowest financial rung of the ladder. They hung with each other so they thought their actions or lack of actions appeared normal. Intellectual mediocrity, lassitude and sloth rarely make for a fulfilling lifestyle.

Such a worm's eye-view ensures definite lifetime limitations. It limits mental and physical travel. It relegates such a person to trailer parks or housing projects. It means factory jobs, stocking grocery shelves, maid work and other minimum wage employment. It means few choices and scant satisfaction.

At my high school reunions, I couldn't help but wonder what would have happened if those dudes and dudettes had chosen to study hard, engage in high school, move on to college and live a more abundant life. Their eyes may have been as bright and shiny as those in our class who chose the eagle's eye-view. Be certain that you get to choose. When possible, choose your view early in life.

The creative process affords, however, that at any life juncture, a mental shift will produce stellar results. It's really up to you how dynamic a life you want to live. It can start at any time you choose to change to an eagle's eye-view.

EAGLE'S EYE-VIEW

For those who choose an eagle's eye-view, hold on to your hats. What a ride! When you put your heart, mind and spirit into the joy of living, you discover a passionate, purposeful and energy-filled life. It's whatever turns you on that thrusts your mind toward mental and emotional zeniths.

I met a young guy named Sandy on my adventure to Antarctica. He carried high spirits, exuberance and friendliness. He worked his way through college to become a journalist and photographer. He possessed buckets of high energy. During his time in Antarctica, he raced in the Scott Hut Race in bitter cold. He jumped into the water in the 12-foot thick ice of the Southern Oceans. He raced around the world within 10 seconds at the South Pole.

I've watched him for 13 years. He learned to speak Japanese. He traveled to France to learn how to speak French. He traveled to China, South America, Australia and other regions on the planet. Later, he met a delightful lady. They decided on a family. Today, he's a father and loves it. He skis, rafts, climbs and races in marathons. He lives in the woods of Maine.

Did he receive a special start in life? Not really. He's a country boy from Missouri. He earned everything through hard work and tenacity.

Sandy provides you with an example of an eagle's-eye view of living.

"The outward movement into form does not express itself with equal intensity in all people," said Eckhart Tolle, author of **Awakening to Your Life's Purpose**. "Some feel a strong urge to build, create, become involved, achieve and make an impact on the world."

Does an eagle's eye-view mean you must be excited or filled with high-energy?

Not at all!

Quieter yet equally dynamic people may be called "frequency holders."

"They are more inward looking by nature," said Tolle. "Their role is just as vital as that of the creators, the doers and the reformers. They endow the seemingly insignificant with profound meaning. They affect the world much more deeply than is visible on the surface of their lives."

Another young man I met in Texas on my 2010 bicycle ride across America proved quiet yet dynamic. Davis walked up to me at a sandwich shop, "Are you the one riding that bike that says coast to coast?"

"Sure am," I said.

"Can I buy you dinner?" he said.

"Why would you buy me dinner?" I asked.

"I want to learn how you do it," he said.

As we talked, Davis said, "I don't want to live a boring life. I want to see the world. I don't want to be average."

What did I notice about him? He came across as a quiet 18-year-old with a thirst for knowledge to live a great life. He attends college where he reads and writes prolifically. His mind expands toward the great events of his future. We keep in touch and I look forward to his unfolding life with an eagle's eye-view attitude.

When you decide to see the world from a higher calling, your intentions fly with your thoughts. In other words, your dreams become your reality. Let these concepts move you toward your dreams. You make the call. No matter what the pains of your past, forgive anyone that has ever hurt you and unload your emotional baggage so it doesn't burden your brain or emotions. Your current perceptions color your imagination and fulfillment.

Engage these points to adopt an eagle's eye-view.

1. Write down what will move your dream into motion.
2. Take inventory, improve, build upon and expand your talents and abilities to maximize your potential.
3. Think positively, optimistically, affirmatively and constructively.
4. Delete that other self in your brain that comes on negatively.
5. Identify any trepidation and neutralize it by positive mental decisions.
6. Think and see success, write it down on paper and repeat it aloud.
7. Keep and read affirmations on your desk, fridge, car dash, bathroom mirror and everywhere that will move your mind toward your intention.
8. Hang with others that enjoy your eagle's-eye view.

What does an eagle's eye-view feel like?

When I go skiing, I take the Panoramic Express chair lift in Winter Park, Colorado to the highest point on the mountain at 12,065 feet. Once off the lift, I spread my arms like the wings of an eagle and fly down the mountain with long graceful turns. Out front, the massive 13,392-foot Parry's Peak greets me and the Continental Divide cuts a rugged profile across the cobalt sky above me. Essentially, I am an eagle flying at great altitude.

However, you don't need to live in the mountains to enjoy an eagle's eye-view. You can ride your bicycle while flying down the road for the same feeling. You can choose a positive mental-emotional point of view. You may be scuba diving for that eagle's eye-view or perhaps taking a canoe trip. Whatever your activity, take it to your highest level of attitude and fulfillment.

Proceed toward tomorrow with an eagle's eye-view.

KEY POINTS FROM THIS CHAPTER

1. You may choose an eagle's-eye view or worm's eye-view.
2. Worm's eye-view keeps you below the surface.
3. Eagle's eye-view carries you to personal and physical success.
4. Engage the eight methods that take you to the eagle's eye- view.

Chapter 15

Claim Your Highest and Best

One final paragraph of advice: Do not burn yourself out. Be as I am – a reluctant enthusiast... a part time crusader, a half-hearted fanatic. Save the other half of yourselves and your lives for pleasure and adventure. It is not enough to fight for the land; it is even more important to enjoy it. While you can. While it is still there. So get out there and mess around with your friends, ramble out yonder and explore the forests, encounter the grizzly, climb the mountains. Run the rivers, breathe deep of that yet sweet and lucid air, sit quietly for a while and contemplate the precious stillness, that lovely, mysterious and awesome space. Enjoy yourselves, keep your brain in your head and your head firmly attached to your body, the body active and alive, and I promise you this much: I promise you this one sweet victory over our enemies, over those deskbound people with their hearts in a safe deposit box and their eyes hypnotized by desk calculators. I promise you this: you will outlive them. ~ *Edward Abbey*

4th Practice—Claim your highest and best

When you regularly use your talents, the ideas and creative process become second nature to you. You will discover that new ideas and possibilities fall into your lap even if you don't know what they are at the moment.

Everything becomes clearer as you move creatively forward. Does every person's life turn out to be a fairy-tale ending? That depends on luck, random chance and tenacity. It depends on the right place, right time and right attitude.

By your consistent work and planning, you will move toward your dreams, goals and intentions.

"Most of the important things in the world have been accomplished by people who kept on trying when there seemed to be no hope at all," said Dale Carnegie, author and industrialist.

Many of life's failures are people who did not realize how close they were to success when they gave up.

How did a farm boy from Michigan land in Antarctica? I worked for it, kept trying and it happened. I interviewed with Antarctica Support Services for four years in a row only to be rejected each time. But the fifth time proved a charm. Had I quit after the fourth time, I would never have reached Antarctica.

On the literary front, I sent my book manuscripts into hundreds of publishers for 22 years before enjoying my first published book. Had I stopped at year 21, I would never have enjoyed success.

Therefore, always think, act and feel for your highest and best.

As you may notice all around you, not all people work toward an outstanding life.

For an example, it's been shown that a large percentage of Americans dislike their jobs. They may enjoy the money, but they don't care for the heartburn, headaches, stress and fatigue of an unhappy employment situation. Many others plod onward without hope or enthusiasm. Anyone can change his or her future by taking action in the present moment.

At the same time, some men and women try daredevil stunts. Are they crazy? What do they get out of them? Who are they?

What happens when they have an accident? Let's talk about a man who jumped off a cliff into Lake Powell and broke his back, suffering paralysis from the waist down. I know him. His name is Matt Feeney. He was born with glorious good looks. He possesses charisma and power in his being that most politicians would give their fortune to possess. After breaking his back, Matt didn't sit on his butt and die of depression. He refused to feel sorry for himself. He got back up from the bed and jumped into a wheelchair. In fact, he started racing in wheelchairs.

During the winter, he learned to race on a mono-ski. Still later, he bicycle raced (using his hands to pedal) and water-skied at the Special Olympics. He supervised and taught at the National Sports Center for the Disabled in Winter Park, Colorado. Today, he runs his own adaptive skiing sports camps for the disabled. www.adaptiveadventures.org He's the kind of man and athlete that thousands of people look up to for guidance, power and inspiration. Even as he mobilizes in that wheelchair, he tackles life everyday— with power, gusto, passion and purpose.

It is my honor and privilege to be his friend. He has no idea how much I admire him, his courage and his actions as he leaps toward life. He chose his highest and best under difficult circumstances.

Instead of accepting his condition as a failure, Feeney engaged "metanoia" which means a total consciousness change. He moved from fear and defeat to courage. He moved toward the light.

Bethany Hamilton at 13, a top Hawaiian surfer, lost her arm to a shark attack in 2003. Today, she continues surfing and inspiring kids of all ages by her full participation in sports and life.

No matter what physical, emotional or mental difficulties you face, you can engage metanoia like Bob Wieland, Matt Feeney, Bethany Hamilton and many other persons struggling with difficulties. By choosing your highest and best, you will capture a meaningful life.

The following are possible avenues toward your highest and best:

1. Hunt for new experiences and activities.
2. Take college classes and attend seminars on personal growth.
3. Apply for different part-time jobs.
4. Check out an unusual hobby or interest.
5. Volunteer to help someone else or an organization.

In the end, highest and best means you maintain a positive attitude no matter how difficult the task or assignment. Few people enjoy an easy ride to their dreams. Go to any library and check out DVDs on Leonardo de Vinci, Ben Franklin, Susan B. Anthony, Dolly Madison, Thomas Jefferson, Jane Goodall, Nelson Mandela, Amelia Earhart, Gandhi, Abraham Lincoln, Dr. Martin Luther King, Mark Twain, Oprah Winfrey, George Washington and many of history's great figures. Every single one of them faced daunting challenges. What did they share in common? They all worked for their highest and best.

To cement these concepts, evolve your thinking:

1. Trust your instincts. Move with the flow of ideas. Begin with increasing your mental, spiritual and physical goals.
2. Think of yourself as happy, prosperous and well.
3. One great philosopher said, "Despair means you're looking the wrong way." Look in the positive direction of your intentions for a positive outcome.
4. The Greek word "metanoia" means total consciousness change. Move from fear to courage. Cleanse your consciousness. Move toward the light.

5. The term "universe" means the creative realm of possibilities.

You may like to incorporate one of the best practices for this transformation of thought: affirmative quotes. You see at the head of every chapter quotes from dozens of top male and female adventurers. Choose a quote from your favorite person and place it on your mirror to be read each morning before you start the day and at the end of the day. You want those positive thoughts and intentions moving through your brain all day and all night. You can write your own affirmation and read it daily. One writer said, "What you seek is seeking you."

KEY POINTS FROM THIS CHAPTER

1. Think, act and feel for your highest and best.
2. Use these points to move toward your dreams.
3. Trust your instincts.
4. Repeat your affirmations created by you or from your heroes.
5. Metanoia means to change consciousness toward enlightenment.

Chapter 16

Live Brilliantly

Never forget that life can only be nobly inspired and rightly lived if you take it bravely and gallantly, as a splendid adventure in which you are setting out into an unknown country, to face many a danger, to meet many a joy, to find many a comrade, to win and lose many a battle. ~ *Annie Besant*

5th Practice—Live brilliantly

Your life unfolds as you choose. You enjoy abundant opportunities with endless possibilities. Move from limitations and limited thinking to unlimited expectations and actions.

Focus, commit, act and engage.

Live brilliantly with your own special brand of passion, enthusiasm, verve, fervor, zest, gusto or any other name you might call it. Let it boil up in you and bubble over in your daily life. Anything positive can and will happen when you work with an expectant attitude.

Focus on your goal, your idea or your purpose. Few persons ever accomplish anything without focusing on their objective. Drive your mind, heart, body and soul toward whatever you expect to accomplish. Focus on it, write it down, say it verbally, create a vision board, paint it or any other expression you find energizing for your life.

Commit to it by avoiding distractions. It's easy to fool around on your way toward your goal by goofing off, making excuses, or finding someone who takes you off your path. Once you commit, you set your mind toward your final destination. It becomes easier the farther along the path you travel.

Action always speaks louder than anything else. Conviction without action turns into entertainment. Words vanish into thin air. A page full of "I hope to...." won't amount to a hill of beans without action from you. Take action toward your intention. It's simple, straightforward and direct.

For example: when my siblings and I were kids, we marched into the kitchen after playing outside and asked our mother for some cookies.

She said, "If you want some cookies, you make them and you bake them."

Within minutes, we pulled out the recipe, all the ingredients and turned up the oven to 350 degrees Fahrenheit. We happily took action that carried us to our final reward of gorging ourselves on chocolate chip cookies. We gobbled those cookies. Mom didn't do it for us. Unknowingly, she gave us a valuable gift. If you desire something, take action.

Another time, I needed a bike for my paper route. My dad said, "You earn the money and you can buy it."

It took me several months of walking my paper route, but after saving up the money, I plunked down cash for a brand new bicycle. I took action toward my goal of buying a bike. During the time that I worked for it, as well as when I pedaled it on my morning newspaper route, I lived brilliantly with purpose, passion and high expectations.

Other parents give their kids everything they want. They buy them televisions, bicycles, cell phones, sports gear and clothes. That sets up a dynamic for the child of thinking that life will give him or her everything at no cost, with no responsibility or personal accountability. Such an upbringing will create challenges for that child when he or she reaches adulthood.

On the negative side, a lot of kids ask their parents for something and the parents respond with a resounding, "No, you can't have cookies or a new bike or a dress."

When a parent says "no" like that, it means to the child that "life" says, "No!" It doesn't matter what rationale the parent is using. Why? That's all a child understands. That "no" manifests in the child's mind as a negative concept. With endless "no's" a kid may buy into the reality that he or she is helpless to enjoy a cookie or any other yearning. It can also translate into the orientation that they can't do well in school, become a cheerleader or captain the chess team.

Of course, all kids learn that they may enjoy recess only when the bell rings. They can only go to eat when the lunch bell rings. All of us learn about our scheduling paradigms, responsibilities and personal behavior.

At the same time, many young kids today lack a sense of self-confidence. They are told they can't do something. The father might say, "I had a hard time in math class so you probably will find math difficult, too."

Kids respond by accepting that they have no power to succeed or take action. Finally, their outcome is failure or apathy. None of us can blame our parents because the same thing was done to them. It's called "cultural consciousness" or "traditions" of our society.

"Well, that's the way we've always done it around here," said the local man in charge. "If you don't like it, that's tough."

You can change that orientation by understanding what happened to you in your youth. You can rewrite the hard drive in your mind. You can decide to take action. You can move toward creating an edge.

"Edge" means to maximize yourself mentally, emotionally and physically. You may notice all great athletes maintain an edge in their sport. Great tennis players study their opponents on film or in person to discover their strengths and weaknesses. Great golfers see their ball dropping into the cup. Basketball players feel their shot swishing through the net. Great home-run hitters watch the ball all the way until it connects with the bat.

It's no different for you. Keep your edge by keeping a keen mind and concentrating on your intentions, work, play and goals.

Finally, as the starship Captain Jean-Luc Picard in *Star Trek* told Commander Data, "Set a course for the Zebulon sector... engage."

Everything falls into place as you work your mind toward success. You engage your entire being into the process of triumph through these practices.

Do you see a new pattern for your life emerging? While many enthusiastic people create energetic lives for themselves, many other quiet individuals also create fulfilling and happy lives at their levels of engagement. None possess a patent on what it means to live an adventure-filled life. That's why someone who loves to sculpt, play chess, paint or macramé may enjoy just as passionate a life as a mountain climber.

At Iguassu Falls in Argentina, my friends and I stepped beside one of the grandest waterfalls in the world. It's not the tallest, but it proves to be one of the most spectacular. Around the roar of the falls, we watched toucan birds and brilliantly colored butterflies. Near the falls, we watched 10,000 black and yellow butterflies dancing on pink flowers. Can you imagine the color contrast and movement as the butterflies pollinated the flowers?

What made that experience more incredible? A man, sitting at a seven-foot-tall harp, played his music to "flow" with the butterflies. We sat on the grass watching him play while the butterflies danced to his music. Maybe his music danced to the butterflies. His passion translated into an amazing experience for him and for us.

Sure, I get high riding my bicycle, skiing down a bump run, canoeing, rafting and climbing mountains. This guy got high playing his harp with butterflies dancing to the music. By the look on his face, I swear he climbed to the top of his own Mount Everest in the musical realm. He lived brilliantly.

KEY POINTS FROM THIS CHAPTER

1. Live at your highest sense of well-being.
2. Choose to expect good things to happen in your life.
3. Expect good outcomes as a matter of habit.
4. Relish every minute along the way whether work, play or quiet time.

Chapter 17

Total Dedication and Receptivity

Your own words are the bricks and mortar of the dreams you want to realize. Your words are the greatest power you have. The words you choose and their use establish the life you experience. *~ Sonia Croquette*

6th Practice—Total dedication and receptivity

The key to the adventure-car that you expect to drive throughout your life, whether you climb a mountain, raft a river, paint a picture, write a poem, create a sculpture or raise kids—depends on your dedication and receptivity.

Let me repeat this wise saying by the philosopher Goethe to drive it into your conscious and subconscious mind: "Until one is committed, there is hesitancy; the chance to draw back—always ineffectiveness. Concerning all acts of initiative and creation, there is one elementary truth: the ignorance of which kills countless ideas and splendid plans. That the moment one definitely commits oneself to a task, then providence moves, too. All sorts of things occur to help one that would never otherwise have occurred. A whole stream of events issues from the decision, raising in one's favor all manner of unforeseen incidents and meetings and material assistance, which no one could have dreamed would have come his or her way. Whatever you can do, or dream you can do, begin it. Boldness has genius, power and magic in it. Begin it now."

Those words echo the quote at the head of this chapter by Sonia Croquette. You must possess total dedication and receptivity.

Your dedication determines the words that you choose and their use establishes the life you experience.

That means you may change your entire thinking and speaking patterns to expect and receive new ideas and attitudes. You may approach it emotionally or intellectually or both.

You can engage your mental thought waves with the creative energy of the universe.

Once you engage that creative energy, you will discover thoughts and ideas that will facilitate your goals and dreams. What dream has your name on it? That's for you to decide. Once you stamp your name on your dream, take action.

When you incorporate the nuances of these practices along with the concepts, you will find yourself thinking, speaking and acting in new and self-fulfilling ways. You are receptive to new ideas and people with creative and adventuresome lives. As a result, you will interest them and they will interest you.

If you climb a 14,000-foot peak, you will run into people that love the mountains, love adventure and love the outdoors. Without a doubt, it's challenging to climb a mountain. No question that a 100-mile bicycle ride taxes the heck out of you. Nonetheless, you ride with others who love the quest. More than likely they love other quests in the same realm.

Those experiences lead to ever-greater possibilities through your commitment and receptivity to a person, place or thing.

KEY POINTS FROM THIS CHAPTER

1. Your intentions engage your receptivity.
2. Your thinking must be geared toward success at all times.

3. Expect success, live success, feel success and breathe success.

4. Draw people like you to your realm by engaging the energy of success.

Chapter 18

Steadfast Conviction

If you think you can or can't, you're right. *~ Henry Ford*

7th Practice—Steadfast conviction

Back in 1884, Thomas Stevens decided to ride his Penny Farthing high-wheeler bicycle around the world starting in San Francisco, California. It features a huge front wheel and a small trailing wheel. Hence, the name stemmed from the British penny and farthing coins, with one much larger than the other. He pedaled with no gears, little pack, less water and no support. Mounting one of them took agility and the ability to use the peg on the back steel frame to jump up to the seat. All before him had failed similar attempts. However, he wired his brain with attitude, guts, determination and steadfast conviction. On December 17, 1886, he finished his bicycle ride around the world in San Francisco. (Amazon: **Around the World on a Bicycle** by Thomas Stevens)

You may appreciate right now that adventure is not and never will be a walk in the park, a Sunday stroll or a bicycle ride around the lake on a paved path. If you ride a long distance touring bicycle, climb a mountain, canoe rivers, walk the entire Great Wall of China, explore Antarctica, walk the length of the Amazon River, or pack into the Grand Canyon—you must be prepared for some rough slogging, harsh weather, tough times, demonic insects, irritating companions and hard knocks.

When the going gets tough, the mentally and emotionally tough get going. No whining, complaining or feeling sorry for yourself. No sitting around in a pity party crying, "Nobody likes me, everybody hates me—I'm going to eat some worms. Big fat juicy ones, squishy soft greasy ones; I'm going to eat some worms."

Instead, dude or dudette, buck up. Saddle up. True grit. Get moving. It's not the easy times but the hard times that make an adventure most memorable. Some days as I cycled 17,000 kilometers around the perimeter of Australia in 120-degree Fahrenheit heat day in and day out, baking in the desert, with those demonic bush flies crawling into every orifice of my body and not a soul in sight—I felt utter desperation, loneliness and futility. I felt sweat draining out of my pores as I fell asleep in the scorching desert heat night after night. I stunk like a koala bear and suffered from thirst and cottonmouth all day long.

Cycling around Australia may be one of the most miserable adventures of my life. Before I started, one Australian, when I talked about cycling across the Nullarbor Plains said, "Do you know how hot it is across the middle?"

"I'm going for the adventure," I said.

"That only proves one thing, mate," he said.

"What's that?" I asked.

"You must be dead from the neck up," he said.

He may have been right. A few times, I sat beside my tent, sweating like a pig, filthy with grime and so lonely that when I looked up, all I saw was the bottom of the bucket. On Christmas Day, one lady at a roadhouse said, "Wouldn't you like to be home with your friends right about now?"

"Sure, it would be nice to share Christmas with my friends and family," I said. "But then, I wouldn't be on this incredible adventure around Australia. They all wish they were me. I'm happy that I am me and living this adventure. Besides, I could easily jump on a plane and fly home. But that's not what I came for."

My dad once told me that when I put myself into a situation, it came from my choice and either I lived it out or I would regret not finishing what I started. I always call on a deep-down conviction that my dad planted in me at a young age. He implanted the power of steadfast conviction in my heart, mind and body.

During my cycle ride around Australia, I witnessed natural phenomenon and animals unknown to 99 percent of humanity. I witnessed a frilled lizard walk up to my tent and flare his frill at me like a space alien. It scared the daylights out of me. I rode my bike across the Nullarbor plains with a flightless bird named an Emu for two days. I watched kangaroos hop through the bush. I walked among the Pinnacles of Cervantes. I swam with the dolphins at Shark's Bay. I stood in the prison Boab tree in Northern Australia. A crocodile chased me in Darwin. I scuba dived on the Great Barrier Reef. I watched the Southern Cross fill the night sky during the whole journey. I live with those uncommon experiences inside my mind.

Andrew Skurka, the man we met earlier, skied, rafted and backpacked 4,600 miles across Alaska and the Yukon Territory in 2010. He stood his ground against charging grizzly bears. He shouldered a heavy 50-pound pack while hiking up to 20 miles per day. He pushed toward his ultimate destination. Was it easy? What do you think?

It matters little whether you walk across America on your hands or walk around the world or climb a mountain peak. You must engage uncommon tenacity to succeed at whatever your quest.

Those hard times that you experience qualify for adventure rather than someone taking a casual bicycle ride around town or watching a movie about some adventure. Let's talk about what it takes to succeed in your quests.

Returning to Thomas Stevens, few people can comprehend how much dedication it took to ride a Penny Farthing around the world. First of all, it's not easy to ride one. If you brake too hard, you can fly over the handlebars from eight feet above the ground.

Pedaling one of those bikes over sandy, gravel or muddy roads makes for a living nightmare. A rider can carry very little gear on that ungainly bicycle with a little trailing wheel.

Nonetheless, Stevens maintained steadfast conviction to complete the ride. His book astounded me in that he lived through it. He pedaled that bike across sand, gravel and muck. He nearly suffered death many times. He crossed the entire United States. After his initial success, he took off by sailing ship to Great Britain. From there, he cycled across Europe, the Middle East to India and China. He hopped all over the place before finally reaching San Francisco two years later. He maintained a steadfast conviction to complete the ride. Not only that, he later pedaled into Africa, rode a horse across Russia, traveled through India and much more. He faced diseases, polluted water, people trying to kill him and a host of challenges beyond anything imagined today.

As a matter of record, my friend Doug Armstrong spent 16 months pedaling from Cape Town, South Africa to Cairo, Egypt. He almost got killed, too. It's not any safer today.

As a six continent-riding cyclist myself, I have benefited from 21 gears and a derailleur that made mountain climbing easy. I have enjoyed big rubber tires, mostly paved roads and plentiful filtered clean water and food. My travels, for the most part, even in developing countries, have been a party compared to Stevens.

He walked up every hill because a Penny Farthing cannot negotiate much more than a five percent grade, and because of poor brakes, he walked down the other side of mountains. He proved one tough hombre. With my gears, I can ride up 16,000-foot mountain passes on gravel, as I have in the Andes, and coast down the other side. Nonetheless, it's tough busting your butt, and you need true grit in spite of any adversity, to keep going—especially in headwinds, torrid heat or pouring rain.

Thomas, you, me or anyone choosing adventure must employ the same tenacity and determination to succeed in worldwide adventures. It's called "steadfast conviction."

Whether you're working a tough job to earn the money for the adventure or during the adventure, you need steadfast conviction. If you suffer from heat, cold, rain or insects during an adventure, you need to maintain steadfast conviction that you own your success. That's right. You live it, think it and feel it. You walk, run, skip or whatever it takes to get you to your goal.

An old sailor once said, "A smooth sea never made a skillful mariner, neither do uninterrupted prosperity and success qualify for usefulness and happiness. The storms of adversity, like those of the ocean, rouse the faculties, and excite the invention, prudence, skill and fortitude of the voyager. The mariners of ancient times, in bracing their minds to outward calamities, acquired a loftiness of purpose and moral heroism worth a lifetime of softness and security."

No one will care one way or the other if you succeed or otherwise. For the most part, human beings only care about their little corner of the world and their own situation. Some choose personal greatness while others choose average lives. If you choose a life of adventure, engage your own brand of personal tenacity that will carry you to a lifetime of achievement.

Therefore, decide to succeed, and, quite frankly, you will succeed with your steadfast conviction.

KEY POINTS FROM THIS CHAPTER

1. Steadfast conviction becomes your mindset.
2. True grit and determination must become a part of your being.
3. Your success depends on your positive mental attitude.
4. If you think you can't or can, you're right.

Section IV

Nuggets of Wisdom for Daily Living

Chapter 19

What Dream Has Your Name On It?

Most people stumble through their teens, stagger through their twenties and meander into their thirties.

By forty, they suffer a mid-life crisis before bumping into the big five zero.

From 50, they face the last third of their lives with a sense of a downhill slide. Most never lived any great moments or vanquished any dragons let alone navigated a great sailing ship called the Black Pearl like Captain Jack Sparrow. None took off through space like the Next Generation on the Starship Enterprise.

Most Americans enjoy two-week vacations with scant time to climb Mt. Everest or raft the Amazon. Others feel so locked into their jobs that nothing and no one can change their fate.

What if teens and twenty-something's changed the course of their existence by co-creating their lives with a greater power, a higher understanding and a plan to enjoy their way of life?

Captain Jean Luc Picard said, "Time is a companion that goes with us on a journey. It reminds us to cherish each moment, because it will never come again. What we leave behind is not as important as how we have lived."

Breathe that statement into your spirit. Incorporate it into your mind. Engage it with your passions.

What turns you on in your daily existence? What moves you to action? What calls you?

For every human being on Earth, a little engine inside calls for "something" to activate a life calling. How do you find out which path calls you?

What heroes do you follow? Why? What great moments in history move you? How do you feel when you study a certain subject? What books engage your interest? What famous movie role inspires you?

It's my contention that you discover your life path by following the slightest thread of your desires. From there, you make your intentions.

One such young lady wanted to fly an airplane. As she grew up, she used a doll for her co-pilot, which she placed next to her in her "airplane" with two seats in her room. As she grew older, she kept the doll next to her and carried it with her when she attended college. After college, she gained work at an airport, but couldn't afford flying lessons. Nonetheless, she made friends with pilots and trainers alike. At all times, she kept her doll with her to remind her of her dream to fly.

As fate entered the picture, she became an assistant to a veteran airline pilot trainer. She worked hard, showed up on time, stayed late and kept the books in order. After a year of watching her, he offered her some time in a flight simulator. Soon, she showed her adept skills as a pilot that impressed the trainer. He offered to take her up in a single engine plane for flight training. She earned, scraped and saved money for pilot lessons. After two years, she gained her pilot's license. At all times, her doll sat with her in the cockpit.

Soon, she learned how to pilot a twin-engine plane. She flew clients all over the country. With that money, she learned to pilot a 747 with the same trainer who started her out years before. When she received her license to pilot a 747, she earned a job with a major airline. Today, as an international 747 airline pilot, she visits places all over the world. With her, that same doll, that same dream, that same intention rides in the cockpit with her. In fact, she is a friend of mine and wrote a book "Chick in the Cockpit" which publishes later next year.

Ask yourself: What dream has your name on it?

On this long journey of your life, you must co-create your life path with the creative energy within you. You possess all the tools and all the ingenious energy to engage a positive, useful, purposeful and happy life.

Open to possibilities daily, engage the flow, and receive the favors of the universe. Finally, weave your story toward co-creating your dynamic life. Take action toward your chosen destiny.

Chapter 20

Three Profound Secrets to Living a Happy Life

We hold these truths to be self-evident, that all men and women are created equal, that they are endowed by their Creator with certain unalienable Rights, that among these are Life, Liberty and the pursuit of Happiness. ~ *Thomas Jefferson*

Throughout all of human history, ordinary people longed for the mythical ideal to be happy, to live a fulfilling life and to enjoy the fruits of their talents.

For the first time in history via Thomas Jefferson and the founding fathers of America—ordinary people suddenly enjoyed the "right" to pursue their happiness in their own ways, at their own speed and by their own choices.

As an ordinary citizen of America, my life path carried me into amazing places. My choices allowed me to come into contact with some remarkable people who espoused "how" to live a happy life. I share their ideals with you in order for you to incorporate them into your own life—and prosper with happiness.

Henry David Thoreau said, "If you advance confidently toward your dreams, and endeavor to live the life which you have imagined, you will meet with success unexpected in common hours. You will pass through invisible boundaries. You will engage new and liberal laws. And you will live with the license of a higher order of beings."

I read that quote every morning before my day begins. I inculcate the essence of the message into my brain cells and my thought patterns. I make plans, I prepare to carry them out and I pursue them confidently. At first, I met with many obstacles with my dream to bicycle on all seven continents. Those difficulties became stepping-stones to my ultimate success because of my "advancing confidently" toward my dreams. Successes "popped up" in the creative field of life at the most unexpected hours.

Somewhere along your own journey, by incorporating Thoreau's wisdom, you will pass through invisible boundaries. Once you make the transition, you will engage new and liberal laws in your daily activities. Your thought patterns change to increasingly more abundant and creative vibrations. Those vibrations propel you toward living with a higher order of beings—in other words, you transform via your thoughts. You become how you think. You manifest what you imagine.

Jack London said, "I would rather be ashes than dust. I would rather my spark burn out in a brilliant blaze than be stifled by dry rot. I would rather be a superb meteor; every atom in magnificent glow—rather than a sleepy and permanent planet. The proper function of man-woman is to live, not merely exist. I shall use my time."

I read aloud this second secret to happiness daily. I engage the energy of London's wisdom for squeezing every second out of every day. That may mean contemplative thought and grateful moments versus quickening intensity. I understand that each moment of living constitutes a marvelous endowment.

You too, enjoy the miracle of living. By incorporating the first and second secrets, you change the vibrations in your mind, in your heart and in your spirit. You transition into an entirely new and creative realm of thought and creative process. London understood it in his vivacious living and his enthralling literary pursuits. His book **Martin Eden** lives inside me since I read it 40 years ago. London inspired me then and still does to this day.

Goethe said, "Whatever you can do, or dream you can do, begin it. Boldness has genius, power and magic in it. Begin it now."

Actions drive your coveted dreams to reality, which drive your life toward fulfillment. While engaging your mind to harness your dreams, you take actions that connect you to your happiness. By channeling the creative energy of the universe, you live a spectacular life.

Chapter 21

Creating Solitude for Your Spiritual Bliss

Americans living in big cities race through their days with gridlocked traffic, honking horns, cheeky taxi drivers, police sirens and jostling pedestrians racing toward their destinations. At work, they juggle temperamental co-employees, deadlines and ashes-in-the-mouth bosses.

Once finished with work, they race home to spouses, kids and dinner preparations. The working groove consumes them while their responsibilities for daily living press their emotions to the wall. With all the automobiles, appliances and conveniences in America, we oftentimes lack peace and quiet in our lives. As we race through our metropolitan arenas, even optimists admit that science will be hard pressed to replace this precious spiritual commodity: solitude.

How can we step back to an oft forgotten pleasure in our lives, in our hearts and in our minds? How can we refresh our spirits?

John Stuart Mill, writing in 1848 when cities remained smaller, less hurried and enjoyed more community among their residents said, "It is not good for man to be kept at all times in the presence of his species. A world, from which solitude is extirpated, is a very poor ideal.

"Solitude, in the sense of being often alone, is essential to any depth of meditation or of character; and solitude in the presence of natural beauty and grandeur, is the cradle of thoughts and aspiration which society could do ill without."

If you feel the same way in your journey, the quest for solitude grows as you add birthday candles. A certain spiritual bliss accompanies your advancing years. Solitude brings divine calm and intellectual clarity. To abridge your life creates more simplicity in your daily living. Once mastered, you will enjoy an inner peace and an outer joyful countenance.

How does anyone move his or her body, mind and soul into solitude?

- Take a daily walk in the nearest park in your city. Sit under a tree. Sit by a pond. Stare into a patch of flowers. Pull up a long stalk of grass and stick it into your mouth. Suck the green insides of the stalk of grass to feel the heartbeat of the universe pulsing over your tongue.
- When you reach a stretch of grass or forest; take off your shoes and socks. Stick your feet into deep grass or sand or rock. Let your body reconnect with the vibrations of the Earth to re-harmonize your entire body's vibrations with our planet. Many call it "grounding" and it works to refresh your spirit.
- Choose the best time of day for your solitary moments. It may be early before work as you sit by a river, stream or on the beach. It could be a stroll along a quiet walk at dusk where the sun's final glory mesmerizes your spirit.
- While solitude means being alone in the moment, you might be one who loves solitude with another who shares your heart strings about life. By all means, make your solitary moments a couple-thing if that works for you.
- The point of solitude means to be luxuriously immersed in the quiet moments of your own choices. You become fully aware of being alive without being ushered into the scurry of daily living.

In my own hiking times through the woods in acceptance of solitude, I feel the sweet spot of temperature playing upon my skin. I feel the essence of light shining through my eyes. I accept my quiet soul pulsing into the energies of life. Once I reconnect with every blood cell charging through my body, I churn with delight.

Therefore, walk into the woods, the park, along the river or by a pond to discover solitude. You will enjoy renewed strength to enjoy your days.

Chapter 22

Invisible World of Caring

Much of life in every civilization revolves around money, power and status. Some youngsters enjoy security with instant success from their parents while others begin in poverty. Everyone learns the ways of the world by the time they reach eighteen.

They understand the inequities, discriminations and biases. Some let their beginnings define them while others take action to change them. Let's face it; we all make comparisons.

I am reminded of a sewing circle of old Catholic women. All carried great pride in their sons.

The first mother said, "I am so proud of my son. He became a priest so when his congregants address him, they say, "Father."

The second mother proudly spoke up, "My son became a bishop so when his flock addresses him, they say, "Your grace."

The third mother bragged, "My son became a cardinal, so when his followers address him, they say, "Your eminence." (High nobility)

The fourth mother straightened her frock while squaring her shoulders, "Well, my son is 6'2" and a personal trainer. When he walks into a room, the women gasp, "My God!"

No matter what your station or status in life, in America, you can rise from the ashes of your youth to become president of the United States. That's been proven time and again.

What propels such success by individuals? First of all, make the positive assumption and understanding that life supports you. The energies of life and the universe get behind you and assist you in flourishing your well being. Once you understand that fact, you may utilize the powers of living to engage your ultimate triumphs.

What does that mean as far as application?

No matter your origins, whether rich, poor or in-between, you must change your thoughts toward the positive. That, in turn, changes your words to evolving concepts. As you pick up speed with a mind-set and word-set change, you re-arrange the energy of your mind toward fulfillment.

Understand that "good" works in your life. Feel gratitude for your opportunities. Stand for excellence in all you say and do. Open to the healing energy of living. Meditate daily. Accept that you move forward in perfect harmony with living.

While some religions preach wickedness and evil, in the 21st century you enjoy the ability to learn, grow and evolve. Seek the golden thread of truth of the oneness, infinite and divine in you. Remember that thought creates form in your life. The way you think becomes the way you live.

How to proceed toward success and happiness

While many see limitations in their lives, and that becomes a habit, you must engage the "high watch" in your mind. Disengage from the old stories of defeat and frustration. "My parents didn't to this or that...I got beat up...I failed because the teacher disliked me...."

Guide your thoughts until they become positive all the time. You maintain total control of your life's ship and you captain it toward your destination.

Empower your new story by changing your old vision to a new vision. What do you really want to do with your life? What job would give you joy and energy? Create it; live it; realize it. You grow into the hero of your life by your thoughts and actions.

Realize an invisible world of energy moves through you, for you and with you. It thrives with the attitudes and actions of your mind. Tune out negative "old thinking" and move toward greater abundance in your mind, health, work and achievements.

What hero inspires you? Read about his or her trials and tribulations. How did that hero succeed? What gave them the power to triumph? Do you want to find love? Read Marianne Williamson's **A Return to Love.**

Want to live a dynamic daily life? Read Dan Millman's **No Ordinary Moments**.

Take these ideas and apply them to your daily life. You will find that an invisible world of caring propels you to your ultimate happiness.

Chapter 23

Planting a Garden in Your Mind

The words you use define your mental acuity. The thoughts you think plant seeds that grow in your mind. By engaging positive words and thriving thoughts, you propel your mind toward a bountiful harvest of daily living. Plant these ideas into your mind for a renewal of your life, your energy and your outcomes.

In America today, you notice an endless stream of teens, college kids and employees looking down into their Smart phones.

At bars, women line the dance floor with a white light shining up into their faces from their phones as they stare into cyberspace. Many people walk into the woods with ear buds stuffed into their heads to vanquish any notion of a singing cardinal, chirping black bird or rippling of the rapids from a cascading stream.

They use their thumbs to write messages to some other person looking down into his or her phone awaiting communication blurted in truncated words. One aspect they all share in common: they cut themselves off from interacting with fellow human beings, friends and their community.

Such addictions create isolation; ultimately they create spiritual disconnection from life and finally, loneliness from personal contact.

We humans arrived at this juncture in history via a tribe, clan and/or community. We raised our children in the cultural container founded on human interaction, face-to-face and eye-to-eye. In order to function, we need heart connection to our surroundings. We need emotional attachment to other human beings. We need to feel a belonging in order to function positively in the world.

For parents willing to plant vibrant seeds in the gardens of their children's minds, they must leave the Smart phone on the kitchen table. They must play with their children at the park. Laugh while pushing them ever higher on the swing or race them down the slides or spin on the merry-go-round.

Instead of living inside the pitiless confines of a Smart phone, engage a child, stranger or friend in face-to-face conversation.

If you ever notice a seed catalog, the editors show you the results of the seeds via the bouquet of flowers. They invite you to see the results of what you plant in your garden.

The same applies with your mind. If you plant isolation via addiction to a Smart phone, you reap the coldness and lack of personal connection afforded by a face-to-face conversation.

You possess the power of decision. You infuse life with your love, empathy and creative energy. You may bring a message of empowerment by your personal interaction with others.

Therefore, choose what you plant in your mind.

- Plant happiness in your mind's garden and express that flowering in your daily connection with others. A simple compliment to the grocery store cashier about her earrings brings a smile. A compliment to your neighbor about his beautiful lawn ushers special vibrations of happiness.
- Plant joy in your mind's garden by celebrating a windy day by flying a kite in the local park. Share your Girl Scout Cookies with a homeless person on a street corner. Feed the ducks at the local pond or volunteer at the animal shelter.
- Spread good will in your home and community with your words and actions. Attend a city council meeting with ideas for improvements in the downtown area.

Remember that you create the container of community whereby men, women and children flourish by flowers you plant in your mind. When the flowers bloom, your happiness, joy and good will spread to the four corners of the world.

Chapter 24

How to Handle Discouragement

At some moments in our lives, we feel depressed or low from something that happened to us. We might suffer a defeat on the sporting field. We may lose a friend or spouse. At some juncture, we may grieve our circumstance in a hopeless job or situation.

When the world contrives against us, our emotions may thrust us into emotional turmoil where things seem insurmountable. Depression drags us into a rut. Please understand this fact: no one possesses enough money, fame or power to overcome setbacks or failure at some juncture in his or her life. No matter what your station in life: a movie starlit, world leader or the richest person on the planet, a dark cloud may descend upon you at any moment in your life's journey.

That moment may precipitate from:

- You suffered defeat on the sports field, you missed the final shot
- You failed in your attempt at love with someone, you suffered rejection
- You lost your job, missed a raise, got stuck in a bad position
- Someone cheated, or betrayed you, or you failed at your highest calling

Some people dwell on their loss. They feel stalled in a funk of melancholy that affects their daily living. They may groove their unhappiness like a track on a CD until they find it difficult to pull out of the feeling. It can become as critical as suicide or as unhealthy as the angry person who lashes out against others such as loved ones or friends. Discouragement magnifies in numerous ways—most of them negative.

When something, someone or some condition discourages you, breathe-in that feeling. Then, breathe-out that energy in a conscious process to release it from your mind. Because that's where discouragement lingers: in your mind, in your emotions and in your heart.

First of all, try to avoid amplifying a problem that causes your discouragement. Define it, understand where it's coming from and finally, appreciate it. For example, one big movie star, in his screen debut discovered that the director cut him out of the movie. Yet, when he entered the director's office, he thanked the man for the incredible experience he enjoyed acting in the movie in a bit part. The director, so impressed with Kevin Costner, wrote the young actor into the next movie, "Silverado", where he became a huge star. Later, he acted in "Dances with Wolves", which became a western classic.

You can accomplish the same success by how you handle your discouragement. Learn from it; release and grow. In the process, your gifts reveal themselves. Use any failure in your life as a stepping-stone to your own success.

Secondly, realize that life sustains those with a great sense of humor about themselves. They know the game of life offers many forks in the road. So, laugh often at the remarkable opportunities you enjoy during your stay on this planet for success, failure and choices.

Thirdly, in all discouragements, you must release the feelings and embrace your heart. Whether you can do this by talking to a friend or loved one, in the end, you must come to terms with yourself and love yourself. Your heart generates the current of self-acceptance and peace.

By engaging these three points, and allowing a little time for perspective, you grow out of despair into renewal. Engage the concept of honesty toward yourself. It calms your spirit. Shift toward enthusiasm. By taking that course, you cultivate your passionate fire within. Take a conscious mental effort to step off the "discouragement" track by jumping your mind onto a new track or attitude. Replace fear with faith.

Finally, realize that you live on Earth to work, to play and to enjoy yourself like few other creatures—because you possess the ability to live a creative life. You're here to love, express and flow with the energies of life. Make it a great ride!

Chapter 25

Your Life One Step at a Time

The energy of life on this planet strives to organize into relationships. As with water, you watch it thrive in many forms such as snow, rain, ice and vapor. It gathers as clouds in the sky, which eventually, falls as rain or snow. It drains into rivers that gather into the oceans. All of these forms create relationships with the processes that allow life to thrive on this globe.

If you look to the universe—stars, planets, moons and galaxies exist in a symbiotic gathering. They co-exist in a mutual dance based on physics and the "Law of Attraction." Their energy via movement flourishes in every sector of the cosmos.

Throughout all of creation, life sprang upon this planet utilizing the "attraction" process. At some point, humanity manifested, which in turn, became "you" as an entity in the process. What will you do with your precious "moment" on this planet? Will you prosper by using your gifts or will you meander into mediocrity? Will you submit to circumstance or strive toward self-fulfillment?

The courage to be you in 21st century America may be one of the bravest acts of your life. Our cookie-cutter society educates people into "slots" that maintain the engine of commerce. General options include teaching, medicine, construction, salesperson, truck driver, cashier, janitor, waitress and factory worker.

How do you step outside that process if called toward a different path? First, you must engage the quality of your mind and spirit to stand up in the face of fear. Sure, it's difficult to be different, to take an alternative path, to become a singer, artist or dancer.

The one thing you may expect on your life's trajectory: challenge! If something doesn't challenge you, it won't change you. That one factor becomes the conduit for your creativity and opportunity. Challenges force you toward a chance to move into your highest and best—one step at a time.

If you remember some of the greats of history, their lives began by trudging toward their goal: Ray Kroc started out with one hamburger restaurant that led to an "idea" to create a chain of McDonald's fast food joints. Billy Banks, inventor of Tae Bo fitness tapes, couldn't read very well because of his dyslexia, failed in school and couldn't qualify for many jobs. Instead of giving up, he used his gifts to combine martial arts and kickboxing. Oprah Winfrey began in poverty and abuse, but marshaled her talents for interviewing into a billion dollar company. Ms. J.K. Rowling, author of the Harry Potter series, transformed from a food stamp recipient to a $15 billion industry stemming from an idea about a character she wrote on a napkin while eating breakfast.

What did those people possess in common?

- They learned to strive toward their dreams with endless passion
- They maintained relentless enthusiasm for their ideas
- They stood in the space of courage of their convictions
- They stood in the "Eternality of relationship with life" to activate their courage

In other words, they surrendered to possibilities inherent within them. They used their challenges as outlets to a greater good simmering within their minds. As with the "Law of Attraction", they incorporated others into their network. When you gather two or more, you harness creative power.

Finally, each person, no different than you, no smarter than you, no more privileged than you—maintained effort over time. They dreamed their dreams, then, day-by- day; they took action toward their destinies. By applying these concepts, you too, march toward your dreams—one step at a time.

Chapter 26

Live Life on Your Own Terms

In this high-speed society we created for ourselves, Americans live in traffic-congested cities with skyscrapers piercing the sky.

On the ground floor, humans race to catch crowded busses, packed subways and Yellow Cabs. With expressways gridlocked from dawn to dusk, people overflow sidewalks and sirens slash through the air 24/7. The evening news reports accidents, robberies, homicides and a plethora of calamities too numerous for human emotions to endure.

But if you look at all the people living in cities, whether in their workplace or their office cubicle, what do you see on the partition wall?

You see posters of what they would rather being doing: windsurfing, skiing, sunbathing on a beach in the Caribbean, scuba diving, dancing, mountain climbing, camping, rafting, bicycling and a dozen other activities they would rather be living.

If you're one of those people wishing you lived a different life or wishing you could live your dreams, then why don't you go after it?

Why not live your poster instead of wishing you were windsurfing across Lake Tahoe or sunning on the beach in Hawaii?

Did you ever wonder how those people you see traveling around the world with a backpack or bicycle, or climbing mountains or taking a winter off to go ski bumming do it?

They defeat the tyranny of resistance.

Henry David Thoreau said, "The mass of men and women live lives of quiet desperation."

In America, anyone at any station in life, at any age, can renew his or her life by choice, by intention and by action. Such individuals learn how to defeat the "tyranny of resistance."

First of all, what constitutes this modern day tyranny that locks people into cubicle prisons in cities or into humdrum jobs that provide zero meaning?

Such persons yield to an inner resistance to transform themselves because they feel afraid, don't know how to break their cubicle-bonds and, often times, none of their office mates know any better. It's easier to be safe with the constancy and comfort of a paycheck and friends.

Do you remember the TV sitcom "King of Queens" with the chubby boy Kevin James and co-star Leah Remini, who also got flabby in the series, staged in New York City? They never showed any happiness, but mostly conflict. Their jobs: meaningless! They didn't know how to escape their relationship or their jobs.

If you live such a scenario, how can you avoid a lifetime of regrets?

- Find your gift, the work that you love that turns you on to life. Discover your talent, your ability, your genius and your expertise. You can find it by examining what you do in your spare time. Pursue it, love it and live it.
- Practice self-awareness. Socrates said, "The unexamined life is not worth living." Instead of going through the motions, create your own wave and ride it.
- Incorporate your independent will as a course correction on your way to your life's destination. As Jack London said, "You can't wait for inspiration to change your life; you have to go after it with a club."
- Discover your True North in the scheme of your life. That's your soul's true knowing and what you desire most about your life. It's your deepest truth.

Finally, you must engage your physical, emotional, mental and spiritual well-being.

Exercise daily to blow off excess energy in the body to release your mind to express itself. Eat healthy foods to maintain a lean frame. That, in turn, allows you emotional balance that that forms the foundation of your relationship with friends, families and co-workers. For your mental well-being, read books, take classes and express yourself through journaling, painting, sculpting or other art forms. Finally, feed your spiritual being via inspirational books, church or nature, and the peace you find from a walk down a tree-lined path.

You will find the tyranny of resistance fades as you walk or gallop toward your happiness in work, play and friends. You won't wish for what you see in the poster on your cubicle wall, you will live it for real.

Chapter 27

The Race of Life: The Happiness Factor

Bhutan, a small country in Asia, sets the benchmark for living a happy life. Its culture mandates that happiness holds the highest distinction in the realm of daily living. Those citizens living in that country enjoy a much slower and quieter pace of living. They maintain a spiritual connection to their world.

Thus, peace and harmony thrive among Bhutan's citizens. No murders, no headaches, no prescription drugs, no alcoholism, no gridlock, no air pollution, no slums and no social unrest. When I visited that country, I came away with a happiness factor that thrives within me today. I caught what they live and incorporated it into my own life in our high speed, high stress society.

How do they maintain happiness in a world racing toward some kind of destination on the horizon?

America features almost the opposite culture from Bhutan. Nearly everyone exceeds the speed limit on our nation's highways. Most Americans buy the fastest Internet provider on the market. They flip TV channels faster than a Ping-Pong game. Urgency dominates America's fast food joints, laxatives and painkillers.

Pain sufferers buy 131 million doses of popular headache and pain relievers annually.

What makes the difference in the "happiness factor" in Bhutan and the "high stress factor" prevalent in American big cities?

Instead of hell bent to get there, try the Bhutan way of thinking about the quality of your life during your journey. Even if you live in a big city, you may gather Mother Nature around you at your office with plants, fish aquarium and relaxed music.

At home, you may create peaceful scenes replete with flowers, plants and paintings that soothe your spirit. You may create a backyard with a waterfall, birdbath and bird feeder.

You may create a "spiritual sandbox" whereby you may take off your shoes daily and thrust your feet into the "biorhythms of the universe" and re-synchronize your body to the pulse of the galaxy.

You may incorporate four quintessential decisions to shift your life from stress to peaceful living:

- Tell yourself each day, "Life is good." Think primal, pure fountain, universal source and energy. Remember your childhood when you played for the sheer joy of movement. Re-introduce play into your daily schedule. A walk along a trail, a quiet moment in your rocker, a swing in the park and bird watching by the pond. Take delight in a dragonfly landing on a lily pad. Walk away from the dark night of the soul or anything bothering you—by your intellectual choice through practice.

- Understand and appreciate that, "I am capable; I am joyful and I am enough." Inadequacy and comparisons permeate a large swatch of American life—business, school and social gatherings. This world today stems from comparisons with others. You may choose to be at peace with yourself because you no longer compare yourself to or with anyone. You cherish yourself because you are the only you in the world.

- You did not come to this planet to prove yourself. You arrived in grand style to express yourself, laugh with life, create with life and entertain yourself with whatever passion(s) catches your fancy. Once you seek and strike upon your passions—stress, anxiety and pain vanish into your rear-view mirrors.

- Finally, like the Bhutanese people, you gather your happiness factor by engaging your calming factor via your connection to the natural world. You impel yourself into wholeness by the little choices that build on your self-acceptance and finally, your freedom from headaches, pain and anxiety.

What absorbs or thrills you? Okay, engage it. As you do, you feel captivated in life's activities, which, in turn render happiness. Seek that which vibrates within your being. Enjoy the miracle of life pulsating in every cell of your body. As you do, you dwell within the happiness factor throughout all your days.

"Pursuing happiness, and I did, and I still do, is not at all the same as being happy—which I think is fleeting and dependent on circumstances. If the sun is shining, stand in it—yes, yes, yes! Happy times are great, but happy times pass—they have to because time passes. The pursuit of happiness is more elusive; it is life-long, and it is not goal-centered. What you are pursuing is meaning—a meaningful life. There's the hap—the fate, the draw that is yours, and it isn't fixed, but changing the course of the stream, or dealing new cards, whatever metaphor you want to use—that's going to take a lot of energy. There are times when it will go so wrong that you will barely be alive, and times when you realize that being barely alive, on your own terms, is better than living a bloated half-life on someone else's terms. The pursuit isn't all or nothing—it's all AND nothing." *Jeanette Winterson*

Chapter 28

No Ordinary Moments: Your Epic Life

Every week in America, you read stories of amazing moments where ordinary people triumphed over failure. You may watch the "Biggest Loser" where a man or woman cut 150 pounds off his or her body to walk on stage looking fantastic in a suit or dress. Most suffered failure and depression for years concerning their obesity. In life, people from all walks of life suffer failure on many levels.

Back in 1947, Twentieth Century Fox dropped Marilyn Monroe because producer Daryl Zanuck felt she lacked the "attraction factor" to make her a star. Dr. Seuss' first book suffered 27 rejections. Richard Bach's book, Jonathan Livingston Seagull, faced 44 rejections from publishers. Barbara Streisand gave her Broadway debut in 1961, but the house closed after one show.

Frank Sinatra suffered expulsion from school for rowdy behavior. Singer Johnny Cash sold appliances before his songwriting and guitar playing catapulted him to fame. Walt Disney's first cartoon company suffered bankruptcy. Decca Records executive Dick Rowe rejected the Beatles in favor of "The Tremeloes" a band that soon failed. Martin Luther King suffered jail and name calling in his quest to bring equality to people of color.

Oprah Winfrey's boss fired her from her first job as an anchor at a Baltimore, Maryland television station. She faced sexism and harassment. Oprah rebounded to become the number one television talk-show host in America as well as an accomplished actress.

Film academics rejected Steven Spielberg from the University of Southern California School of Cinematic Arts multiple times. They said, "He lacked basic abilities to comprehend the cinematic arts." Spielberg struggled until he directed such movies as "ET" that made him world famous.

At his first screen test, dancer Fred Astaire suffered the words of the director: "He can't sing. Can't act. Slightly balding. Can dance a little." He became the greatest film and dance star of his age.

Struggling author and single mom J.K. Rowling lived off welfare when she began writing the first "Harry Potter" book. She now commands the title of the richest working woman in the United Kingdom.

Stephen King spent 13 years living in a trailer with his wife and kids while he took two hours out every night to work on his writing craft. He rewrote "Carrie" after his wife pulled it back out of the wastebasket because he threw it away in total discouragement. The book became an instant best seller that led to 350 million copies of his books published worldwide including the famous movie, "The Shawshank Redemption."

As you know, every one of these people continued their quests until they became world famous. Their legacies continue to this day in literature, the arts, cinema, music and equal rights. Ironically, they continued following their calling no matter what the failure rate.

Unbeknownst to most people who look at famous names, stars or political leaders—they share one thing in common: they experienced multiple failures on their way toward their success.

Many people who faced failure didn't realize how close to success they were when they quit. They allowed their frustrations, obstacles and choices to defeat them.

Where does that leave you? How do you feel about failure? What can you do about your failures? What can drive you to your ultimate success?

First of all, you must appreciate your own worth and the worth of your quest.

Polly Letofsky at 42, from Vail, Colorado, faced enormous challenges before becoming the first woman to walk around the world, 14,000 miles across four continents in five years to bring attention to breast cancer. She raised over a quarter of a million dollars and enjoyed 2,000 interviews from newspapers around the world.

On October 3, 2013, 64 year old Diana Nayad, a world class swimmer, took her fifth and final attempt to swim from Cuba to Florida, a distance of 90 miles over treacherous ocean waters filled with sharks, jellyfish, waves and winds. After 35 years of trying, she succeeded. She said, "You can choose to live your dreams at any age."

No matter what your age, lot in life or past failures, you enjoy every chance to succeed at your chosen-destiny by your decisions to overcome heartache, turmoil and failure.

In your lifetime, every moment, each choice you make, leads to your epic life because there are no ordinary moments. Each moment makes your extraordinary life by your choices.

Chapter 29

Are You Living a Life Worth Remembering?

Totally blind in his teens, American Erik Weihenmayer became the first sightless person to climb Mount Everest. He continued until he climbed the highest peaks on all seven continents.

Bob Wieland lost his legs to a bomb blast in Vietnam, but walked across America on his hands coast-to-coast. Time: three years, eight months, six days! Later, he hand-cycled west to east and east to west across America. Not finished, he became the first double amputee to complete the Hawaii Ironman Triathlon. He ran the New York, Boston and Chicago Marathons that took him five days to finish each race. At 67, he again hand-cycled coast-to-coast across America.

American Aimee Mullins, 37, without legs below the knees since childhood, races track, models clothing and gives motivational speeches. She said, "True disability is having a crushed spirit." She redefines what a woman can be and what she can accomplish.

Wilma Rudolph, sickly as a child, wore braces, but she became the first woman to win three gold medals at the 1960 Olympics where they celebrated her as the world's fastest woman.

Your choices in life transform you from the banal to the poetic—even to the noble. Wasn't it Shakespeare's character "Shylock" a moneylender in the "Merchant of Venice" who spoke these words that ring out in the 21st century, "If you prick us, do we not bleed? And if you tickle us, do we not laugh? It is our humanity and all the potential within it that makes us beautiful."

With those words ringing into the rafters of your mind, how will you live a life worth remembering?

If you're 20 years old, you enjoy choices to lead an epic life that propels you to heroic memories. By age 30, you burned through your 20s and may relish some epic moments. By 40, you you're half way through. Have you lived a life worth remembering? Or, did the mid-life crisis hit you square in the eyes—leaving you with a panicky feeling? By 70, your after-burners exhausted themselves, leaving you in a gentle glide to your final moments.

If you live on this side of 40, are you creating a remarkable life for yourself? Do you live on any "searing the edges"? Are you carving out some extraordinary physical, intellectual or spiritual expression of yourself?

What made the above four ordinary people overcome their horrific physical conditions? What drove them to greatness?

Remember this: if something doesn't challenge you, you won't change. Therefore, instead of watching an average of 29 hours of television weekly by the majority of Americans, create challenges in your life that propel you to more noble encounters. If you divide 29 hours by 7 days, that equals an extra 4.5 hours daily to think about, dream about and participate in activities or challenges outside your comfort zone.

Opportunities: weight training to build a healthy body, cross training to run a triathlon this summer, or buy a canvas, paints and brush to dabble with a painting roiling around in your ingenious mind. You might enter a pottery class to find your talents at throwing pots with intricate designs. How about becoming a chef?

On the intellectual front, read books that interest you. Enroll in a class in jewelry making. Enter a mechanic's class to repair old cars. Most cities feature "Free University" classes to incorporate dozens of arts, hobbies and other classes to fit your propensities and passions. How about joining the Peace Corps or Americorps?

Discover what makes your life worth remembering. What will they say at your memorial service?

"She (he) lived with exuberance, imaginative energy and a song in her heart," smiled the preacher. "She entered the realm of potential and opportunity to live a grand and glorious life. She wasn't lucky; she chose her destiny. We remember her nobility through her actions."

Chapter 30

The Journey Back: Choose Yourself

My friend Fred sat down in the booth at Woody's Pizza in downtown Golden, Colorado last fall. He represented sartorial splendor in that he wore a suit and tie with Italian shoes. I slid into the booth opposite him.

"Good evening gentlemen," the waitress greeted us. "May I get you some drinks?"

"I'll have a beer," said Fred.

"Water works for me," I said.

A month earlier, Fred drove home with his wife to an upscale housing area when she turned toward him, "I can't do this anymore."

Fred knew exactly what Jackie meant. She wanted a divorce from a marriage that didn't work for her any more than it worked for him. When they married, everyone wondered how a high-roller real estate maven hitched up to a mountain man who loved a tent more than a hotel. Nonetheless, they made it work for eight torturous years. Weeks later, I helped him move into his new apartment.

"Well," said Fred. "I finished moving the last of my things. Thanks for helping me move the big stuff into my new digs."

While he knew the marriage didn't work, the pain of separation caused him emotional anguish. That evening, over a pizza, Fred expressed his sorrows to me, his longtime friend.

As we talked, he ordered a second, third, fourth and fifth draughts—16 ounce big beers. Enough to knock down a buffalo! Near the end of our conversation, I wanted to speak up about his driving home with so many beers in his belly. But, unsure of myself, I remained silent. Fred drove home that night legally intoxicated, but he somehow avoided detection by the police.

Too often in our society, we use different drugs to numb the pain within us. Sometimes, friends watch friends spiral into alcoholism or drugs, or eating disorders without saying anything.

That night, I didn't muster the courage to call for my wife to come down and drive him home while I drove his car back to his house. I failed to gather the courage to call him a cab and insist he use it.

Many times in life, in retrospect, we wish we said something at the time, but regret it later when we didn't.

Two months later, after too many beers, Fred pulled out to pass a car on a two-lane highway, but didn't see the yellow line. A cop pulled him over. The officer gave him a DUI ticket.

With $10,000.00, he fought it in court. He asked me if I could help him with driving him around for a week until he received an interim license because he appealed the ticket.

After a great deal of soul searching, he came to terms with his situation. He took personal responsibility. He understood his personal accountability.

He stopped drinking.

"After that night," he said, "I evaluated my circumstances...I can't drown my sorrow in booze. I can't numb the pain. I've got to deal with it and deal with myself. I must meet it with a clear mind, clear heart and clear understanding. That's what I'm doing. This ticket will cost me a lot of money, but I'm lucky the cop stopped me before I killed myself or someone else. I'm done drinking."

A writer-alcoholic Dina Kucera said, "I felt empty and sad for years, and for a long, long time, alcohol worked. I'd drink, and all the sadness would go away. Not only did the sadness go away, but also I felt fantastic. I was beautiful, funny and I could work math. But at some point, the booze stopped working. Every time I drank, I felt pieces of me leaving. I continued to drink until there was nothing left. Just emptiness."

"Fred," I said. "What made you decide to stop drinking?"

"To be quite honest," he said, "I am going to make it through this divorce. I feel the pain. I am working through it. I felt fine before I got married. I am going to be fine again. I decided to choose me."

Chapter 31

Anger, Gossip and Frustration

Back in high school, rumors started as fast as a lightning storm to destroy any girl's reputation. Often out of jealousy for some perceived transgression, classmates concocted stories to create hurt for another person.

As we grew older, most of us learned through the ears that everyone paddles his or her canoe as best they can on this unique journey through life.

But along the way, in most communities around the world, people talk about other people. They make judgments. They hold verdicts. They render conclusions based on their perceptions.

Someone always gets emotionally damaged by bitter reprisals, anger, gossip and other peoples' frustrations.

It's been said that, "Life begins at the end of your comfort zone."

I once knew a friend who carried grudges against those who wronged him. He piled them into a potato sack that he slung over his shoulder everyday when he traveled to work. When I saw him for lunch one day, he carried on with new additions to his "potato sack full of grudges."

Finally, I said, "Jack, you carry so many negative thoughts about folks who have done you wrong that you keep piling complaints into that sack that you carry around on your back. The more you complain, the more you add to the sack—I think it must be getting pretty heavy and pretty rotten. Have you ever thought of forgiving all those who wronged you?"

"I just can't," Jack said.

"If you did," I said, "it would take a load off your mind and emotions. Give it a try."

"How do I do it?" he asked.

"People can be harsh, unfair, perverse, dishonest and irrational," I said. "Just forgive them anyhow. Forgive them unconditionally in your own mind and heart. They don't need to know it. You don't have to tell them. Just know that you forgave them. In doing that, you forgive yourself. It's really freeing."

Jack seemed to click the solution into his mind. From that day, he let go of his anger, bitterness, frustrations and disappointments he experienced with people. One of the best things he did: Jack associated with people who supported him. He fled those people who remained in his former paradigm. He changed jobs.

The facts: if you grow into a successful person, others may deride you. Forgive them anyhow.

It's possible that if you maintain honesty and speak your mind, others may call you names or betray you. Forgive them anyhow.

You may build a business or work hard to succeed, but someone undermines you. Forgive them anyhow and move toward your dreams on your earned experiences.

If you show positive energy and aliveness, others may be jealous and display their envy. Guess what? Forgive them anyhow.

In my lifetime, I have picked up a half-million pieces of trash from rivers, lakes and streams. Also, I picked up trash in the oceans, along roads and in parks. People keep throwing it. As angry as it makes me, I forgive them anyhow.

You may do good things in the world, but people don't care and forget quickly. Do your good anyhow.

While the world disappoints, frustrates and diminishes everyone along the journey, give the world your best anyhow.

During and at the end of your life, you discover that you define your journey, how you live it and how you maintain yourself in the whirling tempest of living.

Shakespeare's Polonius in Hamlet said, "Neither a borrower or a lender be. For the loan oft loses both itself and friend, and borrowing dulls the edge of husbandry.

"This above all, to thine own self be true, and it must follow as the night the day, though canst be false to any man."

Interesting because Polonius' detractors spoke of him as overly officious, garrulous and impertinent.

Be yourself anyhow, because in the end, it's all between you and the Great Spirit that expresses through all of us.

Chapter 32

Oracle of the Soul: Discovering Gems of Understanding

As you grew up, you experienced different lessons along your life-path. You discovered a hot stove hurt when you touched it. A candle flame caused pain when you passed your finger over it. A rosebush thorn made your finger bleed. A bee sting caused you terrible agony.

From those experiences, you avoided the obvious in your daily meanderings. Marching into your teens, you discovered friendship, jealousy and betrayal. A bully beat you up. A girlfriend undermined you in your pursuit of a boyfriend.

In nature, you learned to run for cover during a lightning storm. When a dog gave chase, you picked up a stick to protect yourself.

You learned life-lessons either by your parents advising you or you learned the hard way by direct experience.

As you grew into your twenties, relationships grew more complicated. You worked a job with acerbic bosses and cantankerous fellow employees. You discovered many different aspects to how people operate in the world.

Along the way, you picked up new understandings and created game plans on how to deal with your circumstances. All the while, you became a better you. But sometimes, you wondered about your choices or predicaments.

I'm reminded of the ancient king who held court each day. He beckoned the local sage for words of wisdom. Each day for a year, the sage brought the king an overly ripe piece of fruit along with a witty statement. When the sage left, the king tossed the fruit into a hole in a pillar where it fell to the basement, untouched.

One day, after the sage gave the king the overly ripe fruit, he turned to exit, but noticed the king tossing the fruit into the pillar.

"What are you doing?" asked the sage. "Did you not know I gifted you with a gem in the middle of each fruit?"

The king made an excuse before the sage exited the throne room. Quickly, the king ordered a knave to recapture the fruit.

The king cut it open to reveal a valuable gem. He said, "I never knew such beauty could be found inside an aged piece of fruit."

The king ordered his staff to recover the gems from all the fruits in the basement. The gems of knowledge enlightened him, which allowed him greater understanding. He became a better king for all the people of his realm.

The great writer Thomas Moore said that every person faces the deadly turpitudes of living: obsessions, addictions, depression, loss of meaning, judging others, violence, anger, hate and prejudice.

It's your challenge to connect with the divine in you. You might call it the "spiritual" within you. Choose to identify with your higher self. That quest creates a transformation that leads to your better well being and better choices.

When bad things happen to you, decode the experience to see the gem. As you discover the synchronicity of the lesson, take advantage of it. Synchronicity coupled with purpose equals "coincidence."

Once you step into the "flow" of life, those synchronicities multiply because your energies coordinate with the natural vibrations of the universe.

Engage these talents: walk in the light, walk tall, walk with a song, walk strong, walk wise, walk with hope, walk with joy, walk with purpose and walk with passion. People notice your demeanor. You attract them to their own higher self.

Take advantage of a bitter experience, betrayal of a friend, unfair treatment by another or any of the overly ripe experiences of life. You will find a "gem" in the rotten fruit that will enhance your life beyond all ordinary understanding.

Section V

Understanding Yourself

Chapter 33

Forks in the Road, Stop Signs, Cul de sacs and Dead Ends on the Highway of Life

While taking a hike down a country road near dusk in my teens, an old farmer, plodding along with his walking stick, abruptly stopped me. His wrinkled-weathered skin did not diminish the energy in his clear blue eyes. Silver locks flowed from his wide-brimmed hat while his peppered beard gave him a majestic air of wisdom.

"Where you goin' sonny?" he asked.

"Just taking a walk to catch a few fire-flies when the night settles in on us," I said. "They seem to show their magic just as the sun goes down, but before the stars come out. I like the way they turn the long grass into street lamps, but none of the city noise to go with it."

"Should be a lot of them out this evening as soon as the red-winged black birds fall silent," he said. "So, if you don't mind my asking, where are you going with your life?"

"My mom wants me to go to college," I said. "She said it will give me a leg-up on living as well as make me a better educated man."

"Good for you," he said. "But what do you want to do with your life?"

"After I graduate from college," I said, "I want to travel the world before settling down to a job. I want to figure out some things about this life."

"Do you mind a bit of advice?" he asked.

"My dad told me to listen to my elders to learn their wisdom," I said.

"The path to your destiny has forks in the road that require the imperfect ability to discern the difference between opportunity and pitfalls," he said. "You will make mistakes in judgment. You will fail often. But remember to make those failures into stepping-stones toward your ultimate success. Never get down on yourself. None of it comes easy, but it gets easier as you travel the path with a good attitude, application by work and your ingenuity."

"My dad said something like that," I said.

"Smart dad," he said. "In addition to forks there will be cul de sac's or dead-end's, where you rest and re-evaluate the route you have taken. Everyone comes to these markers at some point. You will become wiser. Experience is the best teacher. So, if you find yourself going down the wrong road, or the road isn't working for you, turn around and go back. When you return to your original location, strike out in a new direction with the wisdom you learned while you traveled along the wrong road."

"That works for me," I said.

"As a young man, you are heading toward your destiny," he said. "To me the term "destiny" implies a pre-ordained purpose by some higher power. This implies a personal belief in that higher power. That may or may not work for you. It also implies that one's destiny answers the question, "Why am I here?" You will find out on your journey."

"Another thing," he said. "Your mom is right...choose your friends carefully. You will adopt some of their characteristics into your personality. When you hang with the smarter, more responsible folks in your school, you become more like them and succeed like them.

"Additionally, memories of your experiences are what come to you in those future quiet times with yourself. Make sure you accept yourself at all times. Even if you are not sure, assume a sense of confidence in your own talents whatever they might be or come to be.

"Some memories will be filled with regret and some will be joyous. You will have both in your life. You get to choose the number of each by the way you live. And, one final thought from my days of meditation on hay bales and sitting beside a quiet pond with dragon flies, turtles, snakes and muskrats: everything you become, you chose. And, everything you chose, you wanted."

As the fireflies lit the long grass, the old man tipped his hat before continuing on into the gathering darkness.

"Thank you, sir," I said, as I walked through the magic of fireflies and stars twinkling in the sky.

Chapter 34

Cloud Talk: Sitting on a Cloud After You Pass Away

A few weeks ago, a preacher spoke about a new term that I never heard before: "Cloud talk—when you die, you elevate to heaven where you sit on a cloud. You may look down on the planet to see where you lived. You may contemplate what you did with your time on Earth. How did you live? What made you tick? Did you fall in love? What kind of friends did you keep? Did you do anything significant with your life?"

The preacher said, "Your greatest challenge will be your greatest triumph. Where would Noah be without the flood? Who would know Babe Ruth if not for opposing pitchers who tried to strike him out? Where would Oprah be if there were no social injustices? Who would know Albert Einstein if not for the mystery of the universe? Who would Peyton Manning be without an end zone? Who would Michael Jordan be without a hoop?"

Before his death, the Beatles singer-song writer John Lennon related a story about what it meant to be alive.

"When I grew up, I asked my mother, 'What was life all about?'"

"She said, 'To be happy.'"

"When I reached high school, the teacher asked the class to write a paper about the meaning of life," said Lennon. "I wrote that the meaning of life was to be happy."

"The teacher handed me back my paper with the statement, 'You don't understand the question I gave you.'"

"I responded, 'You don't understand the meaning of life.'"

What would cross your mind if you sat on a cloud staring down on your life?

When adversity struck you like the floods hit Noah, did you rise to meet the waters with courage? Did you seek solutions? Did you rise with the "Ark" of your creative mind? Did you let other people thwart your aspirations? Did you argue with them? Did you struggle in the same mud?

An old fable said, "Never wrestle with pigs. You both get filthy and the pigs love it because they brought you down to their level."

Whatever adversity arrives on your doorstep, you may change arenas as to work, friends and enemies. Sometimes "inner adversity" tears at your insides. Your spirit reveals itself at such times.

Remember that critics always deride everyone's efforts but their own. As you look down from your cloud, it's amazing what you couldn't accomplish due to other peoples' verdicts on your aspirations.

Did you accept the call while you spent your seven decades on planet Earth? Did you break out of a confining life or relationships? Like Noah's struggle with the flood, ultimately, waters cleanse your body, mind and spirit during the journey.

As you sit back on that cloud, you may realize that struggles on Earth expanded you, enlarged you and taught you. The Great Spirit coded your DNA for expansion throughout your time on the planet.

Realize that life brought floods such as inner turmoil, rough waters, scary times, breakdowns and betrayals. While living, you dealt with angry waters that arrived from different directions. You may have created some of your own problems and other challenges came from situations or people. Remember that life also brought you happiness in the form of friends, family and your passions.

With each passing year, you learned lesson after lesson. Each flood subsided while you charged toward higher ground. That meant you evolved into a higher consciousness. Life constituted a journey of becoming.

Let's fly down from that cloud. You still live upon this planet. Are you following John Lennon's meaning of life, "To be happy"? Are you fulfilling the creative energy of the universe to grow, expand and discover your highest good?

Lennon also wrote a song titled "Imagine" that rings in my ears today. Imagine what you want out of your time on Earth because you enjoy living and pursuing whatever makes you happy as compared to no one.

Chapter 35

People You Hang With, Define You

In high school, I played three sports. I hung with the football jocks, basketball hoopsters and track speedsters in the spring. Later in college, I played tennis, racquetball and learned how to scuba dive.

Each sport featured different kinds of mindsets. In football, on offense, I learned blocking techniques and pass routes. I liked the strategy, but I didn't like the bumps, bruises and pain that came with hits. On defense, guys that loved violence raged all over the playing field to knock the block off any runner carrying the ball. Everyone spoke about kicking someone's rear-end.

Basketball featured quickness and shooting accuracy. No violence, but plenty of speed and intricate playmaking. No talking on court.

In track, no strategy, no game plan and no court. You competed with your only talent: speed and heaving lungs.

I discovered that different individuals liked different sports. In college, tennis created one-on-one battles with no talking. Racquetball created the same with a 140 miles-per-hour rubber ball flying all over the place. In scuba diving, no words, no speed, just the wonder of the world under the surface.

In classrooms, I discovered intelligent people who loafed, average people who studied hard to earn top grades and people who played cards to do as little academic work as possible.

Each type of person hung with the same persons that satisfied his or her style. Academic geeks hung with their own kind, talked their own language and lived their own lifestyles.

During that journey through college, I learned a lesson: you define your life and your success by the people you gather around you.

You may cultivate three special people in your life at all times if you want to deepen your life's journey.

- Foster a friendship with someone older and successful in the work you enjoy.
- Cultivate friendship with an equal who can exchange ideas with you.
- Enrich your life with someone not as fortunate as you.

For example: Aristotle, Leonardo de Vinci and Galileo challenged themselves with mentors that taught them. Later, they stood on the mentors' shoulders to create profound works of reason, art and science.

Aristotle created the "Academy" to learn from equals and teach beginners, one such being a young boy named Alexander, who later became "Alexander the Great."

One key factor in hanging with friends who pull the best from you: you challenge them and they challenge you intellectually, physical and spiritually. It's not a race of fame, money or status. Rather, you nudge each other to yours and their best efforts. It's called, "The power of two."

Along your journey, follow a veteran climber to reach the summit of a 14,000-foot peak. Train with a seasoned triathlete to garner a spot on the starting line. Follow a veteran backpacker into the wilderness until you get the hang of it. Learn a language or push a brush onto the canvas from a master. Notice how each speaks, how each acts and how each faces his or her daily tasks.

Famous mountaineer John Muir said, "Camp out among the grass and gentians of glacier meadows, in craggy garden nooks full of Nature's darlings. Climb the mountains and get their good tidings. Nature's peace will flow into you as sunshine flows into trees. The winds will blow their own freshness into you, and the storms their energy, while cares will drop off like autumn leaves."

How do you know if you're on the right path and traveling in the right direction in comparison? Simple: visit a corner bar to listen to the locals as they tip brew after brew. Visit a pool hall for a peak into their worldview.

Along your journey, travel, eat and play with the same people who plan, work hard, speak well, think and maintain optimal perseverance.

"To laugh often and love much; to win the respect of intelligent persons and the affection of children; to earn the approbation of honest citizens and endure the betrayal of false friends; to appreciate beauty; to find the best in others; to give of one's self; to leave the world a bit better, whether by a healthy child, a garden patch or a redeemed social condition; to have played and laughed with enthusiasm and sung with exultation; to know even one life has breathed easier because you have lived— this is to have succeeded." Ralph Waldo Emerson

Chapter 36

Life Choices: Optimism vs. Pessimism

Author Christine Larson said, "To think well of yourself and to proclaim this fact to the world, not in loud words, but great deeds. To live in faith that the whole world is on your side so long as you are true to the best that is in you."

Clearly, Ms. Larson punches your ticket for the optimism train-ride through life. She encourages you to step on board with the idea that life offers you enormous creative possibilities.

Throughout history, optimists overcame every human dilemma with their ideas that things turn out well on the positive side of living. Pessimists, on the other hand, expected the worst through choice.

Helen Keller said, "Let pessimism take hold of the mind, and life is all topsy-turvy, all vanity and vexation of spirit. There is no cure for individual or social disorder, except in forgetfulness and annihilation."

She understood the final result that pessimism renders the heart and mind deadened to the possibilities of vibrant living. While being positive or negative toward a certain outcome may not sway the universe in your direction, please consider the "Universe" conspires with your thought patterns when you align with its flow propensities.

Sarah Breathnach said, "Both abundance and lack exist simultaneously in our lives, as parallel realities. It is always our conscious choice which secret garden we will tend. When we choose not to focus on what is missing from our lives but are grateful for the abundance that's present—love, health, family, friends, work, the joys of nature and personal pursuits that bring us pleasure—the wasteland of illusion falls away and we experience heaven on Earth."

You will discover in your optimistic approach to life this key factor: when you think something will turn out well, you live with expectation. For example, when you attend a basketball game, you anticipate your team may become victorious. You choose that emotional idea throughout the game. If you win, you feel the wonder of it all. If your team loses, your expectations feel dashed on the hard rocks of reality.

With a pessimist, he or she expects to lose the game. The question arises: why play or participate or engage life at all? It's all going to turn out poorly anyway.

Reality check: your DNA expects to win. Optimism courses through each cell in your body.

Two things about optimistic thinking and living come to mind:

- How you feel positively constitutes your interpretation of an event. It nudges you toward your own fulfillment.
- The pure act of anticipation gives you expectation, which in turn, thrives within your cells.

While "absolute zero" reality could care less about your positive or negative thought processes, when you think in an optimistic manner, your directed thought patterns manifest in ways you may not understand. It's called "flow of the emerging creative energy of the universe." Once you tap into it and align with its dynamic current, you accelerate or enhance every cell in your body toward living at its highest and best.

Therefore, what good do you find in pessimism? Why would you hang out with pessimists that dwell on the negatives of life? Or, do you hang with optimists who laugh in the face of rain at your garden party?

In my own life, I decided to circle the globe on a bicycle, stand on the South Pole and walk on the Wall of China. So far so good! How did I make my dreams come true? Answer: optimism, effort over time and persistence.

No matter what station in life you started, you can make yourself unhappy with a pessimistic attitude or you can choose happiness with your optimistic thrust. Such a choice allows you to soar with eagles, become a fabulous parent, write the next All-American novel, travel the globe and engage your highest and best. It makes for one hell of an adventure of your body, mind and spirit.

Section VI

Actions That Move
You Forward

Chapter 37

Colossal Dreams Take Colossal Actions

Oftentimes parents ask their kids, "What are you going to be when you grow up?"

Like most children, you didn't possess a clue. You didn't know what you faced when you grew up let alone what you might become as a human being.

Nonetheless, you blurted out, "I'm going to be a fireman or nurse or baseball player."

Everyone smiled when you blurted your answer. In reality, most people don't possess an inkling about their life-purpose. Many lose any chance of pursuing their dreams because they get caught up in life by getting married, raising children and working a job. They chase their dreams after they retire.

What if you could live your dreams while living your life? Any chance you could design your life around your dreams?

Ralph Waldo Emerson said, "Dare to live the life you have dreamed for yourself. Go forward and make your dreams come true."

As you grow into your teens, 30s, 40s and older, explore your natural gifts. You may be able to draw, sculpt or paint. You may enjoy tremendous musical talent with a violin, guitar or French horn. You may be a powerful athlete in swimming, tennis or triathlon. You may be an exceptional teacher.

Take each gift, explore it and apply your time. As you hone your gift, try to align it with your mental, emotional and spiritual power. Explore it from different arenas. For example, you may be able to paint compelling posters of athletic bodies in motion. Or, you might love abstracts. Attend an art museum with its multiple artists in every arena. See what heightens your interest among the many. Return home to apply your talents.

In that application, you may hit a chord in your nervous system, your heart and your intellect. Once you hear the chimes flowing with your talents, pursue them with vigor.

During your pursuit of your dreams, avoid becoming the victim. "Oh, I can't do that; I'm no good at that; I wish I could draw better, I wish I was more athletic," you lament.

A big key to reaching your dreams stems from your sense of the "colossal calling of your life."

- Spend your time with affirmative thought and energy toward your dream. Maintain clarity of spirit and a sense of intention daily.
- Move with purposeful work toward your dream. Everything takes effort over time. There's an old saying, "The harder one works, the luckier one gets."
- Affirm your worthiness every day with meditation, prayer or a daily walk. You must accept and believe in yourself.
- Affirm your newness in the world. Break out of judgment into acceptance. That single act creates a confidence in your mind that drives your dreams forward.
- Speak to your inner self with positive ideas, thoughts and actions.
- Affirm your dreams to yourself, your family, your mate, your friends and to the world.

Finally, assert your partnership with the "creative energy of the universe." Whatever your connection to the Creator, you may think, speak or co-partner with that entity. Think of it championing you toward your destiny.

Accept that the energy that runs through the universe also runs through your body and co-partners with your imagination.

You harness that energy as a purposeful creative process that unfolds every single day of your life.

Along your path, stick your neck out. Sniff the wind. Harness your mind. Call upon your muscles to engage. Gaze upon the horizon with your eyes. Remain alert to the creative process.

Your dream becomes your reality by your relentless, passionate and purposeful actions toward it. Note: many of life's failures were people who did not realize how close they were to success when they gave up.

Always affirm to yourself, "I can! I will! I am!"

Chapter 38

The Creative Dynamo Within You

Six decades ago, a Swiss hiker named George de Mestral hiked through autumn colors with his dog. He crossed fields covered in milkweed, purple thistles, burrs, thorny branches and floating dandelion parachutes.

In the autumn, all plants release their seeds to the winds. Others attach to animals for transport to other locations to begin anew.

When Mestral returned home, he noticed dozens of burr balls with hooks attached to his socks and his dog's fur. It took him 30 minutes to dislodge them from his clothing and the dog.

While pulling them off, he noticed each spine featured a hook at the end that embedded itself into anything passing near the plant. Anything with fur picked up the seed and transported it to new fields. His wool sock picked up the most "hooked" burrs.

He put two and two together! Voila, he created Velcro cloth fasteners. Today, we use Velcro to secure our bicycle shoes, coats, fasten our backpacks and a thousand other uses. He became a millionaire through the "creative dynamo" spinning around in his mind.

You can look throughout history to see innovations and inventions that popped up out of nowhere by average men and women who discovered an idea "out of the blue."

By what process does an invention occur? How can you apply it to your life? What can you do with inventions you create?

Remember that everything must come from an idea before it can move into form.

Ideas fly around the universe waiting for someone to grab them and bring them to form. Your mind constitutes a net that captures ideas. You may remember that tiny, gold, winged ball in the Harry Potter books that flew around the stadium while students chased it on their broomsticks.

When that winged ball flies by your head, grab it! Write down the idea. Process it. Play with it. Move it into form. It might be an idea for a magazine article if you are a writer. It might become a book. If you make jewelry, you may create a stunning ring or necklace. If you create macramé, you may discover a new design. You may create a new painting, poem or sculpture. You might design a new bicycle, airplane, car or boat.

In whatever realm you play, those ideas buzz around your head. Capture them like Harry Potter captured the tiny, gold winged ball.

Never allow anyone to deter you or rain on your parade!

Years ago, a man attempted to make a cooler beach shoe that stayed on peoples' feet. He made it out of rubber with a cinch on the back. He offered it in many colors.

Naysayers said, "That's so ugly; it's a crock!"

So, he named it a "Croc" and you know the rest of the story: billions of people wear his beach Crocs!

In order to engage your own creative dynamo, stay open to ideas via your open consciousness. Realize that form emerges out of the invisible field of the universe. It's the playground of your mind. It's spontaneous and self-generating energy.

It's known as the "Law of Mind." It's the "emerging creative energy of the universe" and it flows through you. You can use it. Uplift your life by up-leveling your thoughts. By doing so, you will partner with the power of the universe.

- Open to the new "yes" in you.
- Fuel your creative dynamo with endless ideas from your experiences.
- Write them down, say them aloud, draw them, and work on turning them from thoughts to form.
- Reframe your sense of self.
- Understand and relish in the fact that you represent an endless fountain of ideas.
- Open to the magic.

The creative dynamo thrives in you by your receptivity. As a writer, I look for new ideas daily. Above my computer on the corkboard for the past 40 years, a small card reads: "The Idea Fairy may strike at any time—so be alert and write her ideas down, so she will feel appreciated and come back often."

Section VII

People Choosing
Spectacular Lives

Chapter 39

Erik Weihenmayer: Turning into the Storm of Life

Ray Charles learned to play the piano as he lost his vision during his childhood. In his 70 years, he scaled musical heights beyond the ordinary. Helen Keller, blind, deaf and mute, learned to read and write as she sped toward becoming one of the 20th century's greatest humanitarians. Having lost both legs in war, Bob Wieland overcame his limitations to walk across America on his hands, race in the Hawaii Ironman Triathlon and hand-cycle coast-to-coast across America three times.

Each of those greats decided to abandon feelings of despair, frustration and defeat. Each turned into the storm of life in order to make his or her own mark on humanity.

In the beginning of the 21st century, another intrepid spirit set out to climb the seven highest peaks on the seven continents of the world. On May 25, 2001, Erik Weihenmayer of Golden, Colorado, became the only blind person to reach the summit of Mt. Everest.

Weihenmayer's mountain climbing quest started in 1995 with his ascent of Mt. Denali in Alaska. He lives in the rarefied air of a scant 118 mountaineers who have climbed the "Seven Summits" which constitute the tallest mountain peaks in the world.

After his successful climb to the top of Mt. Everest, he arrived back in my hometown of Golden, Colorado. He spoke at a movie showing of his quest of Everest.

When he slows down for a few months at a time, Weihenmayer writes books including: **Touch the Top of the World.** Being a mountain climber myself, I read the book three times. I see

Erik with his wife and kids each winter at the "Christmas Parade" along Washington Street in Golden, Colorado. When I shake his hand, I feel like I am shaking hands with someone as famous as Neil Armstrong, Daniel Boone, Ray Charles, Susan B. Anthony, Jane Goodall and Eleanor Roosevelt. Each one of those individuals set out to make a difference in the world. Each succeeded.

Weihenmayer once said, "One of the shortfalls that so many people have is that they allow distractions, fears and doubts to get into their heads and sabotage them. Is there a way to make that difficult thing a catalyst rather than to let it crush you? Yes! I am only one of 118 people to climb all seven highest summits on all seven continents. I am the only one to do it blind. I may not be able to see, but I can show others what's possible."

Additionally, he raced his mountain bike through 100 miles, four 12,000-foot passes and one 13,000-foot pass in the Leadville 100 Mountain Bike Race. It takes 12 hours and nearly 12,000 vertical feet of climbing.

In September 2014, with fellow blind kayaker, Lonnie Bidwell, Weihenmayer kayaked the Colorado River through the Grand Canyon, 277 miles from Lee's Ferry to Pierce Ferry. His awards include:

- 2014/2015 Nominated by National Geographic as Adventurer of the Year with fellow blind kayaker Lonnie Bedwell
- 2013 Presented Annie Glenn Award by American Speech Hearing Language Association
- 2005 Inducted into Connecticut National Wrestling Hall of Fame
- 2002 Received a second ARETE Award for the Superlative Athletic Achievement of the Year

Received an ESPY Award
Named Colorado Athlete of the Year

- 2001 Named one of Time's Best of Sports
- 1996 Carried the Olympic Torch for the Summer Games in Atlanta
- 1995 Received ARETE Award for Courage in Sports

Erik Weihenmayer inspires me, a fully sighted man. I am carried by his courage. I am inspired by his heart. I am driven by his true grit.

"A spark of greatness exists in all people, but only by touching that spark to adversity's flame does it blaze into the force that fuels our lives and the world." Erik Weihenmayer

While Weihenmayer taught English and math in Phoenix, Arizona in his twenties, he continues his teaching skills with his "No Barriers Mindset" for kids. Join him on his website.

Meet Erik Weihenmayer in his books or listen to him on his website. You, too, will discover the courage to face your own challenges and "Turn bravely into the storm of life."

Erik can be reached at: www.touchthetop.com

Books: **Turning Everyday Struggles into Everyday Greatness** and **Touch the Top of the World: A Blind Man's Journey to Climbing Farther Than the Eye Can See.**

Chapter 40

Bob Wieland: Walking Across America on His Hands

That first morning, I pedaled through heavy traffic for the beginning of my coast-to-coast across America adventure. After dipping my hand into the Pacific Ocean, I cranked the pedals east toward the Atlantic Ocean. The Los Angeles smog irritated my lungs before I pedaled into the Mojave Desert. After crossing the Colorado River, I breathed easier when the air pollution flowed south toward Phoenix. Thankfully, I pedaled into cleaner air in the mountains. Climbing steep grades took hours while coasting down the backside took 30 minutes. Sweat dripped from my nose as it splashed onto the top tube. A relentless sun beat down from a brilliant blue sky. Onward into the desert I pedaled.

In New Mexico, I crossed the continental divide and descended into the desert on Route 380. With a blazing sun overhead, I struggled along a two-lane highway that curled over the mountainous landscape. Sweat dripped from my face and arms. Salty rivulets drained down my backside. Every breath crowded my mouth with what felt like dry, hot cotton balls. Heat waves rippled over the pavement as I descended further into the barren landscape. Boulders and cacti stood like indolent sentries guarding the land from intruders. The thermometer hit 103 degrees by the time I pedaled to the outskirts of Roswell, New Mexico.

Ahead, a lone figure walked along the left side of the road heading eastbound. I found it difficult imagining anyone walking down the highway in those torrid temperatures.

"I wonder what that guy's doing walking in this heat?" I muttered to myself.

"Looks like he's got a dog with him, too."

A minute later:

"That's not a dog!" I gasped, doubting my eyes, and straining harder to make out what I saw.

The smaller figure proved not to be a dog, but another man walking on his hands! Within a few seconds, I realized why: no legs!

Less than forty yards away, the lone figure walked and read a book while the other man walked on his hands. A camper van awaited on the shoulder a half mile ahead. I rode up even with the two men. Something inside made me stop and drop my bike into the gravel.

I couldn't help crossing the road, knowing that whoever this man was, he possessed inconceivable courage. Why on earth would anyone be walking on his hands, in this heat, along this road and in the middle of nowhere? He saw me and stopped. He lowered his body down to the ground, resting it on a leather pad that covered his two severed legs just below the groin. His Paul Bunyan upper arms led down to his hands, which grasped two rubber pads. Sweat soaked his T-shirt. His sandy hair framed a tanned, round face punctuated by a pair of clear brown eyes. He flashed a beautiful smile.

"Hi, how ya' doin'?" I said approaching with my hand extended.

"My name is Frosty."

"Glad to meet you," he said shaking my hand. "I'm Bob Wieland and this is my friend Paul."

"Pleasure to meet you," I said. "I gotta' tell you Bob, I'm more than a bit curious seeing you out here in the desert."

"The same could be said about you," he said. "What are you doing out here?"

"I'm riding my bicycle across America."

"That makes two of us," Bob added. "I'm walking across. I'd bike but my legs are too short for the pedals."

I laughed. His humor proved natural. We bantered a few minutes about the weather. Bob gave me a short history of his journey. He started on the West Coast. He crossed over many 6,000 to 8,000 foot passes. His friend fixed meals, but often, people asked them into their homes for the night. If no one offered a night's lodging, both men slept in the back of the camper pickup. His friend drove the vehicle ahead and came back to walk with him. His companion read a book while guiding Bob down the left side of the highway. While in Vietnam, Bob lost his legs in combat. I asked him about his start time.

"I've been out 19 months and have completed 980 miles," he said.

"At my speed, I can finish this adventure in three more years, maybe less."

"Why are you doing it?" I asked.

"There's a lot of adventure out here on the road. I suppose I could sit back and get fat watching TV for the next fifty years, but I want to do something with my life. I want to make a difference. I have to make do with what I have left. You know the old saying, you only go around once."

"You have my greatest admiration," I said, shaking his hand again.

It became one of those moments where you don't quite know what to do or say, or how to act. I just met the most incredibly courageous man in my whole life who looked up at me from the pavement. He lost his legs in that terrible war. While still a man, he stood only three feet high. His hands had become his feet. That gray leather pad protected his bottom like a baby diaper. Those rubber pads on his hands gave him wheel tread for his arduous journey. I gasped inside myself at the enormity of his quest.

"Guess I better get moving," I said, reluctantly.

"Take care," Bob said. "Have a good ride. I'll get there one of these days."

"There's no doubt that you will reach the Atlantic Ocean," I said.

While turning away from that amazing human being, tears filled my eyes. I started crying half way across the road. What he attempted staggered my imagination. My friends called me nuts for taking a transcontinental bicycle trip, but they had no understanding about the ease of my task compared to Bob Wieland's.

After crossing the highway, I pulled my bike out of the dirt. I guzzled a half bottle of water. I stepped onto the pedals. I pressed my iron steed eastward into the hot morning sun. I cried for miles at the senselessness of war. I cried for Bob and I cried for humanity. Miles and years down the road—that moment colors my mind as vividly as the day it happened.

Most human beings possess handicaps in one way or the other—physical or psychological. Most importantly, it's how they handle their limitations. Wieland concentrated on what he could do, not on what he couldn't do. Instead of giving up, Bob pushed forward into the unknown not only determined to succeed, but also expecting to succeed.

George Bernard Shaw celebrated people like Wieland when he wrote, "This is the true joy of living, spending your years for a purpose recognized by yourself as a right one...to be used up when they throw you on the scrap heap of life. To have been a force of nature instead of a selfish little clod of ailments and grievances complaining that the world will not devote itself to making you happy."

Bob Wieland pushed himself through 3,400 miles of hardship that few people could comprehend. He gutted his way up mountains, sweated his way across deserts, and fought through raging storms. Every labored breath drew him closer to his goal—the Atlantic Ocean.

Two years later, while I listened to NPR radio during breakfast one morning, the reporter said, "Bob Wieland reached the Atlantic Ocean thus succeeding in his quest to walk on his hands coast-to-coast across America. It took him three years, eight months and six days...."

In 1996, he completed a 6,200-mile bicycle circuit, using his hands, twice across America. In 1994, People Magazine awarded him one of the six "Most Amazing Americans" in the past 100 years. He's the only double amputee to complete the Ironman Triathlon in Kona, Hawaii without a wheelchair. He ran and completed the New York, LA and Marine Marathons. The list continues to grow!

I sat at the breakfast table crying like a baby because that man gave me courage to face my own struggles from that one meeting in the New Mexico desert many years ago. I'm sure he touched thousands more on his remarkable journey across America. Here's to you, Bob Wieland, to your courage, your humor, your passion and your life.

No matter what the hardship, Bob Wieland lives a spectacular life!

Chapter 41

Robin Emmons: Sow Much Good

If you look back on your life, do you feel like you're missing your calling? Do you continue on a path that fails to inspire your heart, mind and body? Do you find yourself going to work each day with an uneasy feeling on your shoulder? At some point, have you asked yourself, "What am I doing here?"

Guess what? If you walk down the wrong path toward your destiny, but keep walking, you will end up with your dissonant fate. However, no matter what your age, you may turn around — and proceed in the direction that calls your heart.

Robin Emmons graduated from McColl Center for Visual Art's Innovation Institute. She continued with a degree from the University of North Carolina in Political Science.

Many of us get banged around on our journey toward our futures. Emmons woke up one day after 20 years in corporate America to ask, "What am I doing in this job?" She quit.

One week after quitting, Emmons helped her brother find residence in a mental health facility; however, while being treated, he became unhealthy due to the consumption of canned and sugary foods. Robin, a gardener, donated produce to the facility and her brother's physical health improved dramatically.

From that point in 2008, Emmons found her passion: "I used food as a vehicle to promote social justice on important issues such as food access in marginalized communities."

Today she advocates for healthy foods and nutrition. She began as a gardener and now, farmer. She dug up her entire backyard and sowed the seeds for a nonprofit organization.

She dedicated herself to eliminating systemic barriers in the food system that disproportionately affect the working poor and underserved populations.

Since launching Sow Much Good, she said, "I want to raise awareness about inequities in the food system that eliminate the basic human right of a significant number of people to access clean, healthy food through workshops, farm stands and speaking opportunities."

Emmons' work arrives at a time when obesity plagues children and adults across America. A mind-numbing 65 percent of Americans suffer obesity and 30 percent of that number explodes into gross obesity.

In May of 2014, Emmons launched, Farm Fresh To Go. She said, "It is available to those living in the communities and neighborhoods we serve who lack transportation or otherwise simply can't make it to the market during regular operating hours."

Weekly **Farm Fresh To Go** CSA shares are available for pick-up or delivery. Delivery is available to individuals and families living well outside of the Urban Farm and Market footprint. Weekly pick-up is encouraged for residents living in the Sunset, Oakdale and Statesville Avenue neighborhoods, with special delivery consideration given to elderly and homebound customers." (She lives in Huntersville, North Carolina.)

In honor of her extraordinary work, TED Talks invited Robin Emmons to speak. She inspired, encouraged and enthralled a capacity audience.

In your life, what path do you walk? More importantly, how good do you feel about it? Are you walking in the right direction that fulfills your sense of purpose, your sense of humanity and your spiritual expansion?

Take a hint, take a clue and directional pointer from Robin Emmons to change your path at any age, any moment and for all the right reasons. Life's energy pulled at Emmons; she answered.

Life's energy tugs at your apron strings; it begs you to enter a new dimension in your life. It calls your heart.

Like Robin Emmons, take courage and take a chance to fulfill your calling by walking down your life-path toward your chosen destiny. Emmons sows much good because her heart blooms and grows. www.SowMuchGood.org

Chapter 42

Anna Harrington: Walking Across America for Little Children

Rebecca Solnit said, "For Jane Austen and the readers of Pride and Prejudice, solitary walks express the independence that literally takes the heroine out of the social sphere of the houses and their inhabitants, into a larger, lonelier world where she is free to think: walking articulates both physical and mental freedom…it connects one to the Earth."

When you take a walk, especially in the woods, you feel a connection to nature that transforms your energy, quiets your body and soothes your mind. Walking allows you to enhance your thoughts, feelings and ideas. Magic follows you on a walk.

But what if you decided during one of your walks to make a greater stroll into the world? What if you garnered a purpose for your journey? What if that trek carried you over 3,000 miles across North America? What if you turned out to be a woman? What if you walked for the children of the world?

Anna Harrington, 42, of Meridian, Idaho took a walk one day that gave her the courage to walk over 3,400 miles across America.

In the spring of 2014, Harrington launched herself from a beach on the Pacific Ocean in Astoria, Oregon with a goal of Boston, Massachusetts on the Atlantic Ocean. Her reason: she crusades to raise funds to help Shriner's Hospitals for Children.

She looked back on the amazing care for her nephew when he developed scoliosis in 2005. She said, "Shriners medical care doesn't cost the families anything, but is funded in part by Shriners' clubs fundraisers, including the Shrine Circus."

A slim, curly-haired redhead with an infectious smile, Harrington averages 20 miles per day. She wore out one pair of hiking boots at the 1,000-mile mark in Utah. She wears bush pants and a shirt. She carries a large water canteen.

I met her at the Buffalo Herd Overlook in Golden, Colorado on Route 40. As we snapped pictures of the newborn bison babies, Anna walked up to us, "Could you guys give me directions to get into Golden?"

"Sure," I said. "Just take that paved road straight down for five miles until you reach a red light. Take a left. Ask for more directions."

"Thanks," she said.

"Where you coming from?" I asked.

"The Pacific coast in Oregon," she said. "I'm headed to the Atlantic."

For the next 15 minutes, I took photographs and learned more about her walk across America coast-to-coast.

"A few years ago I read somewhere that they were considering the closure of a couple of the Shriners hospitals, and I didn't want that to happen," Harrington said. "So I tried to figure out what I could do to raise money for Shriners. And then I recalled the walk — I've always wanted to walk cross-country. So the two came together."

The long journey:

"When you're out there on the road you feel very vulnerable," she said. "I had no idea what to expect. I have people come up to me, and they hear my story, hear what I'm doing, and they put me up in their home for a night, prepare me dinner or they get me a room for the night."

At other times, Harrington breaks out the camping gear she carries in her three-wheeled stroller. She deals with female challenges on the road. Like in the barren desert of Utah.

"There's no tall sage brush," she said, chuckling. "I'm like, seriously, I'm getting a tent or something that I can go into."

Along the route, Harrington expects to visit nine of the 22 Shriners Hospitals in North America.

After leaving Denver, she faced the Great Plains with a thousand miles of nothing but prairie, wheat fields, small towns and the horizon. She faced burning prairie heat day after day.

"What do you like the most about the walk?" I asked.

"The people," she said. "They are so funny, so kind and totally blown away by my journey."

"Probably inspired to make their own journeys," I said.

"Everyone faces obstacles in life," Harrington said. "Just pull up your shoelaces and get moving."

As she grabbed her cart, she looked back at us with a huge smile on her face. "Thanks," she said.

"Safe journey," we called out.

I couldn't help but realize that Anna makes the world a better place for children. She inspires other women to pursue their own dreams. She touches people, encourages them and inspires them by her actions.

As you read her story, Anna heads into a bright new day. She's out there right now with the wind flying through her hair, her legs striding across the Earth. She feels connected. She renders her passion for the children of the world.

At the time of this printing, she walks across Africa to bring fresh water to adults and children.

Her website for support: www.annaswalk.com

"I've come to believe that each of us has a personal calling that's as unique as a fingerprint – and that the best way to succeed is to discover what you love and then find a way to offer it to others in the form of service, working hard, and also allowing the energy of the universe to lead you." — *Oprah Winfrey*

Chapter 43

Anne Miltenberger: Trans-Atlantic

In the summer of 2006, I met Anne Miltenberger in Boulder, Colorado. She planned on rowing the Atlantic Ocean from North America to Europe. In 2009, Miltenberger joined 11 other women in the Woodvale Challenge to make that dream come true.

While growing up in Colorado, she accompanied her father to the top of her first 14,000-foot peak at the age of eight. She camped, hiked and rowed her way through college.

She loved endurance sports.

"I enjoyed the mental high you get and the rhythm of running and the singularity of it," she explained. "Your goal is very clear—get to the finish line first."

After college, she pedaled her bicycle from Washington State to the Atlantic Ocean in Maine. Along that route, she inspired and was inspired by countless people who crossed her path.

"My various adventures have taught me how to think on my feet, go with the flow and accept what comes at me," Miltenberger said. "Does that mean that I'll always respond appropriately? Not necessarily. But I know that when I come around, all the obstacles that were difficult and stood in my way, and all those problems that I had to overcome, will make me smarter and stronger."

During her Atlantic crossing saga, Anne discovered the tedium of repetitive rowing during her shift. Her hands suffered from an ailment known as the 'claw-effect' from rowing for hours on end. She taxed her arms, legs and back. She faced salt-water sores, 100-degree heat, sweating profusely and a pretty rough rear end. She slept in short cycles in very cramped quarters with her crewmates who all held the same goal—to mark the fastest time across the Atlantic in a rowboat in their class.

"I could keep going on about how miserable it was," she said. "But I would totally do it again. I saw surreal sunrises and sunsets while on the Atlantic. I witnessed the ever-changing dynamics of the waves which created awesome perspective along with moonless nights and skies brimming with stars."

Once she followed her inner adventure voice, she found ways to sail in the Caribbean and in New Zealand.

Today she works as a products manager for Kelty. It allows her time for her adventures while inspiring more women to pursue their own dreams of adventure around the planet.

Website: www.rowingfortheenvironment.com

SECTION VIII

NUTS AND BOLTS OF WORLD ADVENTURE

This section offers you everything you need to know about preparation for travel, gear and contact information. You will discover how to use your conscious and subconscious mind to create an action plan for realizing your intentions. If you need more ideas, you will find them from other writers that provide a plethora of information. This section gives you ideas for your bucket list of travel and adventure options.

Chapter 44

Action plan

Every man or woman ought to be inquisitive through every hour of this great adventure down to the day when he or she shall no longer cast a shadow in the sun. For if he or she dies without a question in the heart, what excuse is there for continuance? ~ *Frank Colby*

By now, you have read a number of my adventures from around the world via different kinds of exploits. Most prove mild while a few could have gotten me killed. Many other high-risk adventure-seekers make my escapades look like a walk in the park. Again, no comparison as everyone chooses his or her own level of risk and adventure.

Review and inculcate all the concepts and practices in this book. You want to live your own adventures. How do you make your life work out the way you want it? How do you guide your life in the direction you want to travel? You need to create, plan and fulfill your intentions, dreams or goals.

USE YOUR BRAIN: THE MOST POWERFUL COMPUTER IN THE UNIVERSE

Let's imagine three levels across your head, all parallel and evenly spaced. Just imagine your brain with a first level, second level and third level.

1. First level—your conscious mind or creative mind operates on the top level. That's where you come up

with ideas. Let's say that you imagine a ski trip. It may be a canoe trip, a mountain climbing expedition or riding a bicycle 100 miles in a day. It could be anything that you love or intend to experience such as a painting, sculpture or creating other works of art.

Essentially, your top level may be considered the architect that draws the plans for a weekend adventure, weeklong adventure or year around the world adventure. Again, you may be trying to win a dance contest or triathlon event. Whatever your adventure, it births in the conscious level of your brain.

The architect draws everything into the plans for a successful adventure. It includes times, routes, gear, people, support, transport, shots, passport, visas and everything you need to enjoy a successful adventure.

During your waking hours, you prepare for the adventure by working a job, buying equipment, training, obtaining a passport and all other preparations needed to step into the adventure. In other words, you complete all the necessary details created by your architect mind on the top level.

You research books that cover every detail you need by those who have gone before you. Fill in the blanks by following checklists promoted by clubs, organizations and other entities that help you prepare for your adventure. Once your architect draws up the plans, you let them germinate in the second level or sub-conscious.

2. Second level—let's move to the second level or subconscious. Once you make a definite plan to

engage a certain adventure or piece of artwork, your subconscious works on it while you sleep. You engage your subconscious mind or whatever you care to call it. You work with the creative flow.

As you sleep, your subconscious mind works on the details by making sure you move toward your goals or dreams—however you interpret them. As your subconscious works, you will pick up more ideas and think of things that will move you toward your goals.

Whether it takes you a week to prepare for a mountain climbing trip, skiing trip or canoeing trip—you learn what it takes by starting small and, with time, moving toward more ambitious adventures. You gain knowledge and know-how as you proceed through each check-down.

3. Third level—the third level becomes your fruition level where you live the adventure or finish a painting or run a race. During that experience, you gain valuable insights and understanding of what you did or didn't do to make your adventure successful. With each successive adventure, you may choose greater experiences in whatever arenas interest you.

KEY POINTS FROM THIS CHAPTER

1. Your conscious mind creates the idea or intention.
2. Your subconscious mind works on the details.
3. You fulfill the steps to make your dream a reality.
4. You live your dream, adventure or intention.

Chapter 45

Adventure Lists for Consideration

It takes a lot of courage to release the familiar and seemingly secure, to embrace the new. But there is no real security in what is no longer meaningful. There is more security in the adventurous and exciting, for in movement there is life and in change there is power. *~ Alan Cohen*

Your lifespan provides as many adventures as you care to pursue. You may participate in some of the wildest, weirdest, craziest and zaniest activities ever invented by humanity. You will not live long enough to do everything on this planet, but you can make a huge dent in your bucket list.

While I cycled through Tasmania, Australia, I met a British man who had traveled through 181 countries out of the 193 or so countries on the planet. Well past 80, he inspired me. One lady, Elizabeth, also from London, England, hiked through Nepal with us. At 72, she carried her pack along with the rest of the group.

You may travel, scuba dive, climb mountains, raft rivers, surf, cliff dive, explore caves, camp, ride horses, sail, compete in triathlons and about a gazillion other activities. Suit yourself as to the kind of adventure as well as intensity, frequency and danger.

Several years ago, Morgan Freeman and Jack Nicholson played two guys suffering from terminal cancer. Because they didn't want to drop into their graves without having done something amazing with their lives, they created a bucket list of adventures to pursue while they still lived. That list included sky diving, stock car racing, traveling to the pyramids, climbing the Great Wall of China, visiting the Taj Mahal, visiting Machu Picchu, climbing to the base camp of Mount Everest, taking an African safari and more.

At one point, as Freeman touched the blazing red finish of a 1965 Mustang, Nicholson asked, "Are you going to race it or buy it a dress?"

"Just getting to know each other," Freeman replied, running his hands across the finish.

"Do you hate me?" Nicholson asked.

"Not yet," Freeman said.

As they sashayed around the globe on their bucket list of adventures, at one point, Nicholson said, "We live, we die. The world keeps going round and round."

No question, you possess only so many minutes on this little blue-green planet somewhere in the outskirts of space. When it's over, it's over. No rerun, no second chance, no mulligan, no do-over and no re-take. You're out to capture the whole enchilada while you're living on the planet.

BUCKET LIST IN NO PARTICULAR ORDER

1---Raft trip down the Colorado River through the Grand Canyon. Lee's Ferry to Diamond Creek takeout or Lake Powell.

2---Hike the Appalachian Trail, 2,175 miles.

3---Climb all 54—14,000-foot peaks in Colorado. Climb all 14,000-foot peaks and higher all the way to Denali in Alaska at 20,329 feet.

4---Bicycle across America. Bicycle seven continents.

5---Ballooning across America. Ballooning in New Mexico, Colorado and a dozen other states.

6---Mountain biking in Moab, Utah on Slickrock. Race in the Leadville 100 Race Across the Sky either by foot or bicycle. www.raceacrossthesky.com

7----Ride the Triple Bypass in Colorado. Ride the Rockies. Ride the RAGBRAI in Iowa.

8---Scuba dive the five Great Lakes. Dive in all the famous places in Florida and the Gulf of Mexico. Dive in the Galapagos Islands. Dive the Great Barrier Reef in Australia. Dive in all the oceans and seas of the world.

9---Bicycle tour Nord Cap, Norway to Athens, Greece in five months. Bicycle 17,000 kms around Australia in six months. Bicycle from the Arctic Ocean in Alaska to the bottom of South America in Ushuaia. Bicycle the North Sea Cycle Route.

10---Train ride on the Orient Express. Train over the highest railroad pass in the world from Lima, Peru to Juan Kio at 16,000 feet. Train ride across Canada. Train ride across America coast-to-coast. Train ride all over Europe. Endless opportunities await you anywhere in the world on a train.

11---Bag all seven of the highest peaks on all seven continents. Trek in Nepal, where you will visit ancient people, an ancient culture and astounding scenery.

12---Visit 193, give or take a few, countries in the world by any means you can discover.

13---Surf the big ones in Hawaii, Australia, Bali, Panama and just about anywhere big waves crash on any region of the planet.

14---Horseback ride across America or any continent. For more information: www.thelongridersguild.com

15---Ski the Andes, Pyrenees, Alaska Range

16---Safari in Kenya, Tanzania or anywhere in Africa. Ride a camel around the pyramids or a horse.

17---Parasail, hang-glide and sky dive anywhere in the world. Bungee jumping for kicks.

18---Travel to Antarctica. Watch whales, penguins, seals and skua. Work and live at McMurdo Station.

19---Climb Half-Dome at Yosemite National Park. Hike all of Yosemite and the Sierra Range.

20---Hut to hut mountain ski trips in Colorado and many other states. www.huts.org, www.sanjuanhuts.com

21---Camel trek in Morocco, Africa. Additionally, you can cycle from Cape Town to Cairo, Egypt in about 16 months.

22---Bicycle tour the profile of the boot of Italy.

23---Play golf courses in all 50 states.

24---Raft the Nile River.

25---Explore the Amazon River, South America.

26---Walk the Congo River, Africa.

27---Raft the Yangtze River, China.

28---Climb Everest, K-2, McKinley, Kilimanjaro, Cook, Matterhorn, Rainier, Fuji, Vesuvius, Huascaran, Popocatepetl, Kenya, Ararat, Bromo, Grand Tetons, Baldy.

29---Dive in a submarine.

30---Fly a blimp, airplane, jet, and hot air balloon.

31---Ride an elephant, camel, ostrich and wild bull.

32---Play a piano, guitar or horn.

33---Become a globetrotting photographer.

34---earn unlimited numbers of languages.

35---Stand on the North and South Poles.

36---Walk around the world.

37---Read all the classics.

38---Ride or run Monument Valley at sunrise or sunset.

39---Backpack into Chicago Basin, Colorado.

40---Walk or run the Boulder Bolder in Boulder, Colorado.

Top 110 adventures in the United States

Alaska

Complete a NOLS course
Explore ANWR
Heli-Ski the Chugach Mountains
Tree-climb Chilkat
Float the Tatshenshini-Alsek River
Trek Wrangell-St. Elias National Park & Preserve
Climb Mount McKinley
Camp with Alaska brown bears
Canoe the Yukon River
Bicycle the Richardson Highway
Bicycle the Dalton Highway across the Arctic Circle

Arizona

Row down the Grand Canyon
Hike Buckskin Gulch (& Utah)
Bicycle Monument Valley

California

Surf the Lost Coast
Bike the Death Ride
Hike Half Dome
Hike the Sierra High Route
Paddle Santa Cruz Island
Mountain Bike the Tahoe Rim Trail (& Nevada)
Bodysurf the Wedge
Raft the Forks of the Kern
Ski Mountaineer Mount Shasta
Hike the John Muir Trail

Colorado

Bike From Durango to Moab (& Utah)
Climb Ouray
Ski Scar Face
Hike the Colorado Trail
Run the Trans-Rockies
Ski Silverton Mountain
Race the Leadville Trail 100
Backcountry Ski the 10th Mountain Division Huts
Bag 54—14ers, pack into Chicago and American basins
Climb the Diamond on Longs Peak
Run the Bolder Boulder, Colorado

Florida

Kite-board the Keys
Paddle the Everglades
Swamp Tromp in Big Cypress National Preserve
Dive freshwater caves
Fly-Fish for the Florida Keys Slam
Scuba dive in John Pennekamp Park in the Keys

Georgia

Canoe the Okeefenokee

Hawaii

Kayak the Na Pali Coast
Hike the Muliwai Trail
Kiteboard Maui's North Shore
Parasailing around Diamond Head

Iowa

Bicycle RAGBRAI

Idaho

Hike the Salmon River
Snowkite Camas Valley
Raft the Owyhee River (& Oregon & Nevada)

Kentucky

Climb Red River Gorge

Maine

Kayak the Maine Island Trail
Canoe the Allagash

Michigan

Sail the Manitou's
Windsurf the Straits of Mackinaw
Bicycle the 'Mitt' of Michigan, especially in spring or fall

Minnesota

Dogsled the Boundary Waters
Wreck dive Lake Superior
Race the Arrowhead 135
Canoe the Boundary Waters
Hike the Superior Trail
Canoe the Mississippi River from Lake Itasca

Missouri

Paddle 340 Miles of the Mighty Missouri—Nonstop

Montana

Hike the Bob Marshall Trail
Climb Granite Peak
Ice Climb Hyalite Canyon
Fly-Fish the Spring Creeks of Paradise Valley
Backpack Glacier National Park
Bicycle start for the Continental Divide to Mexico

Multistate

Get fit at a Navy SEAL Immersion Camp
Bike Across America
Learn to fly a wingsuit
Backpack the Pacific Coast Trail
Bike the Continental Divide Trail
Backpack the Appalachia Trail
Run Ironman triathlons in several states

North Carolina

Paddle the Outer Banks
Learn Paddling at Nantahala Outdoor Center

North Dakota

Bike the Maah Daah Hey

New Hampshire

Ski Tuckerman Ravine
Hike the Traverse
Bicycle through the covered bridges

New Mexico

Fly-fish the Pecos
Horsepack the Gila Wilderness

Nevada

Heli-Ski the Ruby Mountains

New York

Canoe the Adirondacks
Climb the Gunks

Oregon

Kite-board the Columbia River Gorge (& Washington)
Ski the Wallowas
Bicycle tour the coast line

Tennessee

Hike the Roan Highlands
Raft the Ocoee

Texas

Float the Big Bend of the Rio Grande

Utah

Raft the Green River
Scale Red-Rock Towers
Paddle Lake Powell
Backpack the Hayduke Trail
Canyoneer Grand Staircase-Escalante
Hike the Zion Narrows
Mountain bike Slickrock in Moab
Mountain bike the Kokopelli Trail

Vermont

Ski Inn-to-Inn on the Catamount Trail

Washington

Transect the Olympic
Climb Mount Rainier
Hike Glacier Peak
Sea Kayak the San Juan Islands

Wisconsin

Ski the Birkebeiner

West Virginia

Raft the Gauley River

Wyoming

Hike the Winds
Climb the Grand Teton
Backcountry Ski Teton Pass
Kayak Lake Yellowstone
Hike Yellowstone's Wild Southwest

You may create your own bucket list. You could watch "The Bucket List" on Netflix and jot down ideas that interest you.

1.John Goddard started with 127 adventures on his bucket list. Later, he added 500 adventures to his list as his awareness and interests grew. Your interests evolve as you taste different adventures in your teens, 20s, 30s and beyond. Think of your list as an evolving tapestry of your life.

2. Think beyond your own experiences. Read adventure books or magazines to get a feel and taste of what's out there. Some things will grab your mind faster than others.

3. Think about different aspects of your existence. While travel appears as the most compelling bucket list for adventuring, you may find plenty of adventure in your own town such as: learning to swing dance, ballroom or country & western. You might want to compete in dance contests all over the country. You may take up art and travel all over the country or world to paint landscapes, statues, marine life, etc. You may want to try photography in a variety of forms. Stay healthy so you can live to be 100 and try out as many avenues as possible.

4. Check out the Internet for ideas on activities that may interest you. You will find an endless stream of adventures and adventure lists on your computer screen. Use Google and the whole world

opens up to you. Try www.43things.com and www.Project183.com for starters.

5. Start out small with easily accomplished adventures. Go with someone who might teach you survival skills, camping, mountain climbing or parasailing. Join clubs to get a feel for your limits. Move with your strengths, gather your confidence and grow your skills. As you progress, you may create bigger and more compelling adventures.

6. If you work a 9-to-5 job, you need to make your intentions for weekends. Then, take one, two and three week vacations. If you love triathlon, you may rise at 5 a.m., swim, bike, run and weight train before you go to work. Try to avoid, "One of these days, I'm going to run a marathon." Get your butt out there, train and run it. Make time, take time and move toward your adventure intentions.

7. If you get off on blogging, take time to post your upcoming adventure. Talk about it. Prepare for it. If you're a quiet and reserved person, write it down for yourself.

8. It's a good idea to write down your intentions for whatever adventure you anticipate. Set some timelines to anticipate the event. I write down and plan my major bicycle adventures two years in advance. That gives me time to earn money and prepare myself mentally, emotionally and physically. It also allows friends who might be going for some or all of the adventure to make their plans. I hold myself to my goals. I move toward each adventure with steadfast determination to stand on the starting line or present my ticket to the airline attendant.

9. Little adventures and big adventures. You need to work them back and forth according to your needs, your money, your time, your age and your condition. For kicks, grins and giggles, make

sure you keep that list in a notebook or hanging on the wall. Each time you finish an adventure such as "The Leadville 100 Mountain Bike Race Across the Sky," cross it off. Save your race placard from your bike as a memento on your "memory shelf." It's a heck of a rewarding feeling to know that you lived it and now, you're on to the next adventure.

10. Laugh, love and smile along the way. Beam good thoughts daily to all you meet and to every challenge. Worry? Intentions and goals come to fruition when you move them into action. Remember that failures provide you with stepping-stones to success.

KEY POINTS FROM THIS CHAPTER

1. Work with your interests to create your bucket list.
2. Talk with friends to gain their ideas for exciting adventures.
3. Read adventure books that interest you.
4. Start out with small adventures and work up to bigger ones.

Chapter 46

Adventure Books to Inspire You

A man does not climb a mountain without bringing some of it away with him, and leaving something of himself upon it. ~ *Sir Martin Conway*

These books may give you ideas, inspire you, enthrall you and educate you. At the same time, you may resonate more with men and women who jumped into life with their own particular zeal in different arenas from sailing, to mountain climbing, to scuba diving and spelunking. These men and women answered the call to a life of adventure. One or several of these books may be the inspiration you need to move into your own life of adventure that best fits you.

1. **The Worst Journey in the World** by Apsley Cherry-Garrard (1922). The author volunteered to go with Sir Robert Falcon Scott in 1910 to reach the South Pole. He met incredible challenges from 100-below temperatures, six-month-long Antarctic nights and horrific danger. I read it and I lived in Antarctica to experience the numbing cold and challenges he faced.
2. **Journals** by Meriwether Lewis and William Clark (1814). Can you think of any two American explorers more famous? Their journey took guts, cunning, courage and luck.
3. **Full Tilt** by Derla Murphy (1965). In 1963, Murphy pedaled her bicycle across Europe, Iran, Afghanistan, Pakistan and the Himalayas to reach India on her own.

I have met more than a dozen women on bicycles riding around the world on their own.

4. **Wind, Sand & Stars** by Antoine de Saint-Exupery (1940). Saint-Exupery was the greatest pilot-poet of the air. In the 1920s, he flew the mail from France to Spain across the Pyrenees in all kinds of weather. Also, with bad maps and no radio.

5. **Exploration of the Colorado River** by John Wesley Powell (1875). Powell and his men started on the Green River in wooden boats. Life, death and geology. This book hits on all eight cylinders for rafters.

6. **Arabian Sands** by Wilfred Thesiger (1959). He said, "Fail the humility test, and the desert will surely kill you."

7. **Desert Solitaire** by Edward Abbey (1968). I've read this book three times. It's a classic for all ages. Abbey is the Thoreau of the West.

8. **Miles From Nowhere** by Jessica Savage (1990). She bicycled around the world for two years. She shares great stories about her ride.

9. **Annapurna** by Maurice Herzog (1952). Herzog and Louis Lachenal reached the top. The descent proved fatal for Lachenal. Herzog lost all his fingers to frostbite and nearly died. It's a gripping icy tale of life and death.

10. **West with the Night** by Beryl Markham (1942). Ernest Hemmingway said, "It's a bloody wonderful book." Markham takes you through Africa where a lion mauls her. She said, "I have lifted my plane from the airport and have never felt her wheels glide from the earth into the air without knowing the uncertainty and exhilaration of firstborn adventure."

11. **Into Thin Air** by Jon Krakauer (1997). The author takes you on one of the most tragic moments on Mount

Everest when 12 people died because of poor judgment and stupid mistakes. I've read this book and remember my time in Nepal as I gazed upon the summit of Mount Everest "The Earth Goddess" at 29,029 feet.

12. **Travels with Marco Polo** by Marco Polo (1298). Polo tells of his 27 years traveling through Asia. He will inspire you toward your own adventures.

13. **Farthest North** by Fridtjof Nansen (1897). In 1893, Nansen purposely froze his ship into the Arctic ice. When the ship neared the North Pole, he guided his dogsled team to reach the Pole. The book proves to be an epic tale.

14. **Terra Icognita** by Sara Wheeler (1996). She writes about her year in Antarctica. I read her book twice. I wrote a companion book to hers. **Antarctica: An Extreme Encounter** by Frosty Wooldridge.

15. **The Snow Leopard** by Peter Matthiessen (1978). The author never saw the endangered snow leopard and neither did I when I trekked in the Himalayas. Nonetheless, I enjoyed peace and spiritual bliss while hiking through eternal beauty and amazing moments.

16. **Roughing It** by Mark Twain (1872). America's favorite writer traveled out west in 1860. This book records a bunch of hilarious characters and events. Twain brings the "funny" of adventure to your front door!

17. **Two Years Before the Mast** by Richard Henry Dana (1840). He describes a sailor's life out of Boston Harbor in the 1800s. This book gives you an idea of adventures on the oceans and seas around the world.

18. **South** by Sir Ernest Shackleton (1919). Shackleton's story must be the single greatest story of perseverance in the world. He and 28 men survived two years on the

ice in Antarctica under mind-boggling cold future. I read it. I loved it.

19. **Endurance** by Alfred Lansing (1957). The author interviewed many of the survivors of Shackleton's attempt to walk across Antarctica. Lansing rivets readers to their seats as to the sheer guts and determination to survive minus 100 below zero Antarctic nights that lasted for six months. This is the greatest survival book I have ever read. I stepped inside Shackleton's hut near McMurdo, Antarctica.

20. **A Short Walk in the Hindu Kush** by Eric Newby (1958). He walks into Afghanistan, climbs mountains and explores the Middle East. He runs into people who said, "Here, we shoot people without permission."

21. **Kon-Tiki** by Thor Heyerdahl (1950). He sailed from Peru toward Polynesia to prove that the South Pacific was settled from the east.

22. **Travels in West Africa** by Mary Kingsley (1897). Kingsley shows that women can adventure with gusto, drive and uncommon determination. She fought off leopards, crocs, bugs and more as she tramped through Africa.

23. **Seven Years in Tibet** by Heinrich Harrer (1953). He escaped a prisoner-of-war camp in India. This Austrian headed for Tibet and met the young Dalai Lama.

24. **The Spirit of St. Louis** by Charles Lindbergh (1953). He became the first man to fly across the Atlantic Ocean. His plane hangs in the Smithsonian in Washington, DC. He said, "Death is the last great adventure."

25. **Journals** by James Cook (1768-1779). Captain Cook sailed around the world and is known for sailing into the Southern Oceans of Antarctica. He is one of the world's greatest adventurers.

26. **Home of the Blizzard** by Douglas Mawson (1915). He marched into Antarctica in 1912 and suffered horrific misery. Heck of a read if you enjoying frostbitten hands while you read the book.

27. **The Voyage of the Beagle** by Charles Darwin (1839). This is the voyage where Darwin cemented his book on the theory of evolution. He explored the Galapagos Islands. Since I spent two weeks in those islands, too, I saw what he saw. You will read about incredible wildlife.

28. **The Seven pillars of Wisdom** by T.E. Lawrence (1926). If you're a desert rat, this is the Lawrence of Arabia of all time. Dry, hot, camels, sand and misery.

29. **The Right Stuff** by Tom Wolfe (1979). Wolfe features Chuck Yeager and America's race to the moon.

30. **Travels in the Interior District of Africa** by Mungo Park (1799). The author traveled through Africa for two years on horseback. He shares his wild adventures in Africa.

31. **Sailing Alone Around the World** by Joshua Slocum (1900). At the age of 50, this man sailed around the world three years and 46,000 miles. He tried it again in 1909, but like Amelia Earhart, he vanished.

32. **The Mountain of My Fear** by David Roberts (1968). He said, "The deepest despair I have ever felt, as well as the most piercing happiness, has come in the mountains." He adventured in Alaska in his twenties and writes a heck of a tale.

33. **First Footsteps in East Africa** by Richard Burton (1856). He spoke Arabic and traveled in disguise around Africa.

34. **The Perfect Storm** by Sebastian Junger (1997). He writes about 50-foot waves and higher. It's a great ocean-going adventure.

35. **The Oregon Trail** by Francis Parkman (1849). This book addresses hard times and rough living on the Oregon Trail by early pioneers.

36. **Through the Dark Continent** by Henry M. Stanley (1878). He found Dr. Livingston, but the good doctor wasn't lost. Stanley runs the Congo River and lives to tell about it.

37. **A Lady's Life in the Rocky Mountains** by Isabella L. Bird (1879). This lady traveled the world and wrote about it. This book inspires women of all ages of life.

38. **In the Land of White Death** by Valerian Albanov (1917). Two dozen men suffered being frozen in the Arctic ice in 1912. Eleven frozen guys tried to walk out and only two made it. This tale freezes your eye-lids.

39. **Scrambles Amongst the Alps** by Edward Whymper (1871). He became the first to climb the Matterhorn, but his four buddies died. He's hardcore and his book remains one of the classics of climbing.

40. **Out of Africa** by Isak Dinesen (1937). Karen Blixen was her real name. She said, "The civilized people have lost the aptitude of stillness and must take lessons in silence from the wild."

41. **Scott's Last Expedition: The Journals** by Robert Falcon Scott (1913). Scott said, "Oh God, this is an awful place!" Scott and his men died after reaching the South Pole second to Amundsen the Norwegian dog musher.

42. **Everest: The West Ridge** by Thomas Hornbein (1965). Great mountain climbing adventure!

43. **Journey Without Maps** by Graham Greene (1936). Liberia in 1935. Greene dared to walk into an area of cannibals and mosquitoes that carried Yellow Fever. We're talking about an ugly, yucky and deadly adventure.

44. **Starlight and Storm** by Gaston Rebuffat (1954). Rebuffat climbed all six of the toughest north faces in the Alps. He's high energy and positive beyond measure.

45. **My First Summer in the Sierra** by John Muir (1911). In the summer of 1869, Muir traveled through the Sierra Nevada with a shepherd and his flock. Muir became the first environmentalist of the world. He was a genius of inventions and wrote compelling poetry and prose. I love the man. You will, too.

46. **My Life as an Explorer** by Sven Hedin (1925). This Swedish explorer of Central Asia set out with four men to cross 180 miles of enormous sand dunes. Temperatures drop. A camel dies. The ink freezes in his pen. It's desert adventure at its best.

47. **In Trouble Again** by Redmond O'Hanlon (1988). He is a naturalist who ventures into the northern Amazon Basin. He tells a funny story.

48. **The Man Who Walked Through Time** by Colin Fletcher (1968). The author backpacked through the Grand Canyon. Since I have backpacked and rafted it, I can tell you that he's a great writer and this is a wonderful book.

49. **The Savage Mountain** by Charles Houston and Robert Bates (1954). K2 tops Everest in climbing difficulty. People suffer, die and triumph.

50. **Gypsy Moth Circles the World** by Francis Chichester (1967). He sails around the world at the ripe old age of 64. Why? Find out.

51. **Man-Eater of Kumaon** by Jim Corbett (1944). Corbett was an Indian-born hunter who killed human-eating tigers.

52. **Alone** by Richard Byrd (1938). Spent an Antarctic winter alone in a small shed. That would drive any man insane. I think it did.

53. **Stranger in the Forest** by Eric Hansen (1988). The author walked across Borneo. Tribes, gators and jungle. Good times if you like to tempt death.

54. **Travels in Arabia Desert** by Charles M. Doughty (1888). He lived the life of Bedouin tribesmen in the desert.

55. **The Royal Road to Romance** by Richard Halliburton (1925). He bicycles, climbs, hikes, hunts and raises heck across the world.

56. **The Long Walk** by Slavomir Rawicz (1956). The author and six men escaped from a Siberian prison camp in 1941. They walked across Mongolia, Gobi, Tibet and the Himalayas. They endured astounding hardship.

57. **Mountaineering in the Sierra Nevada** by Clarence King (1872). King was a Yale man, a lady's man and a geologist. He climbed a lot of mountains.

58. **My Journey to Lhasa** by Alexandra David-Neel (1927). At the age of 55, French woman David-Neel crossed the Himalayas in midwinter and entered Tibet.

59. **Journal of the Discovery of the Source of the Nile** by John Hanning Speke (1863). Speke located and named Lake Victoria as the source of the Nile. My friend Pasquale Scatturo became the first man to raft the Blue Nile from Ethiopia. Read his book **Mysteries**

of the Nile. He also shot a movie for I-Max. Scatturo also took the first blind man to the summit of Everest. Eric Weihenmayer became the first blind man to climb all the highest peaks on seven continents.

60. **Running the Amazon** by Joe Kane (1989). He paddled from the high Andes all the way to the Atlantic. I raise a toast to his squabbling group of rowdy adventure seekers.

61. **Alive** by Piers Paul Read (1975). He and fellow rugby players crashed an airplane in the Chilean Andes in 1972. Horror, intrigue, death and survival in one big ugly and fascinating package.

62. **Principle Navigations** by Richard Hakluyt (1590). Hakluyt writes over a million words. His book is an encyclopedia of adventure.

63. **Incidents of Travel in Yucatan** by John Lloyd Stephens (1843). The author hacks his way through thick jungles. He suffered from malaria.

64. **Shipwreck of the Whale Ship Essex** by Owen Chase (1821). Herman Melville turned this tale into **Moby Dick**. A sperm whale sank the Essex by ramming it. The men escaped in rowboats.

65. **Life in the Far West** by George Frederick Ruxton (1849). He traveled the American West to write this account of the mountain men. Very good reading.

66. **My Life as an Explorer** by Roald Amundsen (1927). He sailed the Northwest Passage first and he was the first to reach the South Pole. He said, "A strange ambition burned within me to endure those same sufferings." I read the book cover to cover.

67. **New from Tartary** by Peter Fleming (1936). He set out from Beijing for India in 1930 via the forbidden Xinjiang region.

68. **Annapurna: A Woman's Place** by Arlene Blum (1980). This book, above all, inspired and inspires all women climbers. Powerful, compelling and all female.

69. **Mutiny on the Bounty** by William Bligh (1790). Rebellious sailors force Bligh and 18 loyal sailors onto four 23-foot longboats for a 4,000-mile survival trip.

70. **Adrift** by Steven Callahan (1986). Callahan's sailboat sank in the middle of the Atlantic. He spent 76 days drifting, fighting off sharks and starving before reaching land.

71. **Castaways** by Alvar Nunez Cabeza de Vaca (1555). Three hundred men land near Tampa, Florida in 1528. Only four survive to make it to Mexico. How they lived is anyone's guess.

72. **Touching the Void** by Joe Simpson (1989). He and a buddy descended a hard route through the Andes. They experienced terrible suffering.

73. **Tracks** by Robyn Davidson (1980). She traveled alone across 1,700 miles of Australian outback on a camel. One hardcore, tough lady.

74. **The Adventures of Captain Bonneville** by Washington Irving (1837). He wrote this memoir from a mountain man's notes.

75. **Cooper's Creek** by Alan Moorehead (1963). This Australian epic adventure takes you across the Outback. Since I cycled it, I know it's one miserably hot, forever desert with emus, camels, kangaroos and wombats. Two mates on the adventure starve to death. Life is tough in the Outback.

76. **The Fearful Void** by Geoffrey Moorhouse (1974). He traveled 2,000 miles across the Great Sahara Desert. Like loneliness? Follow him.

77. **Through the Brazilian Wilderness** by Theodore Roosevelt (1914). Teddy Roosevelt became a true adventurer on the River of Doubt. He takes you for a thrilling ride.

78. **The Road to Oxiana** by Robert Bryon (1937). He forges into Afghanistan. Great read for anyone that loves the Middle East.

79. **No Picnic on Mount Kenya** by Felice Benuzzi (1953). He escaped a prison camp to climb Mount Kenya.

80. **Minus 148 Degrees** by Art Davidson (1969). Three climbers ascend Denali, Alaska, the highest mountain in North America at 20,325. As they descend, Mother Nature feeds them a blowtorch of deadly blasts.

81. **Travels** by Ibn Battuta (1354). He spent most of his life traveling throughout Asia. He was sometimes wealthy and sometimes poor. He faced danger often.

82. **Jaguars Ripped my Flesh** by Tim Cahill (1987). He tells a great yarn.

83. **Journal of a Trapper** by Osborne Russell (1914). How would you like to fight a wounded grizzly bear? Like to starve to death? This book will take you back to the mountain man-days of the 1800s in America.

84. **We Die Alone** by David Howarth (1955). Norwegian commandos sailed into a Nazi trap on the northern coast of Norway in 1943.

85. **Kabloona** by Gontran de Poncins (1941). He crossed the Canadian North Country. He said, "If you see a man in a blizzard bending over a rock, you may be sure it is me and I am lost."

86. **Carry the Fire** by Michael Collins (1974). Collins piloted Apollo rockets to the moon. Want to explore space? Follow this man.

87. **The Mountains of My Life** by Walter Bonatti (1998). He writes about mountains, clouds and nature's bliss.

88. **Great Heart** by James West Davidson and John Rugge (1988). This book recounts the tale of a failed 1903 expedition to Labrador.

89. **Journal of the Voyage of the Pacific** by Alexander Mackenzie (1801). This Canadian traveled across North America ten years before Lewis and Clark.

90. **The Valley of the Assassins** by Freya Stark (1934). Stark crosses vast places in Persia as she dodges bandits and passes from "fear to the absence of fear."

91. **The Silent World** by Jacques Cousteau (1953). I read this book in 1962. It inspired me to dive all over the world in oceans, lakes, rivers and seas. Cousteau is my environmental hero.

92. **Ultimate High: My Everest Odyssey** by Goran Kropp. He bicycled from Sweden to Nepal with a load of 170 pounds of gear. Upon reaching Nepal, he climbed unassisted to the summit of Mount Everest. He pedaled his bicycle back to Sweden.

93. **Letters and Notes on the Manners, Customs and Conditions of the North American Indians** by George Catlin (1841). He spent six years among the Plains Indians. His paintings are world famous.

94. **I Married Adventure** by Osa Johnson (1940). She married wildlife photographer Martin Johnson. He took her to Africa and the Pacific Rim for a very exciting life.

95. **The Descent of Pierre Saint-Martin** by Norbert Casteret (1954). He takes readers into the world's deepest cave explorations. It's a thrilling story for spelunkers.

96. **The Crystal Horizon** by Reinhold Messner (1982). Messner climbed Everest alone and without oxygen. He was the first to climb all seven highest peaks on seven continents.

97. **Grizzly Years** by Doug Peacock (1990). He became the model for the eco-terrorist Hayduke in Edward Abbey's novel **The Monkey Wrench Gang.** Peacock writes about grizzlies as if his head is stuck in the mouth of one of them.

98. **One Man's Mountain** by Tom Patey (1971). As John Muir said, "Climb the mountains to get their good tidings. Your troubles will fall away like autumn leaves." This book does the same thing for your spirit.

99. **Spell of the Yukon** by Robert Service (1890). This man spun poetry like a spider spins webs. Brilliant, compelling, enthralling, funny and historical. You'll love his work. He defines the wilderness. Additionally, Jack London's **Call of the Wild.**

KEY POINTS FROM THIS CHAPTER

1. These books offer you emotional, intellectual and common sense growth toward your own adventures.

2. These books give you new ideas about yourself and your potential.

Chapter 47

Top female and Male Books to Inspire You

Choose to use your gifts and live the adventure of this lifetime. Step into the larger scheme of following your dream. Let's deluge the world with the ultimate dancers, people who feed their souls with work and feed their work with soul. ~ *Tama Kieves*

Let's say you read this book cover to cover. While you gained a great deal of knowledge, information and perhaps inspiration, you feel the need for more. It's possible that some other adventure writer, male or female, might resonate with you better. Whatever gets you to your dreams, go for it.

Many women think it is more challenging to take adventures than men. Let's not sell female adventure seekers short. You read about amazing women and their books listed in the preceding chapter. You may appreciate that prior to 1965, women took a back seat to men because of limited opportunities and a culture of being ladylike, i.e., you can't do what men do. Since 1970 and Title IX athletic programs in schools across the United States, women have gained tremendous impetus from being able to compete like never before in many athletic arenas formerly denied them by the dominant male culture.

Today women box, play soccer, football, hockey, basketball, row, ski race, mountain bike race, wrestle, climb Everest, sail around the world, row across the Atlantic and play every sport men play.

Since I am a man, I cannot know all the challenges women face. However, I have read several excellent books in which some of the finest women present new ideas, energy, enthusiasm and determination to females. These books below may unlock the door for you. They may inspire your own highly successful life as to adventure and daily living.

Books for Women:

This Time I Dance by Tama J. Kieves. This lady is funny, highly metaphorical and charged with wisdom. She gives women a whole new understanding of their power, creative potential and ability to realize their dreams. You will become fearless by reading her book. I loved it and I'm a dude. I met her and she is wonderful.

Travel Tips for the Sophisticated Woman by Laura Vestanen. This woman lays it down totally and with perfect command. You will be so hungry to travel after reading her book, you will take a car trip the next weekend or backpack or bicycle—just to try out her ideas.

Gutsy Women and **Best Girlfriend Getaways** by Marybeth Bond. She takes you to where you want to go. You'll love her style and energy.

Wanderlust and Lipstick by Beth Whitman. This lady shows women how to be successful and happy travelers. Be prepared, move toward your adventure and enjoy yourself.

Bicycle Bliss by Portia H. Masterson. If you like to ride and tour on a bicycle, this lady makes it fun and fabulous—in fact, bliss.

The Girlo Travel Survival Kit by Anthea Paul. She offers more ideas to make your travels successful. She's an inspiration just because she got out there and adventured on her own.

A Woman Alone: Travel Tales from Around the Globe by Faith Conlon. She describes her travels around the world. She loved it.

Adventures in Good Company: The Complete Guide to Women's Tours and Outdoor Trips by Thalia Zepatos. This book will get your feet wet in the company of tour guides. Later, you may strike out on your own.

Eat, Pray, Love by Elizabeth Gilbert. It's an international best seller. She traveled the world to work out her troubles. She suffered self-doubt and worked through it. She found love. She's funny. She may inspire you to explore, love, eat and pray.

Unstoppable by Cynthia Kersey. This lady features dozens of women from every walk of life that chased their dreams and caught them. I cannot say enough for this book. I refer to it often. Your spirit will soar with possibilities.

The Life You Were Born to Live by Dan Millman. While he's a guy, this book offers amazing paths toward what you really love to do in life. It cuts away the mistakes and allows you to find your optimum propensities, work and life path. I've known Dan for 20 years and he provides some of the most powerful and compelling ideas for 21st century living. You might also read **Sacred Journey of the Peaceful Warrior.**

Power of Intention by Wayne Dyer. Again, another man, but his book transforms both men and women to live within a new paradigm designed to bring personal success heretofore unheard of in earlier times.

Books for Men:

The Life You Were Born to Live by Dan Millman. This book will put you years of ahead of stumbling around trying to find your path and work in life. I highly recommend it for men and women.

Way of the Peaceful Warrior, Sacred Journey of the Peaceful Warrior, No Ordinary Moments, Warrior Athlete and **Four Purposes of Life** by Dan Millman. Those books will give you a leg up on successful living.

Power of Intention by Wayne Dyer. Dyer shows you how to accomplish your intentions.

Seven Habits of Highly Effective People and **First Things First** by Stephen Covey. When you engage the skills, habits and methods of successful people, your life will become highly effective, positive and thriving.

Touch the Top of the World: A Blind Man's Journey to Climb Farther Than the Eye can See by Erik Weihenmayer. I met this remarkable man who suffered blindness early in his life. He became the first blind man to climb Mount Everest.

The Adversity Advantage: Turning Everyday Struggles into Everyday Greatness by Erik Weihenmayer. If you are disabled in any way, Erik will show you the way to your own personal greatness.

Self-Reliance by Ralph Waldo Emerson. Uncommon spiritual wisdom and abundant understanding of life and all its promises.

Walden by Henry David Thoreau. One of the greats of American literature.

Travels in Alaska and **A Thousand Mile Walk to the Gulf** by John Muir.

Call of the Wild by Jack London. A man of adventure and imagination.

Some of my favorite authors for your consideration

Richard Bach wrote **Jonathan Living Seagull**. It's still a classic on the bookshelves 47 years later. In the book, a seagull named Jonathan tries to fly faster and farther than all the rest of the seagulls. They ridicule him. He suffers, but keeps flying. Day in and day out, he flies faster and faster. He crashes often, but he dusts himself off and lifts into the wild blue yonder. He learns about his weaknesses and he uses his strengths to improve.

Finally, he learns to fly really fast. He catches the attention of an elder seagull named Chiang.

"Well, Jonathan," said Chiang. "You fly pretty fast. You fly with great passion."

"What happens from here?" said Jonathan. "Where are we going? Is there no such place as heaven?"

"No, Jonathan, there is no such place as heaven," Chiang said. "Heaven is not a place, and it is not a time. Heaven is being perfect. You will begin to touch heaven, Jonathan, in the moment that you touch "perfect speed." And, that isn't flying a thousand miles an hour, or a million, or flying at the speed of light. Perfection doesn't have limits. Perfect speed, Jonathan, is being there." Richard Bach

Once I read Bach's book in my youth, it guided me toward that perfect speed that Chiang talked about. You can interpret it any way you like so long as it works for your ongoing quest to live a spectacular life and a life of adventure as you define it.

Author Dan Millman presents a peaceful warrior's way to turn your ideas into actions, your challenges into strengths and your life experiences into wisdom. You can live like a warrior, yet enjoy the wisdom of spiritual and mental bliss as you face daily challenges that greet you at every stage of your life.

I have seen many friends beat themselves up with such mental torture long after they left home. Those negative concepts stick in the craw of a person's mind. Millman's books will help you erase those scripts. Once erased, you may write new scripts of success, happiness, joy and drive. It's up to you and your choice.

One of the challenges many human beings struggle with arrives in the guise of negative self-concepts, insecurity and a feeling of lack. How did that happen? Usually, one or both parents instilled parent-scripts like: "You're not athletic; I wasn't good in science so you won't be either; you're awkward, just like I was…." Millman talks about it through his character named Socrates.

"But life energy must flow somewhere," said Socrates. "Where internal obstructions lie, the energy burns, and if it builds up beyond what an individual body-mind can tolerate, it explodes. Anger grows into rage, sorrow turns to despair, concern becomes obsession, and physical aches become agony. So energy can also be a curse. Like a river, it can bring life, but untamed it can unleash a raging flood of destruction."

Millman expresses what happens when so many carry their hang-ups and insecurities to the self-destructive side of life. The key is to clear the obstructions from your mind. It's better to understand them and take your energies toward a meaningful life. Choose a life of adventure or artistic expression or sports or family or whatever you choose for your time on this planet. Each day of your life offers unlimited potential and creative process. It depends on how you design it.

Choose your positive-self and avoid listening to your opposing-self. Like anything you want to accomplish, it takes practice. Delete this sentence from your mouth and mind, "I can't do this, I can't do that, I can't...."

Replace it with, "I can, I will, I am...."

KEY POINTS FROM THIS CHAPTER

1. Women from all walks of life have adventured around the world.
2. You can make your life as exciting as any of the authors in this chapter.

Chapter 48

Details

Some people go on an adventure to see something; I go on an adventure to do something. ~ *Steve Boyka, world traveler*

Let's cover a variety of travel items in order to give you some information in various areas. Use this list of options as your starting point for total preparation. If an item applies to you, write it down and make it a part of your own customized list for "things to do before I leave."

Let your adventure desires carry you toward your dreams like Bob Wieland. Instead of lamenting what you can't do, focus on what you can do. Even if you suffer disabilities, you may find ample help at: www.disabledtravelersguide.com, www.disabilitytravel.com, www.access-able.com, www.NSCD.org

I recommend visiting Winter Park, Colorado to enjoy disabled skiing where I have been a volunteer ski instructor for 20 years. Tell them you want Frosty to take you up in a bi-ski or mono-ski for a day on the slopes. During summers, Winter Park also features wheelchair camping, horseback riding, sailing, bicycling and more for the handicapped at the National Sports Center for the Disabled. www.NSCD.org

While traveling, be sure to carry health insurance for national and international travel. Contact www.aaa.com in America and www.caa.com in Canada. Learn more from those organizations for international travel.

Tourist Bureaus and Information Centers

Be sure to carry theft insurance for your car, camera, bicycle, kayak, canoe and gear if you travel in developing countries. You might suffer theft at the hands of any number of situations. Some individuals prove cagey and resourceful to separate you from your pack, bike, camera and passport.

When traveling to exotic countries, check out alerts issued by the United States government at the U.S. Department of State. Visit www.travel.state.gov

You may find out what countries to avoid. Here's another site: www.cia.gov/cia/publications/factbook.gov, which will give you the lowdown on everything you need to know, i.e., danger, water, food, terror, etc.

If you're a woman, you need information to be safe. Try www.forwomentravelingsolo.com and www.thorntree.lonelyplanet.com

Guidebooks are a must. Get the most out of your journey with guidebooks from Lonely Planet at www.lonelyplanet.com. This publisher covers every country on the planet in books by travelers that traveled through them. You can also try www.MoonHandbooks.net for a ton of information about countries all over the planet.

If you're up for blogs telling the real deal, go to www.technorati.com

You may travel at any time of the year anywhere in the world, but you may like to enjoy certain cultural festivals around the world. Check out: www.earthcalendar.net for tons of information.

Try www.Travelingwomen.com for women that need exact information from most regions in the world they wish to travel. Also, for gay men and women try www.GayTravelNews.com

Best guidebooks: **Eyewitness Travel Guidebook** series. It's excellent.

Love great eating? Try www.roadfood.com, www.chowhound.com, www.citysearch.com, www.zagat.com

European dining guides www.viamichelin.com and www.ginkgopress.com

Don't want to get lost? Obtain a map. www.mapquest.com/mobile and www.wideworldtravels.com

Booking travel flights? Book well in advance. Try three months early for cheaper rates. Book smart and use the Internet. Not sure? Go to a travel agent.

To work the deal yourself for the cheapest fares: www.Site59.com, www.expedia.com, www.orbitz.com, www.travelocity.com, www.southwest.com, www.frontierairlines.com, www.jetblue.com

Be sure to check on any website if they have a lock-icon at the bottom of your browser, usually on the right side, to make sure your information remains confidential.

Sometimes, you can obtain cheaper flights or cheaper bookings by waiting. You might try www.farecast.com and also, for a plethora of information on transportation companies, try www.bts.gov

Two websites that will look for the best deals on transports are: www.kayak.com and www.sidestep.com

Do you like globetrotting? You may enjoy e-tickets in most developed countries, but will have to go the old-fashioned way in developing countries. www.whichbudget.com

If you want to start early, you might procure a credit card that gives you free flights. I carry a credit card for free flights, after purchasing enough products to provide me flight points.

Good deals? Try www.priceline.com

My friend Brenda takes courier flights for free to carry time-sensitive materials to foreign countries. She's traveled all over the globe on such tickets with www.aircourier.org and www.courier.org

Always arrive at the airport two hours in advance in developing world countries and the same two hours in advance in developed countries. Better to be two hours early rather than one minute late. I could tell you a few horror stories, but suffice to say, avoid making them your own.

Before you leave

1. Suspend newspaper delivery.
2. Hold mail or divert to a trusted address.
3. Make sure any bills get paid by a trusted person or automatic bill pay at bank.
4. Change your greeting on your home phone and place out of office message on email.
5. Confirm flights and shuttles.
6. Pour gasoline stabilizer in your gas tanks and run through carburetor.
7. Make sure someone waters the yard and mows the lawn.
8. Place luggage tags outside and inside your gear.
9. Talk to neighbors to look after your home and lawn.
10. Pets off to a friend or the vacation kennel.

CAMPING AND HOSTELS

Today, hostels offer inexpensive accommodations—at least, relative to motels and hotels. Visit www.internationalhostels.com and www.hihostels.com to obtain a registration card, directory and the keys to the front door of hostels in just about every country around the world. You must carry a sheet or satin or silk sleep sack for your sleeping bag or they will make you buy a heavy linen sheet. Beat them to the punch.

The YMCA also gives good value for travelers at www.ymca.int

Bed and breakfasts also offer friendly accommodations, but can be pretty pricy for a lean wallet.

For camping travelers, the best and cheapest way to travel is stealth camping. If you're backpacking, riding a Euro-rail, motorcycling or bicycling—slip off into the woods, a cozy corner of a hay field, behind a building, in a shaded glen, beside the still waters of a lake or anywhere you like where no one can see you. Many times, you can ask a farmer for permission to camp and he will not only allow you to camp on his land; he will invite you in for dinner and breakfast. You never know until you ask.

For those who like security try www.koa.com, www.goodsams.com

For touring cyclists, you may enjoy a free night's sleep, showers and friendly conversations from folks that like to host you for an evening at www.warmshowers.com

HOME SWAPS AND EXCHANGES

If you're retired and own a home, you can exchange with people from all over the globe. It's a great way to enjoy a country or a continent.

Find out: www.homeexchange.com, www.intervacus.com, www.seniorshomeexchange.com and www.gti-home-exchange.com

You can host world travelers at your house for amazing experiences with travelers at www.globalfreeloaders.com

If you love to see farms or travel around the world to farms try www.wwoof.org

HUT TO HUT AND RAILS TO TRAILS

In Colorado and many other states, you may use their hut systems in the summer and winter. In Colorado: www.huts.org

For hiking and biking: www.railstotrails.org all over the country.

In Europe, you will find a ton of hut-to-hut systems at dolomitesport.com/2009/09/europes-mountain-hut-culture/

BICYCLES, MOTORCYCLES, RECUMBENTS

If you travel by bicycle, you can take your own by boxing it up, or you can buy or rent in different countries at www.bikefriday.com

Men and women who motorcycle may find unlimited opportunities to rent in many countries. www.globeriders.com, www.imtbike.com, www.motodiscovery.com

For motor homes in USA: www.cruiseamerica.com

For motor home rentals in Europe: www.autoeurope.com, http://www.worldwide-motorhome-hire.com/

Germany: www.motorhomerental.de

PREPARATION EQUALS NINE-TENTHS OF SUCCESS: START YOUR "TO DO" LIST

A passport and visa open most doors to most countries around the world. Make certain your passport carries an expiration date at least a year beyond your stepping into any country. If your passport is close to its expiration date, you may not be given entry into some countries.

Make sure your passport offers at least four blank pages for stamping.

You can obtain a passport at more than 7,000 post offices across the USA. Give yourself at least eight weeks before departure; better yet, obtain your new passport three months before departure. If something comes up, you still have plenty of time to correct it.

A passport remains valid for 10 years. You need two passport pictures, which can be taken at any drugstore and some U.S. post offices. You need a birth certificate, driver's license and any other forms of identification they might require. For more information try www.iafdb.travel.state.gov

In order to renew an expired passport, you may fill out a DS-82 and send it in with your old passport, recent pictures and money to cover the cost of the passport: www.travel.state.gov

If you're anxious for quick service, you can pay extra money to receive your expedited passport.

Canadian citizens may apply for a five-year passport at www.ppt.gc.ca

Follow the protocol in order to obtain your passport.

Caution: Your passport is your ticket to the world. Guard it at all times by keeping it in a waterproof pouch around your neck 24/7. You snooze and you lose. For emergencies, make five photocopies of your passport and keep two copies in different areas of your pack or belongings. Keep the others in a money belt, pouch, zippered pack, or elsewhere. If you should lose your passport or have it stolen, you may be able to show your photocopies to a U.S. Embassy for possible replacement, or at least you will possess a record of your identity with the passport photo and information.

Additionally, if a hotel requires your passport, give them a photocopy in order to guarantee that you have your original passport on you and not in someone else's hands.

VISAS

Some countries require a visa to enter their country for a specific number of days. You need to get that completed before you leave your country. Check **Lonely Planet** for such requirements. You can visit the website for countries you intend to visit. Call the consulates for information, but make sure you have your visas before you leave home. Otherwise, you will suffer some hard lessons on your dream trip.

Make sure you have all your ducks in a row before you leave town.

TRAVELING BY CAR OR MOTORHOME

If you intend to drive in a foreign country, you need to obtain an "International Driver's License" in order to be legal. Visit www.aaa.com or your local American Automobile Association office to fill out the forms for the license. If you need a motorcycle endorsement, make sure you get it stamped on the license. Be sure to carry at least 10 passport-sized pictures for emergencies. You will need one of them on the "International Driver's License."

In Canada, contact your Canadian Automobile Association for your "International Driver's License."

PHONE HOME AND CONTACTS

Make sure you carry plenty of contact numbers of loved ones or trusted friends back in your country so you have someone to call if you should suffer injury or illness or if any other emergency should arise.

Carry a little address booklet or even your notebook computer so you can write postcards to your friends.

PLANE TICKETS AND RESERVATIONS

Keep your passport, personal papers and money with you at all times. Keep reservation and confirmation numbers with you at all times.

Make photocopies of flight reservations, e-tickets, boarding passes, car-rental reservations, shuttle reservations, directions to your hostel or campground from the airport, directions to restaurants and directions to airports.

Today, with Internet cafés in just about every nook and cranny of the planet, you can scan all your important documents and email them to yourself so you can pick up anything you need by heading to the computer bank at the local café. Scan your passport, other ID, reservations, addresses, phone numbers and anything else you might need on the road.

TAKING CARE OF DENTAL WORK BEFORE YOU LEAVE

Before leaving home, make sure you undergo a thorough dental examination. If the dentist thinks anything seems "iffy," get it drilled and filled. You want to avoid a dental problem in a foreign or developing country. Let me repeat that statement with vigor: **YOU WANT TO AVOID AT ALL COSTS A DENTAL PROBLEM IN A FOREIGN COUNTRY.**

BILLS TO PAY BACK HOME WHILE YOU'RE GONE

If you're young with no property, no rent, no nothing—yahoo—take off and enjoy the ride. But, if you leave home with bills, loans or other responsibilities, take care of them or make sure your parents or someone you trust 100 percent will take care of them. If you cannot find someone, you can secure a bank that will pay your bills automatically at a specific date each month. Make sure you keep enough money in your account for your time away from home.

Make sure your car insurance or payments run on auto-pay or other means. You can suspend your car insurance for the duration of your trip.

Before leaving, let your two main credit card companies know that you will be traveling so they will be alerted that you will be charging from far-off places. Additionally, in most banks today, you can set up a debit account that will allow you to withdraw money in the local currency by using your credit card. You can use that credit-debit card for Euros or local currency with the best exchange rate. Otherwise, you will lose a lot of money with traveler's checks via cashing charges. (However, take enough traveler's checks for emergencies.) Always take $200.00 to $300.00 in $20.00 American bills with you for quick exchange.

SHOTS, MEDICAL RECORDS, PRESCRIPTIONS

Check with your medical care people about the shots you will need for whatever country you plan on visiting. Make sure you take all the proper malaria pills before you leave for the South American jungles or Africa—and keep taking them for the prescribed period. You want to avoid malaria at all costs. If you contract malaria, it's yours for life.

Additionally, get your rump ready for Gama globulin shots to make sure you miss the hepatitis express. Bend over. Say please. The nurse will fill your wish in both cheeks.

Take skin creams for rashes, poison ivy and infections. Ask your doctor.

Get your tetanus shots and whatever else you need to make sure you don't die or come back with some nasty stuff. When you do return home, get a urine, blood and fecal check to make sure you don't have parasites or other nasties in your body. If you do, you can get them treated immediately.

If you travel to South America, be certain to take a good tent so you won't be bitten by the "Kissing Bug" that injects the Chagas parasite into your body. If you sleep in cheap hotels or other places, be prudent to protect your body from that little bug. Once inside your body, it attacks your heart and other organs. That parasite affects 14 million people in South America and kills 50,000 annually. Once you get it, there is no cure. Be smart, be safe and protect yourself from its bite.

Face it, on the road, you will suffer sickness. Be prudent, smart and cautious.

Carry your shot record and passport in a sealed plastic bag for safety. Those small sealed plastic bags will keep your important items waterproof.

Medications? Take what you need and carry prescriptions if you will be in a foreign land. Carry extras if you're traveling in remote regions. Take duplicates of everything by photocopy.

Do you have a special condition? Make sure you carry that information in your records as you trek across the planet. Check with www.medicalert.com about an instant record check for yourself.

Check for immunizations and records at Travel Health Online: www.tripprep.com

PERSONAL STUFF YOU CAN DO YOURSELF

First Aid Kit:

1---Sunscreen-30-50 SPF

2---Antihistamine

3---Decongestant

4---Pain medication

5---Mosquito repellant

6---Acetaminophen

7---Ibuprofen

8---Laxative

9---Anti-diarrheal

10-Antifungal and antibacterial ointments

11-Hydrocortisone cream

13-Band-Aids, bandages

14-Tweezers—usually found in your Swiss Army knife

15-Moleskin for blisters—don't leave home without them

16-Cotton swabs for your ears or a wound

17-Alcohol wipe pads

18-iodegradable soap and/or hand-sanitizer

19-To keep mosquitoes off, you might bring a nylon mesh mosquito net that drapes down over your head from a hat. Buy one that fits you for keeping the little buggers from making you miserable. That goes for Australian bush flies, which are the next best thing to the devil himself. Also, those nasty little "no-see-ems" in the higher latitudes will make your life miserable. You may wear a nylon hooded jacket and pants in place of insect repellant. One note: always carry a pair of lightweight between-the-toes shower sandals to wear in foreign shower rooms so you avoid catching athlete's foot or any other kinds of creepy stuff that might grow on your body.

COMMON SENSE PRACTICES FOR KEEPING YOUR HEALTH WHILE TRAVELING

Keep your health by practicing good personal hygiene:

1. Wash your hands before you eat anything.
2. Stay away from cold foods from outdoor vendors, especially meats. Once you see how developing countries leave milk, cheese and meat out for the flies to feast upon—you may decide to become a temporary vegetarian while you travel.
3. When using bathrooms, wash your hands and then, use the toilet paper or a paper towel to open the door and throw the paper towel in the trash. Or use your foot or elbow to open the door. You want to avoid all the nasty stuff that others carry around on them or inside them.
4. When you're in questionable situations, like an elevator, push buttons with your elbow or even the end of your Swiss Army knife.
5. If—well, let's just say when—you suffer from "Montezuma's Revenge" or whatever they call a massive case of uncontrolled rectal evacuation in the particular country you're visiting—take Kaopectate or other anti-diarrhea medicine. At times, you'll be ejecting out of both ends and you will be miserable beyond anything you've ever experienced. But once your guts acclimate to a developing country's food, you will be fine.
6. Always use a water filter and carefully fill your water bottles to make sure you don't allow one unfiltered drop into your canteen. Just one drop can make you sick if the bad guys get into your system.

7. Take a small container of tea tree (melaleuca) oil to cover a cut or scab to keep out infection. You will be glad you did.

8. Maintain hydration by drinking water regularly. Always make certain you drink clean water. Again, take a water filter with you everywhere you travel to make certain you enjoy clean, safe water. Be prudent, be forever alert, be smart and stay healthy.

9. On long airplane flights, get up and move around. Keep your blood circulating so you avoid suffering cramps or other problems while on your journey. If you're older, you want to prevent deep-vein thrombosis, which is a blood clot that forms in your legs from long periods of inactivity. You can mitigate your risk by carrying compression socks that reduce the swelling. Check www.christinecolumbus.com for socks. In the end, good nutrition with a low-fat intake, water and exercise give you the best results during travel. Some folks suffer jet lag more than others. I take melatonin upon arriving at a destination that may be eight time zones away from my normal sleep routine. You may also try chamomile at www.nojetlag.com

KEY POINTS FROM THIS CHAPTER

1. Preparation is nine-tenths of success.
2. Use these resources to be prepared.
3. Learn by doing, making mistakes and correcting them.
4. Create your preparation list and follow it.

Chapter 49

Particulars

I see my path, but I don't know where it leads. Not knowing where I'm going is what inspires me to travel it. *~ Rosalia de Castro*

HEALTHFUL EATING ON ADVENTURE HIGHWAY

All countries and cultures offer amazing foods around the world. In developed countries, you may enjoy a plethora of culinary experiences. My mouth waters when I think about fabulous cuisine in Rome, Italy and Madrid, Spain and Bergen, Norway and Rio de Janeiro, Brazil and Seward, Alaska with sourdough pancakes. Your mouth will water and your mind will remember the great places where you dined amid the cultures and people who welcomed you.

At the same time, once you cross into countries without standards, health regulations and reasonable personal hygiene, you face disconcerting conditions. Be smart and alert.

1. Always take your Swiss Army knife to peel the skin off fruits to get to the fresh, clean inside of the fruit or any vegetable.
2. If you're not certain about silverware or glassware—use your own from your pack or your bags (don't leave without them). For extra precaution, you can take an alcohol wipe and clean your silverware and glassware yourself. If it really feels dangerous, pull out your own cook pot and utensils. Always eat hot food that has been

cooked well enough and long enough to kill any germs, insect larva or worms.

3. Since I've been sickened by what I saw in some countries as to their leaving food out for all the flies to land on, I became a vegetarian early in my life. You may consider becoming a short-term vegetarian in developing countries.

4. My friend Doug did not take this advice and he suffered worms crawling up from his stomach through his throat. He spit them out of his mouth. He visited a doctor to obtain a poison to kill the little buggers in his gut.

5. Accept that you most probably will get sick from eating, but once you've gotten sick, your gut may work with the new foods it finds itself digesting and you will be fine in your new environment.

FOR WOMEN ON ADVENTURE HIGHWAY

I have lifted my plane from the airport and have never felt her wheels glide from the earth into the air without knowing the uncertainty and exhilaration of firstborn adventure. *Ms. Beryl Markham, African bush pilot*

Please note that several of my long time lady friends gave their ideas for this section:

1. As a woman, you need to be prepared differently than men.

2. In developing countries, women take a backseat to men in any number of ways. Some male behavior will appall you. You must be alert and never travel alone at night, and in many cases, never travel alone.

3. If you travel in Islamic countries, you will need to cover your entire body and head. In many other countries, you may want to avoid tight jeans or short dresses. Avoid tempting your destiny with short skirts or provocative clothes.

4. Avoid responding to catcalls and whistles from local boys.

5. While on the road, through stress or food or other circumstances, you might miss your period more than once. It's not uncommon. If the situation continues, you might want to visit a doctor for advice.

6. You may need to carry extra tampons or sanitary napkins in many countries that do not sell such commodities. Be prepared for some rough sledding in developing countries when it comes to your menstruation. If you run out of sanitary napkins, you might check with your doctor back home so you can engage a protocol that works for you. For enterprising female travelers, you can check with Diva Cup at www.divacup.com for a soft silicone lip that collects menstrual flow.

7. Using the pill? Be smart as to any encounters on adventure highway. Make sure your friend wears prophylaxis and wash afterwards. Sexually transmitted diseases run wild all over the world. While the movies may be wonderfully romantic with an Italian or Brazilian lover, STDs are not.

8. In case you contract a yeast infection, prepare ahead by obtaining vaginal cream. You may have to see a doctor.

9. If you contract a bladder infection, try drinking cranberry juice, lots of water and see a doctor if needed.

Traveling while pregnant? Best time would be in the second trimester so you're not suffering from morning sickness and you're not susceptible to the discomfort of your third trimester or premature birth. See doctors about immunizations of all kinds and their effect on your fetus. Some countries demand different vaccinations, etc., so be aware that your growing child may not tolerate such things.

Further pregnancy information: if you're headed into a malaria-infested country and you're taking chemicals, or if you don't and you become infected with malaria—your unborn child can be severely affected. Choose the safe side for the life of your child.

If you get sick or suffer an injury in developing countries, seek out the best hospitals and doctors available. The International Association of Medical Assistance at www.Iamat.org will guide you to English-speaking competent doctors and sanitary conditions; along with safe food.

WHAT KINDS OF SICKNESSES TO EXPECT ON ADVENTURE HIGHWAY

First of all, be gentle with yourself. Take care of the little things and the big things will take care of themselves. You may consult a number of books for many ideas and you will find some of them added to the end of this book so you may gain greater details—especially if you're a woman.

1. Be smart and avoid getting cooked in the tropical sun in southern climes. Always carry a long-sleeve shirt or blouse, brimmed hat, sunglasses and long pants to make certain you protect your skin.
2. Riding a bicycle over the years, I have caught a lot of sun radiation. Today, I keep covered in sunglasses, tights, long sleeve jerseys and gloves. I wear a bandana

draped under my helmet and down over my ears and neck. I coat my face with 50 SPF sun block. It may look cool to sport a tan, but you will pay a severe price years down the road with skin cancer and premature aging of your skin.

3. Always wear broad-spectrum sunglasses to protect your eyes from radiation damage.

4. Expect diarrhea because you most likely will suffer from it. Take the appropriate medications and most likely you will live through it. Oh yeah, and you will be able to tell your friends some really uncivilized stories. You can tell them how you hurled your guts out, cramped and hit a 103-degree fever. You may give an account of nausea and doing your sleeping bag. They'll laugh depending on how animated you become while telling them about your bout with diarrhea as you hiked the Inca Trail. They'll still be jealous because you hiked the Inca Trail and have pictures to prove it.

5. Ever suffered from a case of amoebic dysentery? You will wish to heaven that you never ate the wrong food or drank bad water again. How do you avoid it? Always drink filtered water, cook your food, peel your fruits, and boil your water if you don't have a filter, wash your hands, keep clean with baths or showers, and avoid contact with persons in questionable areas.

6. One of the best ways to kill your adventure would be to contract giardia. It will take you down like a rock falling off a mountain. It's a parasite and it is nasty. Again, practice the highest personal hygiene that I have repeated numerous times in this book. If you do suffer from it; try drugs like Flagyl, Furoxone, Quinacrine, and/or Tinidazole. Most countries carry those drugs.

If no drugs are available, eat garlic morning, noon and night. None of it is fun.

7. In jungle areas, you may run into mosquitoes that carry malaria. I've got a buddy who caught malaria in Africa. He suffers from debilitating attacks that put him down for days. Check with your doctor for the latest prophylactics. You may avoid being bitten by wearing Gore-Tex clothing from head to toe, use a mosquito net over your head and gloves on your hands.

8. While I cycled through the Amazon jungle, I suffered horrible bites from numerous insects that made my legs bleed. I finally covered my legs with my nylon rain gear and wore a Gore-Tex jacket. I perspired more, but I didn't get bit anymore. Keep any bites clean with antibacterial cream.

9. Another nasty is hepatitis "A" which is caused by contaminated food; hepatitis "B" is transmitted by sexual activity; hepatitis "C" is transmitted through blood transfusion; hepatitis "E" is caused by bad food and water. Make sure to get vaccinations for "A" and "B."

10. Obtain booster shots for tetanus and diphtheria. They last for 10 years.

11. Why do you want to cover yourself in the tropics head to foot? Answer: Dengue Fever. It is mosquito-borne, so cover yourself. There is no treatment or prophylaxis.

12. More goodies: Yellow Fever—you will find it in Africa and South America. You may receive a vaccination to avoid this disease.

13. Finally, millions suffer from and have died from HIV, which turns into AIDS. Be certain to stay protected while engaging intimately. Better yet, avoid intimacy. But even then, it could be scary. It spreads through

bodily fluids. Can you catch it from kissing someone who suffers from HIV? Beats me, but I never attempted to find out in all my worldly travels. Stay away from needles, tattoo parlors and medical facilities that may not maintain standards.

MORNING CONSTITUTIONAL IN THE WOODS AND AROUND THE WORLD

Most Americans might be amazed that somewhere around 2.5 billion of the world's humans lack a toilet and have never used toilet paper, but do use their fingers to wipe their butts. Afterwards, maybe—and that's a big, maybe—they rinse their hands. But they may not. Okay, now don't get all freaked out by this new realization. Toilet paper arrived on the scene less than 150 years ago, so you must figure that humans have practiced wiping their bums with their fingers for eons. They may have used a big maple leaf or they jumped into a stream.

In many countries, whether you squat between two bricks to hit a hole or enter a stinking outhouse full of flies and spiders or squat in a latrine in the woods with a million mosquitoes using your bum for a refueling zone—it's up to you to provide yourself with a safe and sanitary bowel-movement experience.

Always carry your TP in a gallon zip-closure plastic bag. Add a second gallon plastic bag, whose use I will explain shortly. You can also carry a lighter or matches.

While camping, carry your TP out to a quiet and secluded area. Dig a six to eight inch hole with your boot or small plastic shovel or find soft sand or whatever you can do to make sure you bury your waste.

Do your business, wipe your butt and roll the soiled TP with your roll of new TP. You need not touch the soiled TP because you're rolling it off the new roll to handle the soiled TP. Place the soiled TP into the second zip-closure plastic bag. Carry it with you to a proper refuse barrel at your earliest convenience. You can carry it to the campfire. If it's safe and you won't be starting a forest or grass fire, you can burn the soiled TP after you have buried your waste. Bury the ashes.

If you don't have TP, take your water bottle with you. Do your business and pour water into your hand and wash your bum with your hand. Wash it until it's totally clean. Bury the waste.

Wash your hands with more water and soap. Use biodegradable soap or hand-sanitizer if you carry some.

Leave no trace of yourself in the wilderness.

If you use toilets in developing countries, you will notice a box beside the toilet with used TP. Throw your TP into the box. Avoid throwing it into the toilet because developing countries' sewage systems cannot tolerate toilet paper. That's when the TP police will swarm down on you with handcuffs and send you off to clean toilets for an automatic two-year sentence. Oh, the horror of it all.

WHAT TO TAKE AND HOW TO PACK IT

Depending on your particular adventure destination or mode, you will need a packing list of important gear for your journey. You will find ample packing lists for summer, fall, winter, and spring in the "Specific Adventures" sections of this book. Customize them to meet your needs. Always prepare months before you leave so you won't suffer a huge case of P-A-N-I-C! Preparation is nine-tenths of success.

Excellent companies for gear, clothes and bikes:

www.REI.com
www.EasternMountainSports.com
www.EddieBauer.com

www.EarlyWinters.com
www.LLBean.com
www.Cabelas.com
www.Travelsmith.com
www.Columbia.com
www.Coolibar.com
www.Golite.com

Just remember this: whatever you pack, you carry. Travel light, travel fast and travel lean. Travel with a smile.

If you load up on the latest fashions, you will curse yourself for every extra ounce in your backpack. "Why did I bring my electric toothbrush and my hairdryer?"

Ladies, wear black undergarments to avoid showing dirt. Also, these days, you can purchase underwear that can be washed in seconds, dries in minutes and lasts through 22 countries.

If you're hankering for an orderly backpack, be sure to use ditty-bags to separate and organize your clothes and other items. You can buy compressor bags that compact your clothes at www. eaglecreek.com

If you carry any liquids in your backpack or panniers, always use those quart or gallon freezer zip-closure bags to keep any liquids from spilling all over the pack.

FOR LADIES

You may like to keep your feminine mystique while traveling. However, when accessorizing, think lean, smart and sassy. You might carry eyeliner, lipstick, one pair of earrings, bracelet and things that make you feel special.

Carry simple jewelry that won't get ripped off your hand or neck. Headscarfs make for elegance or can be worn like a shawl. Bring your own your personal style with you.

I've decided I'm going through this life as my best friend, as my own North Star, best life-coach extraordinaire, and Glinda the Good Witch, complete with wand and tiara. And yes, that doesn't always mean I'll know where I'm going. But at least I know whom I'm traveling with. I'm going to go through this life calling myself "beloved" and rolling out the infinite advantages that kindness offers. The voice I'll listen to inside will be loving—or I won't listen. *Tama Kieves, This Time I Dance*

ALONG FOR THE RIDE: MEMORIES

Make certain you bring a journal, two to three pens and reading glasses, if needed. Write every day about all that happens to you—as if you are writing to your best friend—to allow them to feel, experience, see, taste and smell the adventure as it unfolds. Make it a daily habit before you jump into your sleeping bag or bunk or hostel bed.

Next, a lightweight digital camera allows you the ability to send photos through the Internet and fill in your own website. You can take a zillion shots with 4-GB cards. Bring plenty of memory cards and batteries. Waterproof them at all times. If you have a rechargeable camera, you need to bring the conversion plugs to use it in places like Europe where the electrical current is different than the USA.

Learn how to shoot up close and far away. Learn about framing a picture, bracketing, back lighting, fill-in flash and other techniques to bring your pictures to life for friends. Additionally, you might submit your photos to your local newspaper with a travel story.

Once home, you can create a wondrous travel album of your adventure. It will bring you fantastic smiles and joy down through the years as you look back, and then, spur you toward yet another adventure.

With digital cameras, you can upload online at www.kodakgallery.com and Snapfish at www.snapfish.com to send your favorite moments back home to friends and family.

One caution about photography in foreign lands: in some cultures, people expect you to pay money to photograph them. Others feel it is an invasion of their personal beings. Find out from officials what local people feel about being photographed and respect their wishes.

While traveling, you may bring a voice recorder to document your thoughts, hopes, dreams, ideas and even frustrations. You can refer to them later. These days, you can buy a three-ounce electronic voice recorder that will document all your descriptions as you go.

Another thing you can do while traveling on a bus across the Sahara Desert, Africa, or perhaps bicycling through the Atacama Desert of Chile or some stretch of lonesome road across Death Valley, you might enjoy using an MP3 player, which holds something like 10,000 songs. You can record books to listen to your favorite authors while traveling to make the greatest use of your time. Bring a Kindle eBook with all your downloaded books. Additionally, you can learn a language while traveling. Make use of great technologies to advance your brain or soothe your emotions. Recorded: www.audible.com iTunes: www.itunes.com

Language option at www.rosettastone.com

When packing any of your gear, make sure you either take out the batteries of these devices or flip them to take away their continuity or turn the switch to the lock position so they don't accidently suffer drainage.

Also, bring ear buds or headphones so you can listen to your books, music and or language lessons in the quiet of your own mind. Nothing worse than riding on a bus from Kathmandu,

Nepal to Pokhara with chickens pecking at your feet, babies crying and pigs squealing in the aisles of the bus. Not to mention sick babies hurling their breakfast into your lap. "Oh, the joys of world travel," you exclaim. Headphones at www.bose.com, www. radioshack.com

INTERNATIONAL AMBASSADORS FROM AMERICA

Once you step outside the United States, Canada or any country, you become a traveling ambassador. If you travel with a friend(s), you become ambassadors for your country—whether you like it or not. Your country will be graded, remembered and assessed by your actions. You represent America, Canada, United Kingdom, France, Australia, China, India, Brazil, Germany or whatever country you call home.

Everything you do will be noted by people, groups and organizations while you travel in their country. When you smile, shake their hands, offer aid or eat at a restaurant, you will be showing your best or (otherwise) to the world. Others will judge your country by your positive behavior or otherwise—for a lifetime.

That's why I make sure to learn a little of their language so I can speak in their language such phrases as: "Good morning", "Goodbye", "Thank you", "Please", "Good evening", "Where is the bathroom please?", "How much?", "Miss", "Ma'am", "What a beautiful day.", "You are so kind."

If you get drunk and act like a fool, become argumentative, act inappropriately around women, curse or any other negative behavior—they will remember you and America for a lifetime, one way or the other.

One of the very nicest things you can do is to give a small gift from your state to those that show kindness toward you. My friend Lance, an Australian, whom I met on the way to Alaska, 30 years ago, gave me a small pendant of a kangaroo. I still keep it and I still treasure Lance as a lifelong friend. That one gift brings back marvelous memories of a stranger from a foreign land. You might carry small patches from your state or decals of a grizzly bear if you're from Montana or a sailboat patch from Florida or US flag decals or anything that will give the stranger something good to remember his or her moment with you. You will be rewarded with bright eyes, happy thoughts and incredible memories—because those small gifts will come back to you a hundred-fold.

PACKING YOUR PACK

Load your least utilized gear at the bottom of the pack. Stuff your needed gear like lip balm, lipstick, toothbrush, toothpaste, dental floss, sunscreen, eye glasses, cell-phone, business cards and other often-used gear into the side pockets for easy retrieval.

Load breakable gear into the top; anything liquid should be encased in a zip-closure plastic bag and kept upright. Note: check liquids for a tightened cap before stuffing into your pack. Also, if you unzip a pouch, you zip it immediately. Unzip, zip it back. Make it a habit or pay the price of lost items.

TRAVEL PACKS, BACKPACKS, DAY PACKS, WILDERNESS PACKS

Today, whether you backpack, take a suitcase or lug some mountain climbing gear onto the plane, train or bus—you need to think light, durable, quality and use-specific.

Ladies may go to www.REI.com for female-specific travel packs, backpacks and roll-on luggage. Additionally: www.

EarlyWinters.com, www.EasternMountainSports.com, www.LLBean.com

Ask for a lady counselor and you will enjoy a wealth of information from ones who have gone before you. Additionally, you will find a list of outstanding female-oriented travel preparation books within this tome.

For guys, most top equipment stores carry specific packs for mountain climbing, walking across America, world travel, canoe travel, hut to hut, wilderness travel and more. You can add daypacks that fit your needs. Again, ask any of their representatives for specific information. They will give you first class information because all of them have hit the road themselves.

Special note: always take a specific color yarn or Velcro band to identify your pack or luggage on an airport carousel for easy pick-up from the horde of luggage that is usually all colored dark blue or black.

Not sure what you can and cannot carry onto a plane in these tense times? Check with the Transportation Security Administration, www.tsa.gov, to obtain up to the minute lists for what luggage and carry-on gear you can and cannot take onto an airplane. You can also buy a TSA-approved lock that secures your luggage against employee pilfering, but it can be opened by TSA agents. You can check with Travel Sentry at www.travelsentry.org to buy TSA locks for $20.00. These locks will cause the casual baggage thief to quickly jump to another pack because your zippers were locked up by those little TSA locks.

Be certain to attach an ID tag to your luggage or pack, both outside and inside. If you're staying at a hotel or hostel, you can write the name of the destination on another tag next to your nametag—so if your luggage comes in late, it can be sent to the correct destination. If you're traveling with a cell-phone, place the number on the luggage so they can call you. Are you writing this information on your to-do list? By now you know you must prepare for your trip at least three months in advance.

WHAT TO TAKE AND HOW TO PACK IT

What do you take on a weekend trip, short trip or long trip? What about your gear for backpacking, 14er climbing, canoe trip, day hike, raft trip and other adventures? We will work through exceptionally thorough pack lists in each section of the adventures that you choose.

From there, you can customize your pack lists for yourself. In your garage, keep a notebook filled with pack lists for specific adventures whether a weekend, week, month or year. Each list covers a particular sport. If you need something on a canoe trip that you forgot to pack, take note of that on the canoe trip and add it to your list.

GENERAL PACK LIST FOR MEN AND WOMEN

CLOTHES AND RAIN GEAR

1. Light bush pants with zip-off legs to create instant shorts.
2. Light slacks for women who want more of the feminine touch.
3. Shorts if you don't like the shorts created by the bush pants with zip-off legs.
4. Blouse, tank top, sweater, PJs.
5. Gore-Tex or rain jacket and pants.
6. Underwear, bra and possible other under-garments.
7. Wool socks, cotton socks, bike socks.
8. Bathing suit, swim goggles.

9. Shoes, running shoes, sandals, flip-flops. Bush belt made of nylon for lightness. Foldable cotton brimmed hat, light gloves if needed, bandana. Hiking boots.

Bathroom gear:

1----Soap
2----Deodorant
3----Cream or lotion of some kind
4----Sunscreen, hand lotion
5----Lip balm with 20 SPF or even 50 SPF, sunscreen
6----Brush and comb
7----Hair accessories
8----Medications
9----Feminine products, tampons, sanitary napkins
10---Makeup, lipstick, eyeliner, etc.
11---Birth control pills, condoms, etc.
12---Insect repellant
13---Moist-wipes, tissues
14---Half roll of TP
15---Razor, shaver
16---Toothbrush, toothpaste
17---Bar of soap
18---Dental floss
19---Tea tree oil
20---Anti-fungal ointment
21---Micro fiber towel that dries easily, recommended
22---Washcloth
23---Hand sanitizer
24---Bio degradable liquid soap to clean dishes
25---Nail clippers (must be loaded into hull of the plane)

LEGAL PAPERS, DOCUMENTS, LICENSES

1. Scuba card
2. International driver's license
3. Passport with waterproof container
4. Shot records
5. Credit cards or ATM cards
6. International phone numbers to call if you lose a credit card
7. Leave credit card company phone numbers with trusted friends
8. Twelve extra passport pictures
9. Proof of ownership of your bike or other gear

CAMERAS, ELECTRICAL EQUIPMENT AND OTHER ITEMS

1. Electrical converter devices
2. Silk or satin sleep sack for hostels
3. Watch or some timepiece
4. Cell phone, MP3, iPod
5. Maps and other direction finders like Global Positioning Device
6. Business cards
7. Book or Kindle for reading on flights
8. Language phrase book
9. Camera with chargers or spare batteries and memory cards
10. Notebook and two or three pens
11. Ear plugs (Avoid leaving home without them.)
12. Eye blinders or sunshades so you can sleep with lights on in plane
13. Binoculars (Optional)

14. Small inflatable pillow (Avoid telling the TSA inspector that it's a blow-up pillow.)
15. Small, light, electric travel alarm clock
16. Small miner's lamp flashlight with options like blinking light, red and in LED
17. Candle lantern (optional)
18. Sunglasses, reading glasses, securing cord
19. Camera tripod
20. Foreign currency
21. Plane tickets
22. Health insurance card
23. Leave a legal will in your files so that if something should happen to you, it's all cleared up in your legal papers. Let loved ones know how to find it.
24. Cable lock (Optional)
25. Photo copies of passport and shot card and health card (Recommended)
26. Legal will in your files at home
27. Swiss Army knife (must be loaded into hull of plane)

NECESSARY HEALTH GEAR DEPENDING ON DESTINATION

1. Water filter, tablets
2. Three to five spare plastic bags (5 gallon)
3. Three to five one gallon zip-closure bags
4. Melatonin sleeping tablets
5. Pair of thin rubber gloves from drug store for emergency
6. Stainless steel water container

KEY POINTS FROM THIS CHAPTER

1. Customize these pack lists and to-do lists for your own needs.
2. When you forget something, write it down and place it on your list for the next time.
3. Ask friends for their preparation list and ideas for safe travels.

Chapter 50

Tidbits

Rush boldly and ruthlessly toward your dreams! As you rush toward them, they race toward you. ~ *Unknown author*

MAPS, LAPTOPS, GADGETS AND GOODIES FOR COMMUNICATIONS

Today, you can find an Internet café almost everywhere in the world. You can find them in Antarctica. The penguins use them to talk with their friends on Facebook.

If you carry around a lightweight laptop computer, it will enable you to communicate with anyone back home, send pictures and much more. Use those devices for your diary and remember to send your entries back to your friends so you don't lose them if the computer is lost or stolen.

Just about every place now offers Wi-Fi so you can hook up in remote areas. You can find Wi-Fi places at www.wififreespot. com and www.jiwire.com to list hook ups at airports, RV parks, malls, restaurants and hostels. Make sure your laptop carries a Wi-Fi receiver or card adaptor. Make sure to install the best virus scanners and blockers such as AVG at www.avg.com. Be sure to charge your computer before leaving and make sure you have the correct hook-up converters for all sorts of electrical outlets. You can also bring a multi-prong power plug so you can share an outlet with other travelers at an airport or bus terminal.

During checks at TSA, be sure to keep an eye on how agents treat your camera, laptop or other delicate equipment. Be methodical as you work through the security system to make sure you avoid breaking anything.

MAPS, TOURS AND THINGS

One of the coolest inventions for travel must be the Global Positioning System device. It works like magic. No matter where you are in the world, those little units, that you can hold in your hand, can tell you exactly where you are within a few meters and take you to where you want to be. They work off computers in circling satellites to engage your computer in your handheld unit.

Find out what they can do and learn all about them before buying one. They even offer language translator systems at www. garmin.com

If you want to save money, you may engage audio tours that tell you everything and talk you through a tour: www. ijourneys.com

A tour will provide highlights of your favorite places: Rome, Paris, Madrid, Rio, Beijing, Munich, Bergen, Bangkok and more. Another site for the USA, Europe and more at www. soundwalk.com

You can obtain audio travel podcasts from www. lonelyplanet.com; try www.ricksteves.com for "Europe Through the Back Door."

Today you may quickly access RSS (Really Simple Syndication) feeds for such things as travel alerts, special airfares or other worthwhile information while you travel. You can access RSS feeds through aggregator software available at Internet Explorer, Yahoo, AOL, Mozilla Fox and others. Alerts about the information that you request will be loaded to your home page. Use them and benefit. Save money on travel discounts: www. sidestep.com. Not sure how to operate this subscriber benefit? Ask a friend or a computer store. They will set you up.

Since we live in the computer age, take advantage of eBook guides instead of the published books that add weight to your pack. You can download eBooks to your laptop and/or PDA. Free eBooks can be accessed at www.gutenberg.org and www.ebooks.com

You will enjoy the low prices and versatility. Make sure to download the proper software application in order to view the books.

Want to fire up your imagination about world travel? Give yourself incentives by checking out videos that visually take you to faraway places with great audio complements. Check with www.totalvid.com and www.netflix.com

Be sure to install a media player in your computer to play all those videos.

TRAVEL AND HEALTH INSURANCE

You may find it advisable to buy medical and property insurance for your travels. Otherwise, you could be stuck for untold amounts of money from hospital stays or illness. If you become a victim of theft, you'll be amazed at what it costs to buy a new backpack and gear, or a bicycle with gear.

Check www.travel.state.gov for international and national insurance health providers. Also, www.travelguard.com will cover gobs of stuff you need to have covered. Buy your coverage a month in advance. Again, I hope you're writing a to-do list from this chapter.

In case you get hurt or deathly ill in a remote place, make sure you obtain evacuation insurance for a helicopter ride out. It could cost tens of thousands of dollars. Check out: www.wellnessconcierge.com

MONEY: SAVING IT, SPENDING IT, OUT-SMARTING IT

"I should have been born rich instead of so good looking," said a friend of mine.

"You and the rest of the whole human race," I added.

As stated in previous chapters, money makes the world go around. You need it to feed your travel passion. Whether you work two jobs for a year at 80 hours per week or three jobs at 100 hours a week with no time off or you join the Peace Corps—you need money.

The more frugally you live, the faster you save money. Let me give you an idea of the tenacity of my 18-year-old brother. He worked an entire winter at a pizza joint. He made pizzas, he delivered pizzas and he cleaned the shop. He lived in his car with two sleeping bags covering him in 20-below zero Michigan winters. He took showers at MSU's athletic center. He didn't date, he didn't spend a penny and he didn't waste a dime. His goal: to motorcycle all over Europe. After 10 months of incredible labor, his bank account showed a healthy balance. He and our other brother Rex bought plane tickets to Europe plus two motorcycles. They spent five months touring the entire continent, all its history, all of its amazing architecture and famous places from Norway to Greece.

He discovered that he loved languages. From that first trip, he has traveled to Europe 20 times plus four other continents. He attended language schools in France, Spain, Germany and Alexandria, Egypt and now speaks those languages fluently.

He later graduated from MSU. He then drove a furniture truck 70 to 90 hours a week to save enough money to travel the world extensively. Every year, he sends out Christmas cards from places he's visited. I love the one of him riding a camel with the Great Pyramids behind him. How do you top that? A few years ago, he rode a horse across America East to West and West to East—the only man in history to accomplish that feat. Heaven only knows what his next adventure will be, but you can bet it will be magnificent. Our mother livens up every conversation with her friends as she tells them where her boys traveled during the year.

Make sure that however much money you possess, you calculate a budget for your travels. Determine what your daily costs will be in food, shelter and transportation. Will you motorcycle, bicycle or rent a motor home? Will you take a bus or train? Will you hitchhike? Will you camp out, stay in hostels or live lavishly? How will you know how to budget your money? You may find more than a dozen books in Chapter 47 that will help you.

You will go farther and longer by preparing your own food, camping out and riding public transport. Bicycling can take you to the ends of the world for the cost of your leg power and food to nourish your body. You might try vegetarian eating, which tends to be very inexpensive.

Are you careful with money? You may write an expense account to show you where your money flows. Can you write anything off if you become a travel writer? Yes! Keep receipts of all transactions in a plastic bag in your pack or panniers. Track your purchases in the back of your journal for instant access.

You may purchase the currency of the country you're visiting by visiting your bank. You can also use www.americanexpress.com for more than 50 different currencies.

Take at least two credit or debit cards in order to hit an ATM or any bank to withdraw local currency that will be charged to your cards. Carry some traveler's checks for emergencies: American Express—don't leave home without them. Always keep the numbers of your traveler's checks with you and copies at home. You will need those numbers for replacement if the checks are stolen. Make sure someone at home can answer the phone if you have to call to retrieve those check numbers and any other pertinent information. Again, scan them onto your computer for easy access when all else fails.

Unfortunately, you will get hit with a pretty steep price for exchanging traveler's checks, but that's the way of the world. Shop around for your best deal on exchanging money at the casa de cambio or bureau de change.

Black market exchange rates await every traveler. Avoid the temptation. You can be conned out of money, property and worse. When that shadowy guy asks you if you want to change money, just hurry on your way.

When you leave a country, after paying departure fees, baggage, etc., change your money back to U.S. dollars so you don't waste it once you're out of the country. In Nepal, they let you dump your spare money into a big glass box to save the children of that country. Unfortunately, it actually enriches the man in charge of the lock on the glass box and his superiors.

Bring a couple of hundred dollars in U.S. cash with you. Take clean, crisp, fresh cash with you in $1s and $20s. Keep it in a money belt and always keep it on you. Sleep with it, shower with it, swim with it and walk with it 24/7. That includes your passport.

You can find out the currency exchange rates at www. xe.com and www.megellans.com

HAGGLING OVER THE PRICE IN FOREIGN COUNTRIES

Don't want to pay the full price for a souvenir? Bargain, haggle, quibble, wrangle and barter with the shopkeeper. They expect it. It's their culture. If you fail to haggle, you failed the merchant, yourself and all creation. Avoid spending that dime until you've haggled them down to a price that meets your expectations.

If you want something, go for it. At the same time, please realize that the person you bargain with supports a family. Have fun bargaining, but also understand that just by being able to travel, you're richer than 90 percent of the rest of the world.

If you eat out, or take a cab, or ride a pedal-taxi, or hire a guide—you gotta' tip baby. Find out how much from the Lonely Planet travel books, as it varies all over the world from five percent to 20 percent.

SAVING A BUCK HERE AND THERE

Trying to save a buck? Do it! Those bucks add up:

1. Camp instead of renting a motel or hostel room.
2. Check into a motel where breakfast is included.
3. Share a ride in a taxi with a fellow traveler or two or three.
4. If you never ask, you will never know. Haggle for a better price on goods and services.
5. Always check your receipts for charges so you're not overbilled.
6. Choose the train or bus over the taxi.
7. Don't buy the cheapest; don't buy the most expensive; buy in the middle for good value.
8. Carry your own bags.
9. Seek store items on sale. Check ahead on the Internet for deals. Try www.Craigslist.com and eBay for used, quality gear. Consignment shopping from mountaineering shops can net you great bargains. Many sports shops feature previously owned gear. Buy at a farmer's market for fresh bread, tomatoes, cheese and fruits. Eat on the side of nature's road instead of a restaurant.

Here are more ideas for saving money. In the United Kingdom, you can sleep cheaply in dorms in London at www. westminster.ac.uk/business, www.ucl.ac.uk/residences, www. lsevacations.co.uk

In Germany, "The Tent" is where you pitch your tent inside a big tent at www.the-tent.com

In Switzerland, the Swiss Alpine Club runs more than 150 hiker huts at www.sac-cas.ch

Visit people around the world with Servas, www.usservas. org, a worldwide organization that connects travelers with host families. Some travelers swear this is the best way to see the world.

CouchSurfing is a vagabond's alternative to Servas. More than two million members in 146 countries host fellow "surfers" for free. Check them out at www.couchsurfing.com

For touring bicyclists, check out www.warmshowers.com

KEY POINTS FROM THIS CHAPTER

1. If you can't find the answers in this section, check out other books from the library.
2. Be smart, be aware, be prudent and enjoy yourself.

Chapter 51

Safety

Somebody ought to tell us, right at the start of our lives, that we are dying. Then we might live life to the limit every minute of every day. Do it, I say, whatever you want to do, do it now.
~ Michael Landon, "Little Joe" on Bonanza

PERSONAL SAFETY FOR MEN AND WOMEN

"You're going to get killed by drug gangs," friends warned me before I headed to South America for a yearlong journey from the top to the bottom and back up to Rio de Janeiro.

Most people suffer from a fear induced by headlines from dangerous spots around the world. Okay, I admit it. I avoid war zones, drug cartel zones, mass starvation zones, HIV disease zones and other dangerous areas. You may visit plenty of other places on the planet to explore in a safer mode.

How do you know where to find safe areas? You may find travel warnings at www.travel.state.gov to find out which countries to delete from your bucket list for the time being.

Basically, most of the countries of the world enjoy reasonable safety. But, just like large cities in the United States in some areas, you can suffer unfortunate situations.

Be prudent, be smart, stick with a group, go with a friend and stay inside at night if you're not sure. Darkness provides criminals in any country with the stealth needed to commit crimes.

Women must be smarter, more cautious and cunning as to where they walk, stop and what persons they meet. One single lady traveler friend I know wears a wedding band wherever she travels and keeps a picture of her husband in her wallet. That ring deters many men. If nothing else, it may stop the catcalls, whistles and aggressive behavior of men.

Women need to be aware of their clothing in Asia and other fundamentalist countries such as the Middle East. Showing skin can get a gal in trouble. Be smart rather than fashionable.

To be wise women need to walk with confidence and self-assurance. They must carry an attitude that lets predatory men know that they will meet an abrupt and stern rejection of unwanted advances. For more information, you will be directed to books that give more ideas for traveling women.

When in drug-infested countries and cities, beware not to accept unsolicited rides in cabs or private cars or invitations to parties. You could be set up for a drug bust. Professional criminals can and will plant drugs in your pack. The police will stop you and arrest you, and the only way you can get out of it is to bribe the cops.

Ladies, if you use crowded public transportation, you could be groped. Yell at the groper and stand your ground. Make a scene. They most likely will back off.

If you travel alone, you must maintain close contact with your pack and/or bicycle or other gear—at all times. Lock your gear to you with a small cable lock if needed. Criminals think of many ways to separate you from your pack.

Always keep everything inside your shirt or well protected—such as records, camera, notebook or personal items. The first time you set something down, you will forget and walk off. Within seconds, it will be gone.

You will meet new friends during your travels. At the same time, you must always maintain your 24/7 caution as to your safety and personal property.

CAUTIONARY TALE

While in Quito, Ecuador, I talked to a man shouldering a backpack who walked up the street alone. He said a local person stopped him to ask for directions. While he talked to the man, he felt heavy black oil being poured onto his head from behind. It totally discombobulated him and stunned him. As he turned around with oil dripping down over his face and down his neck, the first guy used a razor blade to cut his camera strap away and took off running. At that point, the other guy ran. Since the 40 pound backpack proved too much to run with, he stood there with oil dripping all over, lost his camera and learned a harsh lesson: never walk alone at night in a strange city, never show your valuable possessions to others, and never walk into large crowds where thieves can grab your gear and go. Stay alert, smart and prepared at all times for a successful experience.

While you remain alert and smart, so much more good arrives on your personal traveling doorstep than you can imagine. Always smile at everyone. Once, in a market in Porta Varas, Chile, we bought a lot of food for our bicycle journey down the Cara Terra Astral. We smiled at a couple also shopping for food items. They talked to us. After we enjoyed much laughter, they invited us to their beautiful home on their private lake. The husband, a successful businessman and his wife an artist, introduced their two college kids. Both their children showed great manners and spoke English. They lived in a one-story sprawling wood-framed home with a glorious deck that overlooked a lake. On the beach, they offered to share their ski boat, windsurfers and jet skis. Let me tell you, we enjoyed fabulous breakfasts, lunches and dinners for three days.

When we saddled up to leave three days later, they treated us like family. They cried when we pedaled out the driveway. We cried. We waved, they waved and our memories remain warm and joyful all these years later. Smile and radiate positive energy to all you meet. Much magic will flow your way.

CONTACT WITH FRIENDS WHILE ON THE ROAD

For the early years of my adventure life, I wrote postcards. Today, anyone can maintain constant communication through Internet cafés around the world.

Be aware that trying to please all your family and friends can become a huge drain on your time. However, if you like to write and you want your friends to enjoy the journey with you, by all means, create a travel blog by accessing www.travelblog.org. Try Blogger www.blogger.com and, for women traveling alone, visit www.forwomentravelingsolo.com

Set up your blog before you leave and learn how to post updates. You will receive lots of responses from your friends as you travel around the planet.

Cell phones provide instant contact with family and friends 24/7. My friend Gary called me regularly from New Zealand on his bicycle tour. His voice and the reception felt like next door. It's a fun deal to hear your friends and their delights on their adventures. To make sure your phone works in a particular country, check out Global System for Mobile Communications at www.gsmworld. com. Make certain your phone uses the technology. Also, access www.mobal.com for a prepaid mobile phone.

Another option: phone cards. Beware that phone booths around the world may become an extinct remnant of the 20th century. Technology kills them daily by the thousands. Whatever will Superman do to change clothes?

With a cell phone, you can text message to your heart's desire.

IF YOU NEED SOMETHING MAILED WHILE ON AN ADVENTURE

While in South America, I broke a granny gear crossing the Andes Mountains. I called my brother to mail me a new one in Santiago, Chile. Be sure to underline your last name.

He addressed it:

F.H. <u>Wooldridge</u>
Post Restante
Santiago, Chile

You will need to show your passport to retrieve your mail. Also, if they cannot find your package or mail, ask them to look in the section with your first name instead of your last name. That usually does the trick.

HOW ABOUT TALKING THEIR LANGUAGE?

The first time my brother Howard biked through Europe at age 18, he noticed that everybody spoke at least three and often, four languages. When traveling, you will make points and find folks really appreciative of your attempting to speak their language.

Before you leave home, buy a phrase book of the languages you may encounter. You can also buy Rosetta Stone CDs to learn a language while still at home. <u>www.rosettastone.com</u> and <u>www.pimsleur.com</u>

You can take language classes at a local college for a year before departing, and/or join a foreign language club in town where folks get together to speak a specific language.

No matter what, when you arrive in a foreign land, smile, laugh, use a warm handshake and realize that they want to know about you as much as you want to know about them. The more you try to speak in their language, the more they will warm to you. We all belong to one big human family.

While you will be hearing different languages, you will also be experiencing different cultures. If you've lived a sheltered life, you may be in for a culture shock when you see some things you have never seen before.

Locals may stare at you for hours. If you eat in town, they will stare at you. You will see blind kids begging for money. You will see disfigured kids with bent arms and bent legs. Their parents did it to them while they were babies to make them look more pathetic. Their disfigurement makes more money from begging. You will see things that turn your stomach, but it's their culture. You're visiting to learn and grow, but not condemn or make any judgments. Try to be sensitive to their behaviors and dress. If not, you may be breaking one of their taboos without knowing it. Please refer to these websites that give information on 75 countries and how to act: www.gacpc.com, www.cia.gov/cia/publications

The most important behaviors you can bring with you on your travels: patience, empathy, quiet acceptance and understanding. After that, more patience will keep you balanced.

KEY POINTS FROM THIS CHAPTER

1. Show your warm spirit; people from all walks of life will respond positively to you.
2. Remember to bring patience, empathy, acceptance and understanding on your travels.

SECTION IX

PREPARATION IS NINE-TENTHS OF SUCCESS

This section offers you everything you need to know to enjoy successful experiences in the wilderness. It covers camping techniques, bear and mountain lion safety, water purification, personal hygiene, cooking, cleaning, human waste disposal and wilderness survival.

By following the rules of the wilderness, you may enjoy years of adventures with great health and safety.

Chapter 52

Weekend, Weeklong and Yearlong Adventures

There are many ways through the Ring of Life. All are constant spiritual movement toward self-fulfillment through growth of the mind and expansion of the senses. They are ceaseless and persistent throughout one's life. ~ *FHW*

How do you begin your life of adventure? Do you purchase tickets to South America, buy a canoe and paddle down the Amazon River 4,000 miles to the Atlantic? How about buying a bicycle and riding around the perimeter of Australia? How about backpacking the Appalachian Trail? Why not sign on to climb Mount Everest? How about renting a floatplane to go fly-fishing in a remote Alaskan lake? How about dropping a canoe into the headwaters of the Mississippi River for a 2,552-mile trip to New Orleans? How about rafting the Grand Canyon with its formidable rapids for a lark?

Bold, to say the least! However, how about starting out easy? You can start with tame adventures, get your feet wet, make the usual mistakes, suffer some blisters on your feet, feel like you will die of thirst and freeze your butt off on a hut to hut skiing trip in January. You can swallow some salt water on a rough scuba diving trip in the Caribbean as part of the learning curve.

It's the beginning adventures that toughen you, teach you and inculcate you into Mother Nature's inner workings. Those first weekend camping trips, hopefully with a seasoned friend, give you the tools to move toward longer trips. That first climb up a small mountain may lead to a 14er or bigger. A day raft trip on Class I,

II or III rapids may whet your appetite for even bigger and more dangerous thrills on Class IV and V rivers. You may be inspired or frightened to death. You may find out that you don't like to scare the heck out of yourself. You may discover that you're cut out for poker or solitaire. You may find that you love danger and the thrill of it all. You're invited to follow your bliss.

Each of us discovers our thrill ratio during those first encounters with the wilderness. I should have been killed by a grizzly in my early twenties because I wasn't prepared. I'm lucky to have survived one of my raft trips because of my inexperience.

That's why I advise little steps that move toward bigger steps. Such fine organizations like www.MeetUp.com all over the USA will put you in touch with people who love to teach or mentor their particular passions. Go with them. You might love fly-fishing. You may love climbing mountains. On the other hand, you may dislike or even fear climbing. A camping trip with mosquitoes may shower you with an endless love of the wilderness or you may prefer a motel. The soft, quiet joy of canoe camping may fit you like a hand in a glove. For that matter, archery may be your niche. Maybe you love to paint landscapes in the wildest of places or take photographs like Ansel Adams. Get out there and find out.

KEY POINTS FROM THIS CHAPTER

1. Start out slow, start out smart and start out with friends.
2. Prepare well, be prudent and learn on each adventure.
3. Utilize www.MeetUp.com to find friends that will guide you.

Chapter 53

Camping techniques, bear and mountain lion safety, safe water, personal hygiene, cooking, cleaning, human waste, leave no trace, wilderness survival

To many Americans, the wilderness is little more than a retreat from the tensions of civilization. To others, it is a testing place—a vanishing frontier where humans can rediscover basic values. And to a few, the wilderness is nothing less than an almost holy source of self-renewal. But for every man, woman and child, the ultimate lesson that nature teaches is simply this: man's fate is inextricably linked to that of the world at large, and to all of the other creatures that live upon it. ~ *Unknown author*

Every time you step into the wilderness, it provides uncommon splendor and beauty. What can you do to preserve it? Answer: "Leave no trace."

By following the established protocol in this chapter—whether you ride a bicycle, backpack, climb mountains, fish, raft, canoe, hike, sail or any other wilderness activity—you will learn to take only photographs and leave only footprints.

My dad said, "Son, when you go camping, always leave the place nicer than you found it."

To this day, I have picked up a half-million pieces of trash in my life, if not more. I volunteer to pick up rivers, roadways, campgrounds, mountain paths and any place I see trash. It's frustrating that many careless people toss their cans, bottles and glass containers without a blink. I also advocate for a 10-cent bottle deposit law like Michigan's to stop the incredible littering of the landscape.

All of us enjoy a stake in our world's well-being and our own as we live this great life adventure. I hope you become one of the people that care deeply. This chapter will show you how to preserve the wilderness.

WILDERNESS CAMPING—EVERYTHING YOU NEED TO KNOW

In the United States, you can always find a campground, motel, hostel or bed and breakfast. You may find ample accommodations in every state and most of Canada. Nonetheless, you always want to be prepared by carrying a tent, sleeping bag and air mattress. Please note that I have met touring bicyclists that carry credit cards for food and motels. If that's your style, enjoy yourself.

Shelter and food take on a whole new significance during an adventure, especially in other countries. If you venture into developing countries, being unprepared may cause you great discomfort.

In developing countries, especially outside major cities, lodging may be difficult to find. That's why you must carry your own tent, sleeping bag and air mattress. For cooking meals, you need a stove, cookware, fuel, water and food supplies. When you're prepared with the basics, adventuring internationally will offer miles of smiles. Nothing beats a good night's sleep on a full stomach.

The most important gear you can carry is a quality tent. It must be big enough, light enough and waterproof. Quick "pitch time" is a nice extra. With so many tents on the market, how do you choose? You may have a friend who knows tents because he or she camps often. Since your friend learned by experience, have him or her go with you to the local camping outfitter to discuss the relative differences of tents. Buy good gear. If you go cheap, you will pay an uncomfortable price if the tent fails and you become soaked in the middle of the night.

If you're on your own, a few tips may help in your purchase. For camping, your tent should be self-standing and six pounds or less. For backpacking, you may find a 4.6-pound half-dome the most durable and dependable. It should have a waterproof floor and sidewalls. Rip-stop nylon is your best bet for durability, or if you can afford it, buy a Gore-Tex fabric tent. Make sure the tent features a loop or loft to hang clothes and candle lanterns from the ceiling. Make certain the tent is taut enough so it won't flap in the wind. Purchase shock-corded poles for easier set-up.

Make certain the rain fly covers the outside edges of the tent. Is your tent long enough? Can you sit up in it? Will you have room for two people and your gear? Is it warm enough for three seasons? A light color will be cooler in the summer and stand up under ultraviolet damaging rays better. Zippers should be YKK plastic. Make certain your tent features "no-see-em" netting. Check for good ventilation flow in the tent you buy. Most manufacturers stand solidly behind their tents with excellent guarantees. Compare for a top choice. Purchase seam sealer and apply to the rain fly and corners of the tent. Seal wherever the fabric has been sewn.

Once on the road, a few good habits will keep your tent in top condition for years of use. Purchase a nylon-backed plastic tarp for a ground cloth. Cut it to fit two inches inside the outside boundary of your tent floor. This will help stop sharp objects from cutting your floor and it will keep out moisture. Cutting it two inches less all around the tent floor will stop rainwater from pooling under your tent in the middle of the night.

Set up your tent every night as if you expect rain. Find a high spot in the land and check for sharp rocks and sticks before positioning the ground cloth. Never leave your tent out in the sun for extended periods of time. Ultraviolet rays will damage the fabric. When taking down a tent, fold the poles and put them in a safe place immediately after you pull them out of their sleeves. This will prevent them from being stepped on. Count stakes each time you put your tent into the stuff sack. If it rains, either dry out the tent in the morning or at the earliest moment. For storage, make certain your tent is bone dry before putting it away for the winter or any extended period of time.

After your tent, purchase a warm, comfortable sleeping bag. You have two choices: goose down or fiberfill. Having used both many times, it's this camper's opinion that for three seasons, a three-pound, 10-degree Fahrenheit, fiberfill mummy bag is your best bet. It dries easier and stands up to usage many years longer. Down shifts and leaves cold spots after a time and the loft breaks down. However, you may have a friend who swears by down for its compactness and lighter weight. I take a down-filled bag on my winter hut-to-hut skiing trips. It becomes a personal decision.

No matter what your choice, buy a quality mummy bag from a reputable company. Make certain it's long enough and features a contoured hood enclosure with a drawstring so you have a small opening for your nose and mouth. When it gets really cold, that's all you want showing so you can breathe. Make certain your bag is designed so the baffle flap drapes down over the zipper from the inside. Gravity will keep that baffle covering the entire length of the zipper and stop any cold air from entering your bag. Expect to pay more for a down bag. Keep it in a waterproof bag or stuff sack when riding, canoeing or backpacking. If you forget, you will be sliding your bare body into a cold, wet bag one night and wonder why you didn't pay attention to these suggestions.

No matter how good your tent and sleeping bag, discomfort stalks the adventurer who fails to sleep on an air mattress. The best self-inflating air mattress on the market is a three-quarter length, one-inch thick Thermo-Rest mattress by Cascade Designs. It insulates against the cold ground. (You may inspect several other brands that might be to your liking.) Buy a stuff sack to go with it. It's the best investment for comfort in the world.

You need cookware while camping. A copper-bottomed stainless steel set with two pots, and plastic cups is light and handy. Additionally, you may like the newer and lighter aluminum and titanium cookware. Some feature no-stick surfaces for easier cleaning. Keep a scrubber and soap in the pot. A plastic fork and spoon are light. If you're traveling in a developed country, go with a propane gas stove and carry two fuel bottles. For overseas touring, carry an MSR International stove that burns any kind of fuel.

Your Swiss Army knife is a vital addition to your cooking utensils. Carry a carrot-potato peeler. Add a small plastic cutting board. Always wash cookware after dinner, especially in the wilds. You want to avoid a grizzly sniffing your toes in the middle of the night.

Depending on how loaded you are and the length of your adventure, a sleeping bag, tent and mattress will sit on your back rack or in your backpack or canoe or kayak. You may have a front bike rack with a platform perfect for a sleeping bag. Be sure to carry a waterproof stuff sack for your sleeping bag. If you travel by water, you need a dry bag. It wouldn't hurt to do the same for your tent and mattress. If you can't find waterproof sacks, you may create your own with plastic bags.

The one thing you cannot count on during an adventure is a campground. Well before you begin looking, about an hour and a half before dark, have water bottles filled and an extra full gallon. If the water quality is questionable, purify with tablets, drops or filtration. Purchase your food in advance. Such things as toilet paper, matches and stove fuel should be secured.

If you find a campground with showers and you're willing to pay the price, enjoy. Try to set up away from dogs and loud music. To be assured of a shower every night, carry a "shower bag" that allows you a three minute shower anywhere you stop.

Often, you are nowhere near an organized campground, or in the case of developing countries, no such thing exists. You're on your own. That's a plus, because it offers you a chance to experience nature, animals and solitude.

The best way to find a campsite is to look for a dirt road that leads into the bush, trees, rocks and out of sight of the highway. Try to find a spot near a river, lake or stream. When you find a suitable spot away from traffic, pitch your tent.

Pitch it every time as if it were going to rain. Exceptions are the Atacama and Sahara deserts. I have broken my own rules a few times and it cost me dearly with ruined camera and miserable nights floating around in my tent on my air mattress. Pitch your tent on high ground. Check for rocks, twigs and roots before laying down the ground tarp. Set the front door away from the wind and possible rain. This will give you a windbreak for cooking. Make certain all stakes are secured and the rain fly is taut. Be sure to keep the ground cloth under the tent. Once the tent is secured, take the gear off your bike or out of your backpack and put it into your tent. Cable lock your bike, canoe or kayak to a tree. A combination lock will allow everyone in your party to use the same lock without using or losing a key.

CAMPING AND COOKING IN ESTABLISHED CAMPGROUNDS

When camping in an established campground, many obstacles are overcome immediately. You enjoy a picnic table, water, washing facilities and seating area at your command. Nonetheless, you need to buy food and load up on water two to three hours before sunset in case you don't reach an established campground. Always check your map for locations.

Making Camp

After finding a spot in a campground, one to two hours before dark, you can:

- Pitch your tent on high ground.
- Roll out the air mattress and sleeping bag.
- Place all your gear into the tent. Always put your gear in the same places, so you know where to find specific items in the dark. Always place your miner's lamp exactly in the same place so you can grab it when you need it.
- Make sure your miner's lamp is on your head and ready to work as darkness falls. Those LED headlamps can be purchased at camping outlets. You may look like a coal miner walking around in the dark, but you will find it very useful.
- Remember to avoid placing food or wrappers in your tent, especially in bear country. Most established campgrounds in bear country offer a steel bear box in which to place your food items. It they don't offer bear boxes: hang food 100 yards from your tent. This applies for all critters that would love to eat your food. That means you may have to cook and eat food first then hang food in trees 100 yards from the final camping site. Don't believe me? Think you can get away with it? I did, too. But when you wake up during the night with a grizzly or black bear pummeling you inside your tent or looking at you when you open the flaps—I gave fair warning. In bear country, always carry bear spray

with you from www.REI.com and other camping stores. It could save your life. I guarantee that you will be scared out of your wits, but you might live.

- If you are not in bear country, you can leave food in your tent as long as you remain in the tent. If you leave or you have food odors in your tent, little critters will eat their way through the nylon and ruin your tent.

- Lock your bike, canoe or kayak to a tree. If you can't find a tree, lock it to your helmet inside your tent. To do this, run the cable through the bike frame, canoe or kayak, then into your tent and lock it to your helmet strap or pack. When you zip up the tent, the cable acts like an umbilical cord between it and your property. If someone tries to make off with your bike or canoe, they won't get far before you notice half your tent being pulled away. At that point, you may need your bear spray to defend yourself.

- Take out your candle lantern and light it on the table.

- Always light the match before turning on your gas burner. Never turn the gas on first, unless you want to make like a Saturn rocket and blast yourself to the moon.

- Set up your food and fixings, cutting board, utensils, pans, water bottles and spices.

- Prepare your meal. Enjoy.

- Wash, clean, dry all your pots and utensils. Replace and secure.

- Secure food in a tree or bear box, or if you're looking for an exciting night of terror, leave it in your tent. You will be able to tell some hair-raising stories when you get home.

Cooking and Food Storage in Established Campgrounds

Before cooking your meal, make good use of the stove burner for heating water for tea or hot chocolate. If you're cooking by a campfire, let the wood burn down so you get an even heat from the coals. You will also have to tackle the problem of balancing pots on the coals.

Once you have prepared the food for cooking by chopping and cutting, place it into the cooking pot. For cooking ease in the US, Canada, Australia and Europe, you may consider rice, pasta, couscous and other packaged meals. As your dinner progresses, keep any eye on the food to keep it from burning.

After dinner, wash everything with soap and rinse with water. Leave no food out for the animals. Keep extra food in a locked food box. You will find a wooden or metal box used in some campgrounds where animals are a concern. If there are no food boxes and you're in bear or mountain lion country, avoid storing food in your tent. Hang your food in a tree 100 yards from your camp. Serious backpackers can purchase heavy-duty plastic bear-proof canisters to store your food.

Leave none of your gear out in the rain. Either store it in the tent or under the tent vestibule.

Camping and Cooking in a Primitive Area

Camping in primitive (wilderness) areas presents several challenges that must be considered. You must be more responsible to your environment, i.e., disposal of human waste, water contamination and generated food and paper waste. You are more susceptible to bears, raccoons, squirrels and wild pigs charging into your camp looking for food. If it's a big old grizzly, he might be looking for you because he perused the latest copy of the "Gourmet Bear in Search of a Bicyclist, Backpacker or Other Dinner Interests." Take precautions when camping in the wilds.

Again, make certain you have loaded up on extra water two to three hours before dusk. Always carry a filter that can purify water if there are ample places to fetch it—such as in the mountains or in lake regions.

Again, look for a campsite well off the road and hidden away from the sight of others. Not only is it a good idea to vanish into the wilderness for personal safety, you will sleep better without hearing traffic all night. Remember your earplugs and use them.

Most dirt roads or trails on public land will lead to a stealth-camping spot. Try to get behind trees, brush, hills or a mountain. You want to be concealed from sight, which includes your fire or candlelight.

Be certain to keep your tent 25-30 feet away from a fire. Keep the tent upwind of the fire. Sparks carry on the breeze and will melt nylon in seconds. Place your tent on high ground. If it rains, you won't wake up feeling like you're being swept over Niagara Falls.

After setting up your tent, place your air mattress inside and unscrew the valve so it inflates fully before you lock it. A key to camping success is having everything where you want it when you need it. That means replacing the same gear in the same pouch every time you use it. Always zip up a pouch immediately after taking out or putting something into it. Make it a habit.

Before cooking dinner, you might want to take a bath first. Do it before the sun goes down and the air cools. Soap, towel and shower shoes are all you need. If it's a swiftly moving stream, be careful with your bottle of biodegradable soap.

A special note on campfires: gather your wood before dark. Gather kindling and larger branches. Stick with dead wood. Be sure the fire pit is a safe distance (25-30 feet) from your tent. Make certain the flames won't catch adjoining grass or overhanging branches on fire. A circular rock firewall is a good safety factor. Place leaves and kindling at the bottom. Light the fire, get it going and keep adding larger and larger wood until you have a good flame. If you cook on an open fire, after cooking, keep your pot in a heavy plastic bag to keep the black soot from smudging your gear. If your campsite is in a dry zone where fire hazards are high, use common sense when building a fire. You may decide not to build one. If you're experiencing high winds, never build a fire. Always put the fire totally out with water or dirt at night and in the morning. Clean the pit and spread the rocks around. Replace twigs and leaves over the pit before you leave.

When you're ready for sleep, use your pack, panniers or ditty-bag for a pillow and/or a sweater to make a cushion. Be certain to check for mosquitoes by shining your flashlight around the tent. If you see one, squash the blood-sucking fiend. Now you're ready for sleep. Or are you? If you camp in deep wilderness where bears or other large meat-eating animals live, put your food in a plastic bag and hang it in a tree 100 yards from your tent. Be certain to brush your teeth and wash your face and hands so no food odor is left on your person. If you even consider fruit in your tent and it's touching the floor, ants will cut the nylon in a few hours. Don't give them the chance. Any time you leave camp for a hike, do not leave food in the tent. Leave it open so chipmunks can get in. If they can't, they will chew holes through your tent.

In the morning, you may need to take your daily constitutional. Just remember the rules of camping. Bury feces if possible. If not, cover it with twigs or rocks. As for toilet paper, wrap it up and carry it out to throw away or burn at an appropriate time. When burning it, use prudent judgment in high fire areas of dry grass. It's that simple. Leave the campsite cleaner than you found it. Burn or carry out the trash and put in a proper disposal. No matter how trashed a place is, you can become part of the solution. Pack it in—pack it out.

When breaking camp, pack your gear and shake out the tent. Pull your tent poles and fold immediately. Avoid laying them on the ground where they can get smashed. Pull your stakes and count them before dropping into the bag. Fold the tent along with ground cloth and place in the stuff sack. If you can't fit the ground cloth into the stuff sack, you may wrap it around the tent and secure with straps. You might try changing your folding pattern periodically so you don't cause premature deterioration on waterproofing and fabric. Strap your gear on the bike or pack or canoe. Walk the bike, canoe or kayak out of the area. Go back to look over everything to see that you have all your gear, including the food bag that you hung in a tree. Don't be surprised if you walk up on a bear scratching his head trying to figure out how to get to your food bag.

When you're satisfied that you have everything secured, it's time to pedal, paddle, hike or climb. If the campsite was beautiful, you may have taken a few photographs for memories of your latest home in the woods.

When you follow a solid routine for camping each night, you wake up refreshed and relaxed. Camping compliments great wilderness adventures.

Making Camp in Primitive Areas

- Secure food and 1.5 gallons of water two or three hours before dusk.
- Look for an abandoned road or trail and vanish into the landscape.
- Pitch your tent on high ground. The site should be safe from lightning and potential washout from a rainstorm.
- Roll out your air mattress and sleeping bag.
- Place all your gear in the exact same place every night.

- Place your miner's lamp near your headrest. Once your tent and gear are secured inside, either lock your bike, canoe or kayak to a tree or run the cable into your tent and attach to your helmet or shoes. Zip up your tent.
- If you build a campfire, make sure it is 25-30 feet away from your tent. If that is not possible, use your stove for cooking. Camp away from rocky ledges or where rocks may fall upon you in the night.
- Spread your tablecloth on the ground outside your tent. Tablecloth can be a square yard of plastic.
- Secure your candle lantern where you can use it.
- Organize all your cooking gear and food in front of you.
- If you are using a stove, make sure it's stable. You want to avoid a scalding injury while away from medical help.
- If you drink coffee, hot chocolate or tea, boil your water first.
- Prepare your food. Eat like a ravenous T-Rex.
- Wash dishes and clean up all traces of food.
- Always leave the bottom zipper of your tent open if you leave camp to take a bath or for any other reason. Whether you have food in the tent or not, curious squirrels or chipmunks may bite their way through the nylon to see what's inside.

Building Campfires Safely in the Wilderness

If you enjoy ashes in your soup and burning embers in your potatoes, make yourself happy—cook on an open fire. It's primordial. Humans enjoyed campfires before they invented the wheel.

You need to remember a few points about making a fire to keep it safe and under control:

- Always check for and obey no-burn rules. Use common sense when camping in a dry area. Avoid building a fire in high wind conditions.
- Build a protective rock ring around the fire. You can wet the ground around the fire ring if you have ample water.
- Keep the fire away from tents and other fabrics. Watch out for your Lycra or Gore-Tex. One flying ember will burn a hole in it.
- Keep your eyes on the fire at all times.
- Build the fire away from overhanging tree branches or dry brush. If you build under some low-hanging branches, you might turn the tree into a bonfire. Explain that to the local fire department chief. Finally, avoid building a fire against a large rock or cliff because it will leave unsightly smoke scars.
- Keep a water supply handy in case you need to douse the flames.
- Let the fire burn down before you place your pots in the embers. You want an even heat on your food.
- If it's windy, eat pork and beans out of a can or a sandwich or energy bars. Avoid the chance of a runaway fire.
- Before hitting the sack, be certain to put the fire completely out by smothering it with water or dirt. If you fail to put it out completely, you could cost people their lives and homes. Repeat with emphasis: put that fire out completely.
- When finished with the campfire, spread the rocks out and return the fire area to its natural appearance. Spread the ashes and place leaves and brush over the fire pit. Really give nature a chance by keeping the wild beautiful. Leave no trace.

No Fire in Your Tent

On those rainy or windy days, your first inclination might be to cook in your tent. Ignore that thought. Okay, you're starving to death and you hunger for hot soup. Again, avoid cooking in your tent.

There are so many little things that can and will go wrong when you burn an open flame inside your tent. I'm as careful as a person can be, but once, I nearly turned my tent into a bonfire. Avoid learning this lesson the hard way.

Candle Lantern

The only flame that can be used in a tent, and I haven't done it in a long time because of miner's lamps with LEDs, is a glass and aluminum-encased candle lantern. Even then, never leave it in the tent unattended. Make sure it's hanging from the roof on a string. You can also set it on a flat surface such as a notepad or book. Please use utmost care if you burn a candle lantern in your tent.

Sanitation and Human Waste in the Wilderness

It's very important to follow a few rules when camping in primitive wilderness situations.

When washing dishes, heat the water and use biodegradable soap. If you're washing in a lake or stream, make sure you discard the soapy water onto the soil at least 15 feet away from the lake or stream water so it drains into the soil. Rinse your cooking gear thoroughly.

Pack out what you pack in. I pick up trash left by careless campers. I honor Mother Nature by leaving a place cleaner than I found it. In the immortal words of the great philosopher Goethe, "Do not think that you can do so little, that you do nothing at all." Avoid burning plastic in the wilderness. Carry it in a bag to a proper trashcan in the next town or wherever it's responsible.

Since no toilets are available in primitive campsites, please follow strict wilderness rules:

- Find a spot 25 to 30 yards away from your campsite and away from a water source. Carry your TP in a one-gallon zip-closure plastic bag and another one-gallon zip-closure bag inside it.
- Dig a hole four to six inches deep. Do your business. Cover your waste with soil. If that is not possible, cover with a rock or leaves. Roll your soiled TP into a ball with new TP and place it into the second zip-closure bag. No, you don't have to touch the soiled TP. Again, leave no trace.
- You may burn your used toilet paper in the campfire. If dry conditions exist or combustibles are present, just carry the used TP in the zip-closure bag and toss used TP at the next proper disposal.
- In Chile, my friend Doug nearly burned an entire wheat field because the flame he used to burn his toilet paper ignited the dry stalks. The next thing I knew, Doug waddled toward me with his shorts around his knees, screaming, "I just crapped in the wrong place." We grabbed six water bottles and ran back to the fire. We squirted it with our tiny water guns. A passing motorist and an old lady stopped to help us. You can imagine her shock and confusion when she saw Doug with his shorts at his ankles and me screaming and squirting at the flames. She didn't know whether to help us or faint. Moral of this episode: be careful where you strike a match to your toilet paper—and pull up your pants before you light it.

- Also, clean your hands with hand sanitizer or soap and water, or at least rinse your hands.

Cleaning and Hygiene

While on tour or any adventure, you're living at a basic level. You're closer to being an animal than you have ever been. Bugs will try to invade your tent and mosquitoes will buzz around your head. Spiders will spin webs across your tent at night and they will be eating their catch when you step out the next day. You may find slugs crawling up your tent in the morning. You'll go to sleep under moonlight and wake up with the sun. The morning alarm clock might be the laughing cry of an Australian kookaburra or a Norwegian cuckoo bird. It's natural, but it's dirty out there cycling or backpacking or mountain climbing or any extended outdoor activity.

That's why you must maintain good sanitation and hygiene practices.

Wash your hands with biodegradable soap in the wilderness. If you don't have any, use any biodegradable soap or hand cleaner, but make sure you use it. Avoid throwing soapy water into a stream or lake.

After any use of pots and pans, make certain to wash and rinse them. Use your camp towel to wipe them or let them dry in the sun. Please honor Mother Nature and she will bless you with wonders around the next bend in the road or turn of the river.

Bear and Lion Country

"Bears are made of the same dust as we, and breathe the same winds and drink of the same waters. A bear's days are warmed by the same sun, his dwellings are over-domed by the same blue sky, and his life turns and ebbs with the heart pulsing like ours. He was poured from the same fountain. And whether he at last goes to our stingy heaven or not, he has terrestrial immortality. His life, not long, not short, knows no beginning, no ending. To him life unstinted, unplanned, is above accidents of time, and his years, markless and boundless, equal eternity." John Muir, hiking in Yosemite Valley, California, 1859

Camping in Grizzly, Black Bear and Mountain Lion Country

The North American grizzly bear symbolizes the wilderness. His domain reaches from Yellowstone National Park in Wyoming to Alaska. To catch a glimpse of this great animal is to fill your eyes with wonder. His wildness defines the wilderness. In his domain, he is king.

Nothing will scare the daylights out of you faster than coming face to face with a bear. Few animals will kill you faster than a grizzly if he or she is so inclined. If she comes in the night, you will feel terror like never before because you have the added uncertainty of darkness. The sound of her grunting will drive your heart into a pumping frenzy and your blood will race around your body like a Formula One racecar at the Indy 500.

I shivered in my sleeping bag while a grizzly dragged his muzzle across the side of my tent one morning in Alaska. His saliva left a mark on the nylon for a few weeks while he left a mark on my mind for a lifetime. I'll never forget the three-and-a-half-inch claws that tore through the back of my tent that day. He let me live so I lucked out.

Bears prove capricious, unpredictable and dangerous. They search for food 24/7. Anything that looks edible to them makes for fair game. They eat berries, salmon, moose, deer, mice and humans without discrimination.

That's why this section deals with camping in grizzly bear, black bear and mountain lion country.

If you travel, hike and camp in remote regions of North America or other areas of the world, sooner or later, you will camp in bear country. It's not something to be feared, but it is something you must respect since you enter his dining room.

The key to your safety and survival in Mr. Grizzly's domain is respect. You must honor the rules of the wilderness. You must follow those rules each and every time you camp, hike or otherwise make your way into his territory. You may not get a second chance.

Imagine looking into a grizzly's eyes, backed by his 800 to 1,500 pounds of teeth and claws. You might plead, "Gee, Mr. Bear, could you give me a break this time…I'm really sorry I left my chocolate chip cookies inside my tent…can we make a deal, like, I'll give you my extra box of bon-bons…please, pretty please…."

Never assume a bear won't walk into your life.

At the same time, you cannot camp in fear. During my many journeys to Alaska, I enjoyed extraordinary moments watching rogue grizzlies fishing for salmon and mother grizzlies playing with their cubs. I enjoyed great wonder and breathtaking moments.

I also had the living daylights scared out of me because of my own carelessness.

By using common sense and following the rules, you can minimize the chances of a bear confrontation. But your safety cannot be guaranteed. You could do everything right and still run into a bear—especially if he's trying to find food for his evening dinner.

However, since I've alarmed you, let me put this in proper perspective. Former Alaska Governor Sarah Palin lives in Alaska. She alleges to have outrun a few grizzly bears. Therefore, if you're camping near Sarah, the only thing you have to do is run faster than her.

If you follow nature's rules, your chances of a bear confrontation are less than a lightning strike. Therefore, go ahead and enjoy yourself. If you do encounter a bear, you will return home with great bear stories that will keep your friends glued to your every word.

Remember: food and food odors attract bears, which makes them overcome their fear of humans. Be smart and keep food odor off your body and tent, and away from your camping site.

Bringing the bear danger home

On July 6, 2011, a couple hiked a popular trail in Yellowstone National Park. They came upon a grizzly mother and her cubs. The mother bear immediately attacked and killed the man and nearly killed the woman before grabbing her cubs and vanishing into the wilderness. Neither hiker carried bear spray nor did they know any defensive techniques for dealing with a bear.

"If a grizzly bear actually makes contact, surrender," advises the US Forest Service. "Fall to the ground and play dead. Lie flat on your stomach or curl up in a ball with your hands behind your neck. Typically, a bear will break off its attack once it feels the threat has been eliminated. Remain motionless for as long as possible. If you move, and the bear sees or hears you, it may return and renew its attack. In rare instances, particularly with black bears, an attacking bear may perceive a person as food. If the bear continues biting you long after you assume a defensive posture, it likely is a predatory attack. Fight back vigorously. Carry bear spray in the wilderness at all times."

Always carry bear spray with you in the wilderness. Have it ready at a moment's notice. Most backpackers carry it in a pouch secured to their chest. They can pull it out faster than a gun slinger.

Remember that you cannot out run a bear. You must stand your ground. Read the directions on how to pull the pin and how to spray the bear. If you're not certain, set up a large cardboard box about 30 feet away from you in your own backyard. Practice by pulling the pin and engaging the lever to the spray can. Make sure you know the nozzle is facing the bear. You must aim at the bear's face. You can watch the stream of spray while you guide it to the bear's face. Most bear spray will continue the stream for over 20 seconds. You may waste a bottle of spray, but you will become a seasoned veteran in case a live bear attacks you.

If you're not sure of yourself, go to REI or any outdoor store that carries bear spray and engage one of the seasoned employees. They will help you or guide you to an instructional video.

Rules for Camping in Bear Country

Camp in an area least likely to be visited by bears. Stay away from animal trails, large droppings, diggings, berry bushes, beehives and watering holes. Don't swim in streams where salmon run. If you do, you may end up running for your own life.

Make absolutely certain your tent has no food odor in or on it. If you have spilled jam or peanut butter—grizzlies especially like crunchy style—wash your tent clean.

Cook 100 yards away from your tent. Wash your gear thoroughly. Avoid sleeping in the same clothes that you wore while eating and cooking dinner.

Avoid keeping perfume, deodorant or toothpaste in your tent. Keep anything that has an odor in your food bag and hang it away from your camp.

Hang your food in a strong 1.5-millimeter thick plastic bag at least 100 yards feet from your tent. That means your camp, cooking and food hanging areas are in a triangle 100 yards apart. If a bear does amble into your sector, he will go after your food bag, and more than likely, he won't bother you. Hang it on a line between two trees and 15 feet high with parachute cord.

Bear-proof canisters that can carry several days of food supplies cost about $100 and can be purchased at most camping outlets mentioned in this book. Carry the canister in your pack.

After you have hung your food, take out a wet cloth and wipe your face and hands to ensure you have no food odor on them.

Finally, brush and floss your teeth. You wouldn't want a tiny piece of food between your molars to be the reason you inadvertently invited Mr. Grizzly to feast upon your tender body at night. Can you imagine the coroner's report in Whitehorse, Yukon, "Gourmet camper was mauled last night because he left one little piece of fried chicken between his teeth."

Also, remember to employ the same sanitation rules you learned in the primitive camping section.

Hanging food: attach one end of a parachute cord to a rock or carabineer and throw it over a tree limb. Use the other end of the cord to tie your food bag. Pull the bag into the air at least 12 to 15 feet above the ground, at least five feet from the tree trunk and at least five feet from the limb where the cord is hanging. Secure the parachute cord by tying it to a limb at the base of the tree or some other tree.

A second method for hanging food: loop two bags over a limb so they balance each other and let them dangle with no tie-off cord. Some bears have figured out to follow the tie-off cord and release it by batting or pawing it—mostly in Yellowstone National Park where so many careless campers visit. This second method should discourage a bear's efforts. Again, keep it 12 to 15 feet off the ground and at least five feet away from the tree trunk.

A third method: throw a line over the branches of two trees about ten feet apart. Throw the same parachute cord over the line and hang your food bag between the trees on the line. Do what works best for you.

Grizzlies do not intentionally prey on humans. A grizzly will attack if you accidently disturb a mother with cubs. As long as they are not drawn to any food odor, you should enjoy a good night's sleep.

If a Bear or Mountain Lion should Confront You

Okay, you've followed the rules, but you wake up to the sounds of a bear outside your tent or something else that's breathing and prowling through the night mist. Your nostrils fill with the stench of something that's got a really bad case of body odor.

You don't carry a gun, but you do have your Swiss Army knife. Yeah, great! The bear would snatch it out of your hands and use it as a toothpick afterwards. If you did carry a gun, it would only upset him. But you kept your bear repellant spray right next to your sleeping bag, so you pull it out. Yes, bear spray will stop a grizzly better than a gun.

At that moment, you wish you could sprint like an NFL halfback or fly like an eagle.

What to do: stay calm. Remember that bears and mountain lions don't like humans. It could be a deer, moose or elk. Unless you're in bear country in early spring, when a bear is just out of his den and hungry, he may only be curious and sniffing around.

I have been told that a good strategy is to play dead inside your sleeping bag if you're attacked by a grizzly. If you're with another person, you may opt to run in different directions. At least one of you would live. Keep that bear spray in your hand. No hard and fast rules exist that guarantee anything in this situation.

During the day, be alert. If you come in contact with a grizzly, try to move out of his area without running. Make a lot of noise by blowing on a whistle if you're hiking. If a bear sees you and charges, turn sideways and do not look at him directly, but do point your bear spray at his face. He may still attack you, but then again, if you are not threatening, he may not. If he continues charging to within 30 feet, spray a stream of bear spray at his nose, and follow the stream with your own eyes until you hit him right on the nose and continue the stream. It should stop him.

Make sure your friend carries a second can of spray to continue the point-blank spraying if needed. If you don't have bear spray and the attack continues, drop to the ground and assume the cannonball position with your hands over your head to protect your head and stomach.

If you run, he most likely will chase you down. At this juncture, you may want to cry, pray, scream or faint. It may not do any good, but it may make you feel better. If you die, you died while living a great adventure, which makes it a bit heroic. It's better to die this way than suffering a heart attack while eating chocolate bon-bons on a couch in front of an NFL game with the remote glued to your hand.

When confronting black bears, you have a much better chance of survival. Stand your ground. Do not drop to the ground or play dead. Don't look into his eyes; stay on your feet and keep that bear spray pointed right at his nose. Don't look scared, even if you're wetting your pants with fear. Maintain your composure until the black bear leaves your area. In any bear situation, you have to "buck up" your mind with a sense of fearless power. In other words, you must overcome your fear in order to think straight and take positive action.

If confronted with a mountain lion or puma, stand your ground and make yourself appear larger if possible by spreading out your hands and/or hopping up on a log or rock. Move away slowly and keep the bear spray aimed at the lion. If you have a child with you, pick him or her up and hold the child close to you. With a cat, you can fight back and it may run away. It also may run if you throw rocks at it. Avoid running away. Again, it's between you and lady luck.

Adventure is not always comfortable, but it is still adventure. I am a firm believer that neither bliss nor adventure is ever obtained by staying home in your rocking chair.

As a final note, be confident that you will make your way through bear country safely when you follow Mother Nature's rules. When you respect her, she will respect you right back.

I can see you sitting around the table with your friends after your adventure in Alaska.

In your journal, "Yeah, I woke up one morning on the Kenai River when I heard a blood-curdling growl...I thought the sun was shining through my mosquito netting, but it was the pearly whites of a thousand pound grizzly...well sir, I didn't have much time to think, so I pulled out my big knife—like Daniel Boone— and stared back into that grizzly's eyes. That's when I gave him a toothy growl of my own. It scared him so badly, he scrambled up a tree where we used him for an umbrella to keep the 24-hour sun from burning down on us while we ate fresh salmon steaks on the campfire."

You made Jack London proud.

KEY POINTS FROM THIS CHAPTER

1. Follow the rules of the wilderness for maximum safety.
2. Develop your own camping and wilderness style based on basic rules.

SECTION X

MAJOR VENUES FOR WORLD ADVENTURE

This section offers you a few of the top sports you may pursue in your lifetime. Because I am a bicyclist, I brought a great deal of knowledge from a life of pedaling around the planet. You may use some or all of it in different venues that you pursue.

Many of these websites will help you in pursuing a dozen other sports. Many other sports exist that you will be able to discover on the Internet for your own exploration.

Chapter 54

Pick Your Adventures from an Endlessly Growing List

I'd rather wake up in the middle of nowhere than a city any time! *~ Steve McQueen, actor*

In this amazing 21st century, you enjoy endless opportunities to experience this planet in the air, on the land, in the mountains, underground, on seven continents, at the North and South Poles, and under all of its lakes, oceans and seas. You may be one of the lucky ones to fly to the moon and Mars before this century ends.

You may become a mountain climber who climbs all of the highest peaks on seven continents. You may scuba dive in all the seas and oceans. You might fly a plane to every country. You may enjoy multiple pursuits as an adventure dilettante who enjoys everything or changes pursuits as you add birthday candles. The list grows beyond imagination.

While you may pick from hundreds of adventures, move toward the ones that turn your crank. The following chapters give you a taste of different modes of adventure. Most likely, you will meet others on adventures that turn you on to sailing around the world or climbing Mount Kilimanjaro in Africa.

Be open, be excited, be enthusiastic and jump into life.

KEY POINTS FROM THIS CHAPTER

1. It's all good.
2. Go for it.

Chapter 55

Mountain climbing

In a sense, everything that is, exists to climb. All evolution is a climbing towards a higher form. Climbing for life as it reaches towards the consciousness, towards the spirit. We have always honored the high places because we sense them to be the homes of gods. In the mountains there is the promise of...something unexplainable. A higher place of awareness, a spirit that soars. So we climb...and in climbing there is more than a metaphor; there is a means of discovery. ~ *Rob Parker*

Climbing mountains allows a sense of freedom, energy, danger and triumph far beyond normal living. Over my lifetime, I ratcheted my body up high peaks in the Andes, Himalaya, Swiss Alps, Alaska Range, Rocky Mountains and even in Antarctica. Each mountain, no matter how big, tall or small—offers challenges, joy and danger.

Some of the most famous mountain climbers who conquered Everest and K-2, died by falling off 30-foot rock walls. You never know what will happen on a mountain climb.

How do you start? Again, begin with a climbing club or buddy who climbs.

You may love rock-climbing vertical walls. You may like 14er climbing that takes endurance, but not a lot of gear. Colorado offers 54—14er peaks. Once you finish all 54, you can tackle 1,100—13ers in Colorado. Some men and women have climbed them all. You might enjoy ice climbing. You might like climbing all of the highest peaks on all seven continents. You can grab all the danger or delight you desire.

Mountain climbing web sites to get you started

1. www.rockclimbing.com
2. www.abc-of-rockclimbing.com
3. www.abcsofrockclimbing.com
4. www.indoorclimbing.com
5. www.climbingatabout.com
6. www.howrockclimbingworks.com
7. www.spadout.com
8. www.newenglandbouldering.com
9. www.climbingaustralia.com
10. www.alanarnette.com/alan/climbinglinks.php
11. www.allwebhunt.com/dir-wiki.cfm/Top/Recreation/Climbing
12. www.elephantjournal.com/2010/01/top-ten-climbing-web-sites-jamie-emerson/
13. www.top20sites.com/Top-Mountain-Climbing-Sites

For 14er climbing gear list:

1. Tent
2. Ground mat
3. Sleeping bag
4. Pillow
5. Camp chair
6. Moleskin
7. Five gallon water container
8. Mess kit
9. Small towel
10. Miner's lamp, flash light
11. Paper towels
12. 50 feet of parachute cord
13. Small ax and saw

14. Gore-Tex jacket
15. Wool sweater
16. Boots/socks/liners
17. Underwear, pants and T
18. Travel kit
19. Rain pants
20. Swiss Army knife
21. Anti-bear spray
22. Compass
23. Sunglasses
24. Adventure hat
25. Gloves/mittens
26. Day pack
27. Sun block/lip balm
28. Notebook and pen
29. Camera/tripod/film/digital cards
30. Plastic trash bags
31. Binoculars
32. Ice axe
33. Books for reading
34. Bandana
35. Food, fruits, energy bars, dinners, oatmeal, trail mix
36. Plastic box with food, stove, water filter, soap,
37. Toilet paper and two one-gallon zip-closure plastic
38. Firewood
39. Spare keys to vehicle, one for each person
40. Add to this list as you see fit from your experiences.
41. First aid kit
42. Two aluminum telescope walking poles
43. Helmet

Chapter 56

River rafting

Something will have gone out of us as a people if we ever let the remaining wilderness be destroyed, if we permit the last virgin forests to be turned into comic books and plastic cigarette cases; if we drive the few remaining members of the wild species into zoos or to extinction; if we pollute the last clear air and dirty the last clean streams and push our paved roads through the last of the silence. ~ *Wallace Stegner*

For anyone who loves the eternal wilderness at the perfect speed, you can raft a river, fish a river, dive into a river, swim a river—and come away with serene ecstasy.

After having rafted rivers on six continents, I feel that few activities beat a river trip for tranquility of the spirit. Nothing beats living by the slow, quiet and peaceful river-time.

Whatever you do in your river rafting life, be sure to take the 17-day Grand Canyon raft trip from Lee's Ferry to Diamond Creek takeout, some 225 miles and 1.7 billion years of geological magic. Few other raft trips offer such dramatic scenery and ecological magic.

Top ten river rafting destinations in the USA:

1. Grand Canyon, AZ
2. Salmon River, ID
3. Arkansas River, CO
4. Colorado River, UT
5. American River, CA
6. Rogue River, OR

7. Glacier National Park, MT
8. New River, WV
9. Chattooga River, GA/SC
10. Snake River, ID/WY
11. Deerfield River, MA

How do you get started?

1. America's Top 10 River Outfitters: http://www.class-vi.com/
2. Rafting America and Canada: http://www.raftingamerica.com/
3. Adventure Connection in California: http://www.raftcalifornia.com/
4. Rafting, canoeing, floating: http://www.wareagleresort.com/
5. Jim Thorpe River Ad ventures in Pennsylvania: http://www.jtraft.com/
6. Blue Sky Outfitters Washington State: http://www.blueskyoutfitters.com/

Chapter 57

Backpacking

How hard to realize that every camp of men or beast has this glorious starry firmament for a roof! In such places standing alone on the mountain-top it is easy to realize that whatever special nests we make - leaves and moss like the marmots and birds, or tents or piled stone - we all dwell in a house of one room - the world with the firmament for its roof - and are sailing the celestial spaces without leaving any tracks. ~ *John Muir*

It's been said that backpacking becomes Mother Nature's way of feeding mosquitoes. You must love it. Millions do love backpacking, whether for a day hike or weekend or for the hard core, a whole summer—such as backpacking the Continental Divide.

Nothing in the world beats a trek into the wilderness, whether mountains or woods or rolling hills. Peace, serenity, campfires, stories and friendships.

How to get started:

1. Information and gear reviews: www. BackpackerMagazine.com
2. Keep yourself abreast of gear and classes: www. TheBackpacker.com
3. Recreation Equipment Incorporated: www.REI.com
4. Trails and maps for your treks at: www.slackpacker.com
5. Ins and outs of light weight backpacking: http://www. backpacking.net

6. Yosemite: www.nps.gov
7. New Zealand: www.backpackerboard.co.nz/directory/worldwide-backpacking.html
8. General info: www.wilderness-backpacking.com/index.html
9. Europe: www.bakpakguide.com/europe/europe101/highlights/index.shtml
10. Australia: www.backpackersinaustralia.com
11. Canada: www.outdooradventurecanada.com

Chapter 58

Sailing Around the World

The pessimist complains about the wind; the optimist expects it to change; the realist adjusts the sails. ~ *William Arthur Ward*

It's been my pleasure to sail and scuba dive in the Caribbean, Indian Ocean and on mountain lakes at 9,000 feet. There's nothing like filling the sails with a brisk wind. It fills your mind, body and spirit at the same time.

Humanity has sailed the oceans of the world from the beginning of recorded history. Whether you sail around the world or sail around the bay—what a glorious way to spend your life for however long you allow the winds to fill your sails.

How to get started:

1. Sailing info: www.sailnet.com/forums/cmps_index.php
2. More sailing: www.sailinglinks.com/
3. Canada: www.sailingforyou.ca/
4. Sailing needs: www.home.ussailing.org/
5. Sailing magazine: www.sailingworld.com
6. World sailing: www.internationalsailingfederation.com
7. Sailing: www.48degreesnorth.com
8. Solo sailing: www.singlehandedsailingsociety.com
9. Sailing: www.latitude.com

Chapter 59

Canoeing

The first thing you must learn about canoeing is that the canoe is not a lifeless, inanimate object: it feels very much alive, alive with the life of the river. Life is transmitted to the canoe by currents of air and the water upon which it rides. The behavior and temperament of a canoe is dependent upon the elements: from the slightest breeze to a raging storm, from the smallest ripple to a towering wave, or from a meandering stream to a thundering rapid. Anyone can handle a canoe in a quiet millpond, but in rapids a canoe is like a wild stallion. It must be kept on a tight rein. The canoeist must take the canoe where he or she wants it to go, not where it wants to go. Given the chance, the canoe will dump you overboard and continue on down the river by itself. ~ *Bill Mason*

For the power of a paddle, give me a chance to power my own canoe. I love the peace, quiet and serenity of canoeing, canoe camping and canoe adventure. As Henry David Thoreau said, "Canoeing is pure nature."

You may enjoy turtles sunning themselves, swans flapping their wings, cormorants spreading their feathers to dry them in the sun, diving ducks and a chance to see loons playing their circle games—all in the quiet of the canoe.

Whether you paddle a lake, the Boundary Waters or the Mississippi River, a canoe gives you special magic.

How to get started:

1. Minnesota: www.redrockstore.com
2. Guide to canoes and products: www.canoeing.com
3. Top canoes: www.oldtowncanoe.com
4. Canoe   Australia: www.canoe.org.au/?page=20186&format=
5. North American rivers: www.nationalrivers.org

Chapter 60

Scuba diving

Scuba diving is sensual. To breathe underwater is one of the most fascinating and peculiar sensations imaginable. Breathing becomes a rhythmic melody of inhalations and exhalations. The cracks and pops of fish and crustaceans harmonize with the rhythmic chiming of the bubbles as you exhale. Soon, lungs act as bellows, controlling your buoyancy as you achieve weightlessness. And, as in your dreams, you are flying. Combine these otherworldly stimuli and you surrender completely to the sanctuary of the underwater world. ~ *Tec Clark*

My dad got me into scuba diving at age 15. After a lifetime of diving in exotic places around the world, including the Great Barrier Reef, Galapagos Islands, Caribbean, Hawaii and Australia's east and west coast—I am ready to jump into any lake, river, sea or ocean to see the magic beneath the surface.

Whether you like wreck driving, a slow drift on the Crystal River in Florida or John Pennekamp Park in the Florida Keys or a sinkhole—scuba diving allows magic and freedom of flight, fancy and beauty.

How to get started:

1. Scuba directory: www.wv-travel-directory.com/scubadiving/view.html
2. Scuba vacations: www.scubasuperpower.com/
3. Scuba products: www.odysseydiving.com/links.html
4. Scuba gear: www.diversdirect.com/

Chapter 61

Skydiving

When the people look like ants—Pull!
When the ants look like people—Pray!

This kid has never jumped out of an airplane with a parachute in his life. But the people who do it love it. If skydiving turns your crank, it may be the sparkplug that lights your fire. Go for it.

How to get started:

1. Learning to skydive: www.skydiving.com
2. Wing suit: www.dropzone.com/
3. Sky diving: video.search.yahoo.com/search/video?p=sky+diving+websites
4. New Zealand: www.skydivingnz.co.nz/
5. Canada: www.vancouver-skydiving.bc.ca/
6. Australia: www.sydneyskydivers.com.au/

Chapter 62

Surfing and Windsurfing

When talking with co-windsurfers and trying to get your shoulders out of your wetsuit, be careful not to also grab your bathing suit strap as you forcefully pull down on the wetsuit. It tends to interrupt the flow of the conversation. ~ *Marcy Kennedy*

As a kid, I surfed in Hawaii off Diamond Head. I couldn't get enough of riding those waves. Years later, as a landlubber, some bright guy stuck a sail on a surfboard and called it windsurfing. It's also known as boardsailing. Either sport, what a rush.

Wild winds may drive your soul. Whether surfing the big ones in Australia, Hawaii or anywhere in the world, you may enjoy surfing and windsurfing as you choose.

How to get started:

1. Surfer Magazine to get started: www. surfermagazine.com
2. California: www.surfingcal.com/surf-links.html
3. Australia: www.sasurfschools.com.au/
4. United Kingdom: www.magicseaweed.com/ UK-Ireland-Surf-Tools/1/
5. Hawaii: www.surfline.com/home/index.cfm
6. Windsurfing: www.windsurfingmag.com/
7. Gear: www.windsurfing-direct.com/

Chapter 63

Hot Air Ballooning and Parasailing

The winds have welcomed you with softness, the sun has greeted you with its warm hands, you have flown so high and so well, that God has joined you in laughter, and set you back gently into the loving arms of Mother Earth. ~ *Known as The Balloonists' Prayer*

You can't help but sense the wonder of rising into the biosphere inside a basket carried aloft by a hot air balloon. Peaceful, joyful and serene. If it's your cup of tea, rise in the morning in a hot air balloon.

If you're into hang-gliding or parasailing, go for it. To soar like an eagle may give you great joy and spiritual bliss.

How to get started:

1. Getting started: www.hotairballooning.com/
2. Director for sites: www.eballoon.org/directory/balloon-sites.html
3. World ballooning: www.hot-air-ballooning.org/
4. Parasailing: www.hot-air-ballooning.org/

Chapter 64

Snow skiing, snowboarding, cross country skiing, snowshoeing, water skiing, wake boarding, knee boarding, disabled skiing

The sensual caress of waist deep snow...glory in skiing virgin fluff, in being the first to mark the powder with the signature of their run. ~ *Tim Cahill*

As one who lived the ski bum dream, it's worth it. You will enjoy fantastic powder runs all your own. First tracks! Busting the bumps! Screaming at the top of your lungs from so much excitement! For two years, I skied 110 times a winter, bartended, danced and played in the powder at Winter Park, Colorado. I enjoyed a fantastic time in my life. Do it while you're young or do it while you're old, but live the life of a ski bum for one winter and you will have made it to heaven before you died.

Also, if snowboarding chimes your bells, go for it. You may like snowshoeing, skiing, hut-to-hut mountaineering skiing and water skiing. Life awaits you in the mountains anywhere on the planet. You're in for the time of your life wherever you strap on a board, skis or any other gear to move you across snow or summer warm water.

How to get started:

1. Ski Magazine: www.skinet.com/
2. Hut to hut: www.huts.org/

3. Ski Utah: www.skiutah.com/winter/index.html
4. Ski California: www.snowsummit.com/ski/
5. Ski Vermont: www.skivermont.com/
6. Ski Europe: www.ski-europe.com/
7. Snowboarding: www.lovetoknow.com/top10/snowboarding.html
8. Snowshoeing: www.snowshoemtn.com/jobs/faq.htm
9. Water skiing: www.usawaterski.org/
10. Disabled skiing: www.NSCD.org

Chapter 65

Many Other Ways to Travel Around the World

There must be 50 ways to leave your lover…hop off the bus Gus, we don't need to discuss much, drop off the key Lee, set yourself free…get out the back Jack; make a new plan Stan; don't try to be coy Roy, just listen to me…. ~ *Neil Simon*

After presenting components of this book along with a slide show at a sports store in Denver, Colorado, an older lady stepped up to me at the end. She said, "You didn't talk about the wonders of RV'ing around the United States. We RV'd for two years and had the time of our lives. Please talk about that travel mode in the future."

Another guy came up, "I liked your show, but what about motorcycle adventures?"

"I'm with you," I said. "Whatever travel mode turns you on is the best way to go."

"Thanks man," he said.

As you can see, this book already stretches beyond 350 pages. I could not cover everything or it would resemble an encyclopedia.

You may like to travel by RV (camper van), motorcycle, plane, sailboat, canoe, scooter, unicycle, Penny Farthing, bicycle, paraglider, horseback and a dozen other travel modes. You may choose to make yourself happy along your path. You may apply the concepts and practices in this book to make your dreams come true.

Chapter 66

Gear, Adventure Companies

You've ridden so long in the rain, you feel like a dishrag. But despite the misery of your soaked body, you look around to see verdant leaves dripping with water. The air enters your nostrils vibrantly clean. To experience adventure, you must be willing to be uncomfortable at times and enjoy loneliness by being happy with your own singing. A song pops out of your mouth…It rained all night the day I left, the weather it was fine…. ~ *The Gourmet Bicyclist in the Washington State rain forest*

A special breed of individuals, adventure seekers require muscles and guts to pedal, pack, paddle, ski, sail, run and climb into nature's inner sanctum. Mountains test your gumption and deserts test your will. Life offers you challenges. Nature tests your character daily. Hardships impact your inner being. At the same time, you experience joys and bliss during sunsets or after a rainstorm when a double rainbow arcs across the sky.

Your quest creates something special in your life and draws magical moments that cannot be generated any other way. You hike, bike, climb, paddle and move forward between personal power and exhaustion. Life mingles with death. Enchanting moments happen. You can't look for them nor can you expect them. You interlock with the forces of nature.

In order to enjoy that charm, equip yourself with the best gear you can afford. The following organizations base their research and development on making camping and outdoor adventuring optimum for you. They guarantee their products. I have utilized gear from all of them and I have never been disappointed.

By contacting their 800 numbers or websites, you will receive a catalog with all their equipment that you may need.

QUALITY OUTDOOR OUTFITTERS

Recreation Equipment Incorporated: This company is popularly known as ***REI*** and offers top quality as well as environmentally responsible merchandise. They offer a money back guarantee on all their products. Additionally, over 100 REI stores across the nation sponsor top adventure experts that educate, inspire, guide and mentor audiences throughout the year. ***REI*** offers backpacks, bikes, canoes, skis, GPS, safety gear, rafting, sunglasses, mountaineering gear, sailing, camping, food, winter gear, snowshoes and more than can be listed in this short paragraph. Additionally, you may become a member and enjoy bonus dividends annually. Call 1-800-426-4840. www.REI.com

The North Face: Top quality gear for every kind of adventure. Excellent guarantees. Camping, skiing, rafting and mountaineering. For a catalog call 1-800-447-2333. www.thenorthface.com

Eastern Mountain Sports: Excellent outdoor gear all around. Guarantees on all products. www.ems.com

L.L. Bean: Excellent selection of clothing, boots and more for the great outdoors. Full guarantees. Call 1-800-341-4341. www. llbean.com

Early Winters Outfitting: High quality, lightweight camping and outdoor equipment. Great service and excellent guarantee. www. earlywintersoutfitting.com

Campmor: Excellent camping store. Latest equipment and fair prices. www.campmor.com

Marmot Mountain Works: Excellent sleeping bags, running gear, camping gear and more. Excellent guarantee. www. marmotmountainworks.com

Go Lite: Exceptionally light backpacks and outdoor gear. Excellent guarantee. www.golite.com

Army-Navy Surplus stores: You can find one in any big city. They feature surplus outdoor gear and reasonable prices. They will stand by their products with a money back guarantee. Look them up in your local phone book. Full guarantee.

Performance: Primarily bicycles, parts, tires, clothing, gloves, helmets, tents, shoes, panniers, rain gear. Excellent quality and full guarantee. www.performancebike.com

Bicycle Village: Primarily bicycles, tires, repair, fitting, shoes and jerseys. Full guarantee. www.bicyclevillage.com

Bike Nashbar: Bicycles, parts, jerseys, shoes, jackets and pretty much everything you need for your bicycle adventures. Full guarantee. www.BikeNashbar.com

Accommodations

American Youth Hostels: If you enjoy meeting travelers on a budget, you will meet the best in hostels around the planet. You will find 5,500 hostels worldwide. You need a hostel sheet, your membership card and a smile. www.AmericanYouthHostels.com and www.YHA.com

Magazines

Adventure Cycling Magazine: For long distance bicycle touring riders, this magazine excels. You will find ideas, innovations, bike reviews and stories from around the world. www. adventurecycling.org

Bicycle Times: This magazine gives you an excellent overall view of touring, commuting and many other great stories about bicycling. www.bicycletimes.com

Bicycling Magazine: This magazine carries a great deal of information about bicycles, clothing, travel, food and fashion. www.bicycling.com

Tandem: This is a great magazine about folks that like to ride two up. www.tandem.com

Mountain Bike Magazine: This magazine gives you everything you need to know about competitions and more. www. mountainbike.com

Outside Magazine: This magazine will take you to adventures around the world. Amazing photographs and compelling stories. www.outsidemagazine.com

Canoe and Kayak Magazine: This magazine will take you into the calmness of canoeing and the wildness of kayaking. www. canoeandkayak.com

Cruising World Magazine: This magazine is for sailing around the world. www.cruisingworld.com

Backpacker Magazine: This magazine gives you the best in trips, tips and stories. www.backpackermagazine.com

Campground Sources

Rand McNally Campground and Trailer Park Guide: Enjoy information about campgrounds in every section of the USA. Also, www.goodsamsclub.com, www.koa.com

National Bicycling Touring Companies and Gear

Austin-Lehman Adventures: First class, inn-to-inn cycling adventures. Offers a guarantee. Bike all over the country and more. Experienced group leaders. www.austin-lehmanadventures.com

Backroads: Class act and a ton of fun. Quality tours and cuisine. For all abilities and all levels. Get your feet wet in style. Cycling, backpacking and many other outdoor adventures. They really offer first class adventures. www.backroads.com

Bicycle Touring Gear: Expedition panniers, racks and bicycle touring gear. Call 1-800-747-0588. Email: wayne@TheTouringStore.com, www.thetouringstore.com

Recumbents, tandems, trikes: Everything you need for bicycling in a variety of styles. www.jayspedalpower.com

Custom Franklin Frame bikes: For incredible workmanship of a custom bicycle, try www.franklinframes.com. I have owned a Franklin Frame custom mountain expedition-touring bike for 21 years.

Hubbub Custom Bicycles: They fit, design and build a bike for you. www.hubbubcustom.com

Classic Adventures: Bicycle tours in USA and around the world since 1979. www.classicadventures.com

Pedal and Sea Adventures: You name it, they will take you there. Austria, France, Germany, Lake Constance at the foot of the Alps, Quebec, Vermont and more. www.classicadventures.com

Women Only Bike Tours: Fully supported, all ages, all abilities, quaint inns, cross country, national parks, Europe and more. Wine tasting. www.womantours.com

America by Bicycle, Inc: Choose 38 tours from five to 52 days. Coast to coast. Highly recommended. www.abbike.com

Alaska Bicycle Tours: Ride Alaska and the Yukon. www.cyclealaska.com

Wandering Wheels: They will guide you coast to coast inexpensively. www.wanderingwheels.org

Historical Trails Cycling: Lewis and Clark Trail, Oregon Trail, the Wilderness Road and more. www.historicaltrailcycling.org

Bike Flights: Bicycle shopping, airline tickets, travel insurance. www.bikeflights.com

Easy Rider Tours: Bicycle Europe and America. They will take you first class. Since 1987, Jim and his wife have been taking folks on great tours. You'll love your time with them. I know them personally and give them a five star rating. Call 1-800-488-8332. www.easyridertours.com

Australian Adventures: Top quality touring company. Thirteen individual tours in the land down under. Call 1-800-889-1464. www.AustralianTours.com

New Zealand Pedal Tours: Local guides, inns, quiet roads, incredible scenery. Twenty years in the business. www. newzealandpedaltours.com

Backpacking trips with "Just roughin it": Top quality backpack trips into the Grand Canyon and beyond. www.justroughinit.com

Backpacking for women with Adventure Chick: These ladies will take you to wild places to enjoy great fun. USA and around the world. www.adventurechick.net

Backpacking in Yellowstone: Play in the wilderness of geysers and waterfalls. www.bigwildadventures.com

Backpacking in Alaska: Huge, wild and amazing. www. trekalaska.com

Backpacking and hostelling worldwide: Around the world. www. abouthostels.com

Backpacking South America: Inca Trail, Amazon jungle, waterfalls. They take you to the best in Central and South America. www.bambaexperience.com

Backpacking and how to get into it: They give you information from A to Z. www.easybackpackingtips.com

Backpacking in Utah: Profound beauty and sunsets. www. excursionsescalante.com

Caribbean backpacking: Water, islands, exotic. www. adventurefinder.com

Backpacking in the USA: They take you into the inner sanctum of nature's playground. www.outwardbound.org

Backpacking Canada: Try a trip in the Yukon. www.yukoneh.com

Backpacking for teens: Hit the Appalachian Trail. www. outdoors.org

Sea kayaking in Alaska: Sea kayak Prince William Sound with whales and glaciers. www.alaskasummer.com

Backpacking in Thailand: Exotic, stunning, beautiful. www. backpackersthailand.com

Luxury backpacking: For those that enjoy comfort. www. luxurybackpackers.com

Backpacking in Australia: Travel down under. www. backpackingaround.com

Backpacking in New Zealand: Packing the Milford Trek or Rootburn Trek. Expect an amazing time in that country. Raft the Shotover River. Bungee jump. Stand on the four billion year old Meroki Boulders. www.NewZealand.com

Backpacking in Switzerland: Whether you bicycle or backpack, Switzerland offers incredible sights and beautiful villages filled with flower boxes. www.backpackeurope.com

Finding partners

For backpacking, camping, hiking, climbing, rafting, cycling, windsurfing, para-sailing, scuba diving, horseback riding and a hundred other sports, you may sign up to enjoy new friends at: www.MeetUp.com

For companions wanted in cycling. You may sign up on line for free. www.adventurecycling.org

Chapter 67

Unlimited Sports Activities

There are so many things to do in this world that you need twenty lifetimes to pursue them all. ~ *FHW*

The more you travel the world, the more you realize that you cannot do it all in one lifetime. However, you can accomplish as much as possible by sticking your nose into everything along the way.

In the final reality, you captain your life, you choose and you live it to your satisfaction.

You may participate in different sports and activities at various stages of your life. When one activity grabs you more than another, pursue it. You might battle on the racquetball court with unending passion. You may climb mountain peaks with a sense of high adventure. You may crash the gates snow skiing.

Windsurfing may have you raging on the water with the wind. You might pursue triathlons with swimming, bicycling and running. Mountain bike racing may hook into your soul. You may turn into a swing dancer and compete all over the country. You may become an artist, screenwriter, sculptor or chef. This life allows you unlimited opportunities to express yourself.

In the end, this book presents you with useful information and techniques that will allow you to adventure around the country or around the world for your entire life. If a Michigan farm boy can chase after his dreams and live them one by one, so can you. May you enjoy your life journey with persistence, passion and action.

Whatever your interest, go for it, love it and live it.

Remember: steadfast conviction, relentless enthusiasm and a sense of purpose will take you anywhere you want to go in this world.

As my dad said, "You can live a spectacular life!"

Now you can say, "I am living a spectacular life!"

The End

About the Author

Frosty Wooldridge lives each day with gratitude, boundless enthusiasm and a sense of purpose for everything he undertakes. He graduated from Michigan State University. He loves mountain climbing, scuba diving, swing dancing, skiing and bicycle touring. He writes and speaks on overpopulation and environmental challenges facing humanity. He has taught at the elementary, high school and college levels. He has rafted, canoed, backpacked, sailed, windsurfed, snowboarded and more all over the planet. He has bicycled 100,000 miles on six continents and 12 times across the United States. His feature articles have appeared in national and international magazines for 30 years. He has interviewed on NBC, CBS, ABC, CNN, FOX and 100 radio shows. His new website will contain more information for anyone aspiring toward a spectacular life:

www.HowtoLiveaLifeofAdventure.com

Facebook adventure page: How to Live a Life of Adventure: The Art of Exploring the World

Acknowledgements

Special thanks to Cynthia Schoen for brilliant copy editing along with ideas for creating a compelling and motivational piece of literature. Thanks to my fabulous wife Sandi for her treasured ideas and daily support. Extraordinary thanks goes to my college roommate and best friend Bob Johannes who brought scholarly ideas, wisdom and constructive criticism to this book. Thank each of you from my heart to yours.

Book cover: Frosty Wooldridge and Al Wilson on top of Homestake Peak at 13,209-feet in the Rocky Mountains in January at 30 below zero with 100 miles of visibility in all directions.

Other books by the author:

Handbook for Touring Bicyclists—Bicycling touring grows in popularity each year. Men and women around the world take to the highways and the "open air" is their kitchen. On the pages of this book, you'll discover how to buy, carry, prepare and store food while on tour. Discover the ins and outs with a "Baker's Dozen" of touring tips that are essential for successful bicycle adventuring. Whether you're going on a weekend ride, a weeklong tour or two years around the world, this handbook will help you learn the artistry of bicycling and cooking.

Strike Three! Take Your Base—The Brookfield Reader, Sterling, VA. To order this hardcover book, send $19.95 to Frosty Wooldridge by contacting him through his website. This poignant story is important reading for every teen who has ever experienced the loss of a parent from either death or divorce. This is the story of a boy losing his father and growing through his sense of pain and loss. It is the story of baseball, a game that was shared by both the boy and his father, and how baseball is much like life.

An Extreme Encounter: Antarctica—"This book transports readers into the bowels of million year old glaciers, katabatic winds, to the tops of smoking volcanoes, scuba diving under the ice, intriguing people, death, outlaw activities and rare moments where the author meets penguins, whales, seals and Skua birds. Hang on to your seat belts. You're in for a wild ride where the bolt goes into the bottom of the world." Sandy Colhoun, editor-in-chief, The Antarctic Sun

Bicycling Around the World: Tire Tracks for your Imagination—This book mesmerizes readers with animal stories that bring a smile to your face. It chills you with a once-in-a-lifetime ride in Antarctica where you'll meet a family of Emperor penguins. Along the way, you'll find out that you have to go without a mirror, sometimes, in order to see yourself. The greatest aspect of this book comes from—expectation. Not since *Miles from Nowhere* has a writer captured the Zen and Art of Bicycle Adventure as well as Wooldridge. Not only that, you may enjoy a final section: "Everything you need to know about long distance touring." He shows you "How to live the dream." You will possess the right bike, equipment, money and tools to ride into your own long distance touring adventures. If you like bicycling, you'll go wild reading this book. If you don't like bicycling, you'll still go wild reading this book.

Motorcycle Adventure to Alaska: Into the Wind—"Seldom does a book capture the fantasy and reality of an epic journey the magnitude of this book. Trevor and Dan resemble another duo rich in America's history of youthful explorers who get into all kinds of trouble—Tom Sawyer and Huckleberry Finn. They plied the Mississippi River, but Dan and his brother push their machines into a wild and savage land—Alaska. My boys loved it." John Mathews, father of two boys and a daughter.

Bicycling the Continental Divide: Slice of Heaven, Taste of Hell—"This bicycle dream ride carries a bit of mountain man adventure. The author mixes hope with frustration, pain with courage and bicycling over the mountains. John Brown, a friend left behind to battle cancer, provides guts and heart for his two friends who ride into the teeth of nature's fury. Along the way, you'll laugh, cry and gain new appreciations while pondering the meaning of life." Paul Jackson

Losing Your Best Friend: Vacancies of the Heart—"This is one heck of a powerful book. It's a must read for anyone that has lost a friend or parent. It will give you answers that you may not have thought about. It will touch your heart and you will learn from their experiences. It also shows you what you can do if you suffer conflict with your friend's wife or girlfriend." Jonathan Runy

Rafting the Rolling Thunder—"Fasten your raft-belts folks. You're in for the white water rafting ride of your life. Wooldridge keeps readers on the edge of their seats on a wild excursion through the Grand Canyon. Along the way, he offers you an outlaw-run by intrepid legend "Highwater Harry," a man who makes a bet with the devil and nearly loses his life. The raft bucks beneath you as Harry crashes through Class V rapids. And the Grand Canyon Dish Fairies, well, they take you on separate rides of laughter and miles of smiles. Enjoy this untamed excursion on a river through time." Jason Rogers

Misty's Long Ride: Across America on Horseback—by Howard Wooldridge (Frosty Wooldridge's brother). "As good as Howard was, sometimes there was nothing he could do about our situation in the burning inferno of Utah. In that agonizing desert, a man's mouth became so dry, he couldn't spit. I felt the heat cook my hooves at ground level where it felt like walking alone in the middle of a farrier's furnace. Above us, vultures soared in the skies searching for road-kill. Yet, Howard pulled down the brim of his hat and pushed forward. I followed this cowboy because he was a Long Rider and I was his horse." For anyone who loves horses and high adventure, Howard's horse Misty tells one of the great adventure tales in the 21st century by galloping across America. You'll enjoy horse sense, horse humor, unique characters and gallop across America.

How to Deal with 21st Century Women: Co-Creating a Successful Relationship—The chapters on the nine key points for creating a successful long-term relationship are the best suggestions for anyone considering marriage. Every woman should read them along with her man. This is the first male relationship book that honors the male perspective and aims for sensible collaboration. I highly recommend this book for men and women." Chelsea Robinson

All books available at: 1 888 280 7715, www.amazon.com, www. barnesandnoble.com, also on Kindle.

Praise for Living Your Spectacular Life

"This book entertains, inspires and motivates. What I liked most about it: Wooldridge offers other motivational writers in each chapter to give you new ideas on living a spectacular life. He wants you to succeed for your sake. If that means you enjoy a greater affinity to another writer, he gives you plenty of choices. He's got six concepts and six practices that provide you with personal courage, self-confidence and empowerment. He offers you dozens of ordinary men and women living spectacular lives in various pursuits from world travel to growing a garden. He kept me reading through every chapter." Jake Hodges

"You learn, you act, you grow from the wisdom of this book. The author grabs you by the seat of your pants and takes you on a ride into self-confidence, self-acceptance and self-motivation. I loved how he educates while he inspires. He shows you ordinary people breaking into spectacular lives through the principles he offers in his book. Effective, eloquent writing! I want to read it again. He gives plenty of examples of women who succeeded." Marie Jackson

"There must be a ga-zillion books published for you to live a dynamic life. There are also thousands of therapists charging $100 an hour to move you into a balanced and productive life. Wooldridge takes you where you want to go much easier and more inspiringly than any therapist. He's a 21st century gut-level John Muir, the most inspiring outdoor writer of the 1800s. Take Wooldridge up on his six concepts and six practices, and you will find yourself living a spectacular life. He gives you the courage

353

to get off your sofa and find out what you truly love—and then, pursue it." Charles Hamilton

"I love people who succeed against great odds. I really love to know how they do it. This book shows anyone how to live a spectacular life. Great read! Got me off my butt! I've got plans for Alaska next summer." Paul Hawkins

"This book gives you a better idea of who you are and where you're headed. Spectacular may not be a big enough term for this book. Stupendous may work better. By plugging into Wooldridge's 12 points, you may lift off to Saturn if you are so inclined. All those people he writes about are just like you and me. If they can live spectacular lives, I can live a spectacular life." Jonathan Franks

"Once you read this book, you can't forget it. It plays with your mind in ways that move you toward discovering your own exciting path on your lifelong journey. Wooldridge offers you countless ordinary people living spectacular lives. What's more, he shows you their secrets and his secrets. Not secrets, actually! Each person shows you how to flip your mind toward living dynamically. Somewhere in the middle of the book, you begin to evolve your thinking. By the end, you're a changed person. And, there is no going back. You're in for a heck of a ride!" Sandra Hamilton

"This book will either exhaust you with its energy or enliven you toward a totally new understanding for living your own spectacular life. No kidding! I couldn't put it down." Len Dawson

Made in the USA
Middletown, DE
22 October 2023

41206247R00227